ROUTLEDGE LIBRARY EDITIONS:
TRANSPORT ECONOMICS

Volume 23

WORK AND WEALTH IN A MODERN PORT

WORK AND WEALTH IN A MODERN PORT

An Economic Survey of Southampton

P. FORD

Routledge
Taylor & Francis Group
LONDON AND NEW YORK

First published in 1934 by George Allen & Unwin Ltd

This edition first published in 2017
by Routledge
2 Park Square, Milton Park, Abingdon, Oxon OX14 4RN

and by Routledge
605 Third Avenue, New York, NY 10017

Routledge is an imprint of the Taylor & Francis Group, an informa business

British Library Cataloguing in Publication Data
A catalogue record for this book is available from the British Library

ISBN: 978-0-415-78484-9 (Set)
ISBN: 978-1-315-20175-7 (Set) (ebk)
ISBN: 978-1-138-70002-4 (Volume 23) (hbk)
ISBN: 978-1-315-20505-2 (Volume 23) (ebk)

Publisher's Note
The publisher has gone to great lengths to ensure the quality of this reprint but points out that some imperfections in the original copies may be apparent.

Disclaimer
The publisher has made every effort to trace copyright holders and would welcome correspondence from those they have been unable to trace.

WORK AND WEALTH IN A MODERN PORT

An Economic Survey of Southampton

by

P. FORD

LONDON
GEORGE ALLEN & UNWIN LTD
MUSEUM STREET

FIRST PUBLISHED IN 1934

Thesis approved for the Degree of Doctor of Philosophy in the University of London

PRINTED IN GREAT BRITAIN BY
UNWIN BROTHERS LTD., WOKING

PREFACE

THIS survey was designed as a contribution to our knowledge of poverty, its incidence, and causes. Poverty is a product of many variables, and the real significance of any ascertained volume of it is apparent only if it is understood as an expression of a complex of economic and other social forces. The study therefore goes beyond the immediate facts relating to it, and investigates some of the factors which have influenced the growth of population, the earning strength of families, and the elements of costs which attract and repel industries. But the investigations were also extended to include an examination of certain socially depressed groups, the composition of family incomes, means tests, etc., as well as certain aspects of retail distribution and crime. For the real strength and weakness of our social services will not be known without a careful study of their operation in economically diverse areas.

Problems of public administration have too often been regarded in artificial detachment from the broad and fundamental influences which have settled the terms in which they are posed, and because this book is in part a plea for more general attention to these wider issues behind administrative policy, it may be regarded as an essay in the economy of cities. To those who are concerned to plan and change, it is a plea for the necessity of a thorough examination of all the relevant data. To the professional economic theorist it may perhaps serve as a reminder that, as Allyn Young remarked, English political economy has largely grown out of efforts to forge instruments that will help us to understand how to deal with the communal problems of organized economic life.

Certain features of this study need explanation. The survey was first planned in 1927–28 and has included a study of 21,000 families, and a random sample household enquiry, as well as a great deal of other statistical work. Surveys of this scope are usually endowed in some way or other, but this had to be conducted with no other assistance than three annual grants from the research funds of University College, Southampton, together amounting to £50; and no special secretarial assistance of any kind was available. The load was a heavy one to carry in addition to full-time University work, and the investigations were hampered in various ways. It was not possible to conduct all branches of the enquiry as a single date. The mass interview was based on a survey in the autumn of 1928; that of house densities in 1929; the second income group in 1931; the study of mentally deficient and the retail distribution map in 1932. The enquiry into the subsequent history of persons disallowed unemployment benefit, which may be read with this book, was made in 1931. It was also necessary to stop short at various points when much would have been gained by pushing the investigation home with further enquiries.

Some of these delays were due to the fact that the *Southampton Civic Survey*, with which the writer was concerned both as contributor and editor, had to be completed by a given date if it were to fulfil its purpose; work on it had therefore to be given preference. Various chapters in that book, including two by the present writer, deal with topics discussed in this book, and with related subjects not here touched upon, from the special point of view of town planning. Those interested in the town itself, or in the methods of investigation used, will find that the two studies are in some degree complementary.

ACKNOWLEDGMENTS

THIS survey could not have been made without the help of those persons who provided information or submitted cheerfully to persistent questioning; and it would be unkind to draw distinctions by mentioning particular names. Those who helped me included officers of the Southern Railway Company, of the shipping companies and the heads of other businesses; the officers of the Borough Council, of the Ministry of Labour and other Government Departments. My thanks are due to the investigators, who carried through the delicate work of the household enquiry with such thoroughness. I wish to acknowledge also the assistance and reasonableness of the hundreds of householders who answered the very personal questions which the enquiry necessitated. If this book should come into the hands of any of those who have assisted, I hope they will find the information it contains on the economic and social conditions of Southampton a due reward for the contribution they made to it. The Southampton Civic Society kindly allowed me to reproduce the map showing "Distribution of Income by Streets" from the *Civic Survey*. Finally, I wish to express my gratitude to the University of London (Publication Fund) and to University College, Southampton, for the generous financial assistance which made publication of the book possible.

CONTENTS

PAGE

PREFACE 5

ACKNOWLEDGMENTS 7

CHAPTER

I. HISTORY 11

II. POPULATION 24

III. INDUSTRIES 34

IV. THE LABOUR MARKET 59

V. INCOME AND POVERTY 91

1. Income Survey 93
2. The Random Sample Household Inquiry 101
   - i. The Earning Constitution of the Family 106
   - ii. The Distribution of Income 110
   - iii. The Poverty Datum Line 112
   - iv. Primary Poverty 118
   - v. Potential Poverty 123
   - vi. Causes of Primary Poverty 128
   - vii. Family Means 131
     - (*a*) Social Service Income
     - (*b*) Supplementary Earners' Contributions
     - (*c*) Miscellaneous Income
     - (*d*) The Composition of Family Income
   - viii. Means Tests 144

VI. DEPRESSED CLASSES 155

1. The Unemployed 156
2. A Group of Applicants for Assistance 159
3. The Mentally Deficient 161
4. The Legal Poor 164

VII. HOUSING 170

CHAPTER PAGE

VIII. CRIME 191

IX. CONCLUSION 199

APPENDICES

1. Definitions and Rules 203
2. Methods of Colouring Street Maps 208
3. Street Records 214
4. House Density and Overcrowding per House 216

INDEX 219

MAPS

1. Distribution of Income by Streets 51
2. Dot Distribution of Accounts of a Local Store in Hampshire and the Isle of Wight *At end*

WORK AND WEALTH IN SOUTHAMPTON

CHAPTER I

HISTORY

THE Southampton of to-day and that of a century and a half ago present a remarkable contrast. At the earlier date, through its various representative bodies, the town owned or controlled the immediate sources of its prosperity. It owned both the foreshore and its mudlands, as far as its boundary (near the West Station); it owned its docks, controlled and drew annual revenue from its harbour. To-day these are in private hands, and the vital decisions affecting the town's economic future are made by non-local companies.

The alienation of the foreshore arose from the failure of the town to develop the docks and harbour, and from the intervention of private enterprise for the purpose. In 1803 an Act was passed for extending the quays and making docks, but the powers were not used, nor were renewed projects in 1810 any more fruitful. The real impulse did not come until a group of persons had considered the construction of both railroad and docks. Since important property rights were concerned, it is useful to trace the development in the minutes of the Council's own proceedings. The record for November 22, 1830, contains the following entry: "The Council received a deputation of subscribers of the intended railway and docks," and it resolved "That the Corporation is willing to treat with the said committee or with any respectable company for making liberal arrangements with a view to the extension of the port." It was the railway which first made progress. Any line which had its terminus near the dock would have to pass over land under the control of the town, and in order to interest the Council in its plan, the railway company took the unusual step of inviting the Town Council to send the Mayor as *ex officio* director[1] of the company during his year of office and the next, a form of liaison doubtless well devised to promote co-operation of the two bodies in furthering the project. In March 1832 the Council granted the company leave to pass over the Marsh, according to a plan presented. The next important stage as far as the Council was concerned, did not come until 1835, when the company sent its chairman and solicitor to request the Council to grant six acres of the Marsh for a station and line, and to sanction a readjustment of the route. The Council had earlier resolved that it would make "liberal arrangements,"[2] and it certainly lived up to its word, for at its next meeting on October 16, 1835, the following remarkable resolution was passed: "It is resolved that this Corporation do approve and consent to the deviation of the line of the railroad . . . and are willing to execute a conveyance of the land applied for both the road and the station for the purpose of the Act for the sum of one guinea; and that the company may take gravel from the shore between the land demised to the late Mr. William Lintot and the shore demised to the proprietors of the baths by the Corporation until Christmas next for the use of the company, they paying five pounds." There were present the Mayor and nine councillors. It was almost the last act of the unreformed Council.

The reformed Council met on the 28th December, and consisted of thirty councillors. It had straight away to tackle the other portion of the project, the dock scheme, now fostered by a separate company. Technically it was fortunate for Southampton that the two schemes had in some measure been conceived together, and that the dock company employed the same engineer, Mr. Giles, as the railway company,[3] for it implied a unity of conception and convenience of layout which might

[1] Wording of Minute, June 22, 1831. [2] Minute, November 22, 1830.
[3] *Southampton Civic Survey*, 1930, p. 40.

otherwise have been absent. Nevertheless, the dock scheme received a much more critical treatment in the reformed Council than the railway scheme had in the unreformed one. In 1836 the dock company applied to the Corporation for the sale of the Mudlands. The struggle over this alienation was as dramatic as the consequences of both dock development and of loss of control of the foreshore were important, and the charges made by the dissenting minority were so unusual that the intensity of feeling breaks through even the cold form of Council minutes. The first statement appears in the minutes of February 19, 1836, when the company asked approval for its plans; on that date the Council resolved that while the whole scheme was of great advantage to the town, it dissented from the application because the plan embraced a larger proportion of the Mudlands than it thought necessary for the scheme, and because sufficient data had not been supplied. A month later, however (March 18th), a deputation of the provisional committee of the intended dock company met the Council. A motion that the Council dissent from the proposals was amended to read that it was willing to assent provided that suitable terms could be arranged. Without further ado, a committee of five was appointed to confer with the deputation, and brought back to the same meeting agreed terms. The Corporation was to receive a rent charge equal to the dividend on 100 shares, which were to be regarded as fully paid up and free from all liability for calls; if the dividend paid were 10 per cent, the rent charge was to equal the dividend on 120 shares; if 20 per cent, to the dividend on 140 shares. The Corporation was to be entitled to ten votes at all meetings of shareholders. In lieu of shares, the Council was to have the option of receiving £5,000, provided that in addition an annual rent charge should be paid if the dividend reached 10 per cent. Thirty members were present at the meeting and the scheme was agreed to, but the depth of feeling of the minority was such that five dissentients took the unusual course of recording in the minutes a personally signed protest at the decision. Four, Messrs. Whitchurch, Hill, Rubie, and Brady, argued as follows:

We protest against the resolution in this day's Council because, in our opinion, the lands and privileges of the town entrusted to the Town Council have been hastily and inadvisedly given away, because the value of the land far exceeds the consideration offered, and because we will not be participators in a scheme which will benefit the company without giving the burgesses of the town those advantages they have a right to expect from their valuable property.

The fifth protest, by Admiral Tinling, was made on the ground that it would be a great misfortune for the docks to come into the hands of a private company whose main interest would be, not low dock rates, but the maximum return on capital; that the Corporation was giving up the only improvable land in their possession, that the Council had enough resources to do the work themselves, and finally that the steps had been hastily taken, and the scheme hurried on by interested persons. The committee appointed at the next Council meeting to scrutinize the clauses of the Bill did not include any protesting member.[1] When their report came before the Council, the dissentients proposed that the opinion of the law officers of the Crown should be taken on a case to be drawn up by a committee of Council as to the course to be adopted. This was negatived, and three of the dissentients, Hill, Rubie, and Whitchurch, again signed a protest against the negativing of this resolution.[2] In May[3] it was proposed that "the Corporation seal be affixed to the Bill now before Parliament." Despite a hostile amendment, this was carried and the seal affixed, whereupon a protest was again entered in the minute book, and personally signed by eight members: J. Lankester, D. Brookes, C. Tinling, J. Joliff, J. Whitchurch, J. Hill, R. Young, and J. Rubie. They protested:

Because no member of the Town Council nor any one on behalf of the Council, has collated the points of the amended Bill with the Bill settled in committee of the House of Commons; because no

[1] Minute, March 25, 1836.
[2] Minute, April 6, 1836.
[3] Minute, May 5, 1836.

member of the Town Council has assured that the letter of the Bill carries into effect the alterations agreed to; because the dock committee has not abandoned the claim to purchase the whole of the Mudlands at a very inadequate price of £5,000.

In June[1] the dock company applied for actual purchase of the Mudlands, and the proposal to confirm the sale was met by a series of hostile amendments, for example, that the Corporation was not prepared to accept money or shares until the whole proceedings of the Council with the dock company were laid before the Lords of the Treasury, and their sanction as to the quantity and price was made known. These were negatived, however, and the original proposition carried by seventeen votes to ten. This was followed by another signed protest, which recorded the "determined opposition of the signatories to the proposed gift or sale of the most improvable lands of the burgesses." The sale was declared to be a hasty and improvident bargain, which alienated lands held in trust for the present and future inhabitants, without the consent of the majority of the burgesses. Consent of the burgesses should be obtained at public meetings after free, fair, and open discussion. Objection was also made that "nothing was known" of the chief promoters of the scheme; that the company had insufficient capital to develop the land transferred, and finally, "that because a majority in the Council, including many members who were directors, shareholders, or otherwise interested in the company have voted away property of the town without calling in the aid of any engineer or surveyor to assist their judgment or bear out their proceedings." Eight members signed this vigorous protest: Whitchurch, Hill, Joliff, Lankester, Young, Rubie, Brady, and Tinling. In the next Council meeting a more direct attack was made by the dissentients, who moved "that in the late meetings of Council, many members who were shareholders and directors of or otherwise interested in making a most advantageous bargain for themselves and the company with whom they were connected, have been the

[1] Minute, June 16, 1836.

means of causing majorities to vote away inconsiderately and inadvisedly the property, rights, and privileges of the burgesses . . . the Council, not wishing to establish a precedent so dangerous, hereby record their opinion that no member of the Council should vote in any decision at any meeting of Council or committee of Council, should be an applicant of any grant or privilege for himself, or when the decision may interest him as lessee or yearly tenant, or if he should in any other way be directly interested in a pecuniary manner in any application so made." This was naturally negatived.[1]

The contest was now carried to the Treasury. Memorials were presented to it by the Corporation, asking for authority to carry on the scheme, by the dock company in support, and by certain town councillors and burgesses "objecting that too large an area was being transferred, and that the price was too low."[2] In view of the importance and difficulty of the case, the Treasury sent an officer to survey the land and to confer with the deputations and others. His report, which the Treasury accepted, was to the effect that the whole of the 216 acres was necessary, and that the sum agreed upon was an ample price, when it was considered that the ground was of no real value until considerable sums of money had been spent upon it; but he also stated that a prompt payment of the £5,000 should be insisted upon. The Treasury's decision respecting the proposed methods of payment suggest the frame of mind induced by an economy campaign. Calling for a return of the Borough finances, the Treasury noted that the annual expenditure of the Corporation was £3,783, and that the income was £1,860, leaving the remainder to be raised by rates. The debt of £9,235 was amply covered by the Corporation property and lands. The Treasury argued that "whatever might have been their view in other circumstances, My Lords consider that they should not be justified in acceding to the proposals of sale for

[1] July 6, 1836.
[2] See long minute of August 19, 1836, which quotes the Treasury's statement.

shares when, in additon to a considerable debt, there exists a large annual deficiency which must be met out of the Borough rate." With certain stipulations the Treasury therefore sanctioned the sale.

There were further alienations of considerable importance. Some was transferred to a rival railway company for a proposed new main station and jetty; another area of eleven acres was leased at £500 per annum for ninety-nine years for the construction of cable works.[1] As regards the dock undertaking, additional Mudlands were transferred for the purpose of dock extension between 1892 and 1896, but these were adjacent to the existing dock property, and involved no fresh sale of the foreshore itself. The transfer of the foreshore and Mudlands which the present dock extension[2] required was in a different category. For not only did it involve the alienation of the remainder of the foreshore and the loss of the amenities of the water front for a considerable portion of the town's inhabitants, but this reclamation will make available some hundreds of acres of land for industrial development, and will also shift the focus of the town in a marked degree. With the passing of the Southern Railway Act of 1924 and this final sale of the foreshore, Southampton completed its transformation from the ancient port and harbour controlled by the town itself to the modern type of control by non-local enterprise.

The relaxation of corporation control which marked the development of the docks showed itself also in the management of the harbour. The principle of outside influence had been conceded as early as 1803, when an Act was passed establishing, after the fashion of the day, a special statutory body, which consisted of the entire membership of the Borough Council with the recorder and ten specific members.[3] Under the Act of 1803 these specific commissioners were life mem-

[1] Minutes, November 23, 1912.

[2] See letter of Southern Railway to Corporation, October 12, 1923, and Section 20 of Southern Railway Act, 1924.

[3] Southampton Harbour Board Commission, Report, 1912, Cd. 6347, p. 7, and Appendix 9.

bers, with power to fill vacancies as they occurred. Into the detailed changes of qualifications, etc., for specific members it is not necessary to enter, but in the latter part of the century such a member was required to have a property qualification in the borough, to be a householder and assessed for the poor-rate to the amount of £30, and in the same year to have paid rates and duties as an importer of goods from any legal quay within the borough. In the middle of the nineteenth century it was alleged of this, as of other local special bodies similarly constituted, that its specific commissioners were lax in attending the Board's meetings, one reason given being that the Council members were always in the majority, and so could and did continually outvote the special members.[1] On the other hand, at a 1912 enquiry[2] into the Board's constitution, it was stated on behalf of the Borough Council that this majority was given to it because it had always claimed the right to receive harbour dues, had never relinquished that right, and had agreed to accept one-fifth only of the dues as part of a bargain.[3] It appeared to be admitted, however, that sometime before the 'nineties it was the Council members who took little interest in the meetings.[4]

In many other ports the question of the appropriateness of local control of a port of national importance serving a wide area arose acutely as the development of trade made the interests served more and more non-localized, and in this development Southampton was no exception. An Act of 1911 was the occasion both of further weakening of Council control and of strengthening of personnel in other ways. The Southampton Harbour Act of 1911 was concerned with the powers of raising money, and when the Bill was heard the House of Commons Committee agreed that enlarged powers should be given only to a reconstituted and strengthened Board, and the

[1] Report of W. Ranger, Superintending Inspector to General Board of Health, 1850, p. 47.

[2] Southampton Harbour Board Commission, 1912.

[3] Southampton Harbour Board Commission, Proceedings, q. 1733–4.

[4] Proceedings, q. 15, 16.

House of Lords insisted on the insertion of a new clause, (Section 11) which instructed the Board of Trade to set up a commission of three members to enquire into the Board's constitution and to make recommendations.[1] All parties—the Corporation, the Railway Company, the shipping and yachting interests—agreed that reconstitution was necessary, but the point in dispute was whether the Borough Council was to retain its majority of members. The Corporation representatives again claimed that while it had sold the foreshore, it had never given up its legal claim to all dues, that the agreement to accept one-fifth only was a part of a bargain, confirmed in every subsequent act, and that it was therefore entitled to a majority vote to safeguard its historic and existing rights. It was easy enough for the opponents of the Corporation to make pretty play with the remote connection between the professions of those who were actually members of the Board and knowledge of the requirements of shipping—to point out, for example, that an important resolution regarding the Bill had been moved by a draper and seconded by an undertaker. And in similar criticism the shipping interests naturally joined. The Corporation raised the fear that if the railway company were given the dominance, they could manipulate dues to their advantage, e.g. by reducing the tonnage dues and raising their dock charges, they could leave the total amount paid by shipping unaltered, but increase the railway revenue at the expense of the Harbour Board revenues; or they could, with the votes at their command, increase the charges at the Town Quay in order to divert traffic to the docks. The commissioners were unconvinced of all the Corporation's major claims, and reported that reconstruction must provide for qualified personnel, for a representation of the shipping and other interests, and for a balance of power between the parties; and that subject to these principles, regard should be paid to history. Their scheme provided for twenty-five members, of which the Corporation had the largest representation—seven

[1] Southampton Harbour Board Commission, Report, pp. 1–3.

members. In this reduction of local control over its port Southampton thus underwent the same transformation as a number of other ports.[1]

Another critical phase of the town's history was the proposal and eventual failure of the scheme for an independent and rival railway access to the Midlands. The history of the definite endeavours to achieve this purpose goes back at least as far as 1845, when an effort was made to establish more direct contact with Manchester and the north. Repeated attempts were subsequently made, but they broke down on the difficulties in raising money and on the opposition of the London and South Western Railway. Matters came to a head in 1873 and 1880 when the Didcot, Newbury and Southampton Junction Railway Acts were passed, empowering the company to construct 34 miles of railway at Didcot, passing through Newbury and terminating by a junction with the South Western system near Cobley Wood, Overton. The line was to be worked by the Great Western Railway. The attitude of the Council was made abundantly clear in a resolution which it passed in 1879:[2]

> That the Council deems it expedient, and active steps be taken, to develop the capacity of the port by an independent direct railway communication between Southampton and the manufacturing districts of the kingdom.

A further development of the scheme was a proposed independent line from the company's line at Burghclere to the town itself. The line was to pass over the South Western system near West Station to the main station on the Western Shore at the end of what is now Bargate Street, and the line was then run to the Royal Pier, where the Company was to have a separate jetty. This proposal was warmly taken up by the town, and the Corporation agreed to convey the Mudlands "between Blechynden and the Town Quay, subject to the consent of the Town meeting." The meeting unanimously

[1] On the whole question, see Report of Southampton Harbour Board Commission, Cd. 6347, and the Minutes of the Proceedings.

[2] March 8th.

passed a resolution supporting this proposal, as well as a further suggestion that the Council should obtain power to subscribe £50,000 to the line.[1] The Company obtained its Act, which authorized the scheme, and despite the opposition of the South Western Railway, thirty-three acres of Mudland were conveyed to the new Company. The work of fencing and excavation was in progress by the spring of 1883, both at Winchester and Southampton, as and when possession of the land could be obtained, and by July 1883[2] the whole of the land required for that portion of the line which was to be constructed immediately had been acquired. The relations between the London and South Western Railway and the Great Western Company, which had agreed to work the Didcot Company's line, were far from friendly. After some years a change of policy and financial reasons led to the Didcot Company's extension into Southampton being abandoned by that Company's Act of 1889. In lieu thereof they obtained powers to make a branch line about two and a quarter miles long from Winchester to the London and South Western Railway's main line at Shawford; this was opened in 1891. The land acquired at Southampton was ultimately disposed of by the Didcot Company. Thus the project miscarried.

There can be no doubt that the future of the port would have been profoundly modified, for good or ill, by the appearance of the competitive railway. Competitive rates and the interest in the port by another railway system with a more industrialized territory than that of the South Western Railway were the advantages on one side of the account. On the other hand, unless the new project had greatly augmented the traffic, it is doubtful whether the dock company would have been able to raise capital enough to make the extensions which the increasing size of the ships demanded. It is the secure knowledge that the gains of enlarging traffic at the docks and

[1] Council Minutes, June 4, 1881.

[2] A detailed statement relating to legal and other aspects of the projects, including a tracing of the plans, were courteously supplied by the Great Western Railway Company.

by rail will not have to be shared with competitors that has enabled the Southern Railway to embark on its policy of systematic extension.

With the transfer of the docks and the Mudlands, and their industrial potentialities, the main sources of prosperity passed out of the control of the town in its corporate aspect, but the local inhabitants in their business capacity were also affected. The most vivid impression of the changed atmosphere can be obtained from an incident in the development of the Union Steamship Company. This Company, following the example of the P. & O. Line, proposed to remove its head office, staff, and even steamers to the Port of London. As far back as 1871 there appears an entry in the Town Council minutes of March 8th, referring to a deputation in which the Council joined to meet the directors of the Company regarding their rumoured removal. The matter came up again later, and a description by a local writer in the *Graphic*, British Association Supplement of 1883, will convey the issues. After claiming that the Union Line was "of purely Southampton growth" and at first was confined to the coal-carrying trade, he goes on to describe the efforts made to induce the Company to reverse its announced decision regarding removal. Proposals were made to establish a new line of Cape steamers, and projects set afoot to improve the port. A defence committee was formed and excited meetings held; the meetings of shareholders, he says, were in favour of Southampton, but the polls of shareholders against it. Questions of law were raised, and while these awaited court decisions an enlarged body of directors, the majority of which were favourable to Southampton, assumed management. Then comes a claim, the implication of which throws into such significant relief the contrast with present conditions:

> The carrying out of the proposed change was thus effectually delayed, and in the meantime there has been such a large acquisition of shares by residents in Southampton that the port now virtually controls the voting power. Hence it is generally supposed that what-

ever may be the result of the appeal to law no removal of steamers will now take place, since the ultimate decision must be with shareholders and that is assured in favour of Southampton.

At present the majority of the greater businesses are either non-local in origin or are non-locally controlled. The large ship-repairing firms, the tobacco factory, and the electrical firms are examples of this, while retail distribution has not been left untouched by this development. Southampton is a rationalized town. The significance of this for our present study is that the town presents a sharp contrast to such a port as Newcastle, where many local men have built up large businesses and fortunes on exporting, shipping, and manufacturing. Most of Southampton's fortunes are derived from sources found in and around any large town, such as retail distribution, building, and estate development, and in consequence it shows a smaller proportion of very large and large fortunes than in other ports where manufacturing or import and export houses run by local men are more prominent. In the sense here implied, Southampton is a gate for traffic and wealth, rather than a point of its origination.

CHAPTER II

POPULATION

THE standard of living of any population depends on the relative numbers of those who are of the industrially productive and of the dependent ages, and these proportions are themselves the consequence of birth, death, and migration rates. Since these are variable factors, a full appreciation of the meaning of any ascertained incidence of poverty involves some study of their strength and of the direction in which they have been moving.

The history of Southampton's growth in population contains nothing striking like the rise of the textile towns in the early nineteenth century or the development of the great London conurbation in the twentieth. The industrial changes of last century offered Southampton no comparable stimulus or opportunity, and in the same way the shift of population in the present has brought it only a moderate increase of numbers. The figures below set forth the chief facts in its development.

It was an insignificant place at the date of the first census, though its rate of growth from that date was consistently faster than that of Hampshire and of England and Wales. From 1801 to 1861 the percentage intercensal increases of the county's population varied between 12 and 19 per cent, and of England and Wales between 11 and 15 per cent, while Southampton showed increases which were never lower than 20 per cent and twice exceeded 40 per cent. The absolute numbers involved were nevertheless small, the greatest addition in any decade up to the boundary extensions toward the end of the century being 12,000.

It will be observed that the greatest rate of growth occurs between 1831 and 1861. Reversals of fortune have shown that its striking physical advantages alone were an insufficient basis for permanent prosperity. The loss of the French provinces

GROWTH OF POPULATION: SOUTHAMPTON AND OTHER AREAS

	1801	1831	1861	1891	1901	1911	1921	1931
SOUTHAMPTON—								
Numbers	7,913	19,324	46,960	65,325	104,824	119,012	160,994	176,007
Increase per cent	—	144·2	143·1	39·1	60·5	13·5	35·3	9·3
HANTS—								
Increase per cent	—	43·2	53·5	55·2	15·6	18·9	5·7	11·0
ALL URBAN AREAS—								
Increase per cent	—	—	—	15·4	15·2	11·1	5·2	4·9
ENGLAND AND WALES—								
Increase per cent	—	56·3	44·3	44·5	12·8	10·9	5·0	5·4

PERCENTAGE RATE OF INTERCENSAL INCREASE IN CERTAIN AREAS

	1901	1911	1921	1931
Present Borough area	30·7	17·6	11·8	9·3
Added areas*	52·0	34·5	18·1	—
Town Planning area†	29·2	17·2	10·9	10·3
Electricity supply area	31·4	19·6	10·1	11·2
Water supply area	27·2	19·7	10·8	12·1
Gas supply area	31·3	19·4	10·5	13·7

* Figures for 1931 not available.
† I.e. borough area, plus area outside borough included in Scheme No. 1.

and the change of the channels of trade which followed the Great Discoveries had destroyed the wool and the wine trade on which its welfare had rested in mediaeval times, and also removed the occasions of the military expeditions which so frequently sailed from its harbour. The short period at the end of the eighteenth century during which it played the role of a fashionable health resort was terminated when the French wars took away the nobility and gentry who patronized it. There was scarcely any real basis for such a development; the chances of history both created and destroyed it. The addition of advantages derived from human invention, the steamship, the constructed dock and a railway line from London, were necessary if it were to have any hold upon the commercial life of the country, and the thirty years referred to must be regarded as its "industrial revolution," though the immediate consequences as measured by the growth of population were modest enough. It was between these census dates that important events in its economic history occurred. In 1835 the Commercial Steam Packet Company was formed, and in the next year the dock company seriously undertook the development of the port. The construction of the railway line from London commenced, the sections from Southampton to Winchester and from London to Basingstoke being completed in 1839 and the intervening gap closed by 1840. In 1851 the inner dock was completed.[1]

The second feature of its recent growth has been the diminishing rate of increase. This is but a consequence of the fall in the rate of natural increase by excess of births over deaths, combined with a modest addition by immigration from other parts of the country. It would not be necessary to emphasize or enlarge upon it were it not for the marked inclination which exists to exaggerate its possible rate of growth, a tendency it has shared with many other towns, both British and American.[2] If we take the growth of population in the present borough

[1] Hearnshaw, *Short History of Southampton*, 1910, pp. 116–128.

[2] Aronovici, "Let the Cities Perish," *Survey Graphic*, 1932.

area, in the areas added by the extensions of 1895 and 1920, and in the various technical areas named, both the absolute and percentage increases have declined. In this respect its experience is common with that of the regions surrounding the other great ports.[1]

To what extent has this increase been drawn from other areas and what proportion is due to the excess of births over deaths? As far as the available data[2] permits, the following table shows the relative importance of these two sources.

GROWTH OF POPULATION BY NATURAL INCREASE AND MIGRATION

Year	*Increase of Population*	*Excess of Births over Deaths*	*Migration*
1873–1880	5,051	6,013	− 962
1881–1890	5,274	7,636	− 2,362
1891–1895	6,435	2,896	+ 3,539
1895–1896	22,400	785	+ 21,615[3]
1898–1901	11,029	5,698	+ 5,331
1901–1911	14,214	13,364	+ 850
1911–1920	11,671	9,147	+ 2,524
1920–1921	31,135	1,615	+ 29,520[3]
1921–1931	15,013	12,167	+ 2,846

It will be seen that from 1873 till 1890, the town was not retaining its natural increase, but actually lost on balance over 3,300 of its own surplus of births over deaths. The turn of fortune takes place in the next decade. By 1895, the loss had been more than made good by the gain of over 3,500 newcomers. The complete period 1891–1901 shows—leaving out of account the increase due to the extension of boundary—a total addition from outside of not less than 8,870 persons, a figure never again reached. Thereafter the gain by migration, though continuing, is at a declining pace. We may compare

[1] Balfour Report on Industry and Trade, "Further Factors of Industrial Efficiency," p. 199.
[2] Census Reports, and information supplied by the Medical Officers of the various authorities.
[3] Extension of boundary.

these figures with those of two other ports, Hull and Cardiff. The former grew both by a heavy birth-rate and a considerable inward migration. Between 1871 and 1891 the natural increase was 47,900, and the gain by migration 30,700; between 1891 and 1911 the natural increase was 69,900 and the gain by migration 7,500. But in the next decade the town actually lost 17,700 of its own increase. In the case of Cardiff, boundary extensions break the continuity of the figures, but for some decades the movement is clear. Between 1881 and 1891 the growth was made up of 18,800 from natural increase and not less than 29,300 by additions from other areas. In the period 1901–11, however, the natural increase of 17,900 was balanced by a loss of 7,000 to other areas, and in the succeeding ten years only 67 persons were added from outside.

From what areas did these migrants to Southampton come? We can get some light on this from a study of the census figures relating to birthplaces, though unfortunately the details for 1921 were not published.

BIRTHPLACES OF THE POPULATION OF SOUTHAMPTON, 1861–1911

(Numbers per 10,000 *of the Population)*

District	1861	1871	1881	1901	1911
South-Eastern	7,920	7,000	7,290	7,130	7,100
South-Western	973	1,306	1,173	947	779
London	327	455	412	468	478
Eastern	68	98	104	142	156
Midlands	190	317	307	396	420
North-Western	42	63	47	127	161
Yorkshire and Northern ..	55	77	93	106	123
Wales, Scotland, and Ireland	266	312	286	281	296
Others, including not stated	159	372	288	403	487

NOTE.—Borough extended, 1895.

The outstanding fact is that consistently about three-quarters of the inhabitants were born in the South-Eastern counties of Hampshire, Sussex, Berkshire, and the extra-metropolitan parts of Surrey and Kent; or, to change the emphasis, that one in every four[1] of the population was born outside these areas, i.e. came in from some distance. Strips of Dorset and Wiltshire are thrust into Hampshire, and these, the nearest points of any county outside the South-Eastern group, are respectively ten and twenty miles distant as the crow flies. If we include these two counties with the others, we can re-state the facts in this form: in 1861 twelve persons in every hundred had moved in from a distance of at least forty-five miles as the crow flies; in 1871 one in five, in 1901 nearly one in four, and in 1911 one in four persons. The mileage would, of course, be greater if road and rail distances had been taken. The consistent prominence of London and the South-Eastern counties as sources of origin is explainable on grounds of proximity and of occupational relationships. A rise of the ratio for any given area is not conclusive evidence of an influx from it, for the proportion would also increase if those born in other districts began to leave the town and return to their homes. A comparison of these proportions with the actual numbers as given in the census reports suggests that an influx from the West Midlands had commenced by 1861; its proportion increased until 1911, though between 1901 and 1911 an excess of males had turned into the more usual excess of females. In 1861 and 1871 the North-Western counties were not important contributors, but their share was increasing, and by 1901 and 1911 their representation had increased and contained more males than females. On the other hand, the influx from the South-Western counties, which had been consistently the most important element from outside the South-Eastern group, rose rapidly up to 1871 and then declined till it presumably ceased between 1901 and 1911, for in the later years not only the proportion but even the absolute numbers declined. This influx, natural on account of the proximity of the source to Southampton, was noteworthy for the fact that it always showed a dominance of females. It

[1] This proportion holds good in two other towns in these counties, Brighton and Portsmouth in 1861 and 1911.

consisted, no doubt, largely of women from rural districts seeking domestic service, and the development of Bournemouth may have proved a more obvious outlet for them. In 1911 Dorset-born people were more numerous in the town than people from any other county outside Hampshire itself, being more than one in every ten of the population; and they were overwhelmingly females (sixteen women to ten men).

The second source of increase is the surplus of births over deaths. The downward trend of the birth-rate since 1870 is as striking in the case of Southampton as for the whole country, but there are some interesting differences between its movement in this port and the country generally, which tend to confirm earlier conclusions. In the period in which it was losing by migration, 1873–90, and for the five years thereafter, its crude birth-rate was consistently below that of the country as a whole. Thus in 1871–75 the average crude rate for England and Wales was 35·5, for Southampton 34·4; in 1891–95, the respective average rates were 30·5 and 30·0. After this date, in its years of expansion, its crude rate rose slightly above that of England and Wales generally, for the next two five-year periods. From 1906 to 1915 it was once again below the rate for the whole country; but there was a slight upward turn in the last year or two. In Hull the birth-rate has been consistently high. It was 38·9 per 1,000 in 1871–75, and since then its quinquennial average rate has been about 4 per 1,000 higher than that of the country generally. In Cardiff the rate has had a similar history, showing an excess of some four or five per 1,000 in 1886–90, though the excess grew smaller in the post-war period. Compared with these towns, therefore, Southampton's crude rate is closely similar in magnitude and speed of fall to that of the country generally, being neither consistently higher, as in Hull and Cardiff, nor consistently lower, as in Bournemouth, nor erratic in movement as in Portsmouth.

The marriage-rate has been maintained, though there has been some postponement of marriage, and a consequent shortening of the fertile period. In 1861, 6·5 per cent of the married persons were under 25 years of age, and in 1921 only 4·7 per cent. (The increased expectation of life would cause some fall by increasing the proportion of persons over 25 years of age.) As a result of these changes, the fertility of marriage has declined, for whereas the crude birth-rate shows between 1880–82 and 1920–22 a fall of 31·4 per cent, the number of births per 1,000 married women aged 14 to 44 years declined by 38·3 per cent.

The bearing of these vital movements on the general standard of life is made clear by their effect on the age composition of the population. The effect on the proportions of the population which are dependent and of working ages can be seen from the figures:

PROPORTIONS OF POPULATION OF DEPENDENT AND WORKING AGE

(*Numbers per* 10,000 *of the Population*)

		Under 10 Years	*10 and under 70 Years*	*70 Years and over*	*Total*
Males	1861	1,234	3,398	68	4,700
	1921	935	3,781	137	4,853
Females	1861	1,244	3,952	104	5,300
	1921	935	4,004	208	5,147

The proportion in the central age group has thus increased by 11 per cent in the case of men and 3 per cent in the case of women. If the limits of the central age group had been 15–65 the contrast between the two years would have been increased. It is important to see Southampton's situation against that of other areas. The figures below compare the proportions of the population of various ages with the corresponding proportions in England and Wales.

It has a greater number of young and fewer old dependents than the country generally, but less young children than Hull and Liverpool, though more than Cardiff. In the case of males, the excess as compared with England and Wales is especially

RELATIVE PROPORTIONS OF PERSONS OF WORKING AND DEPENDENT AGES IN CERTAIN PORTS AND OTHER TOWNS, 1921

(Numbers in each Age Group per 1,000 of the Population)

Years of Age	*England and Wales*	*Southampton*	*Bournemouth*	*Portsmouth*	*Hull*	*Cardiff*	*Liverpool*
MALES							
Under 10	91	93	62	94	99	91	104
10 and under 70	372	378	303	382	377	396	365
70 and over	14	14	21	13	12	11	9
All ages	477	485	386	489	488	498	478
FEMALES							
Under 10	90	93	63	91	99	91	103
10 and under 70	413	401	513	399	397	397	405
70 and over	20	21	38	21	16	14	14
All ages	523	515	614	511	512	502	·522
Number of females to 100 males ..	110	106	159	104	105	101	109

marked in the industrially active years of 30–60; Liverpool, on the other hand, shows a deficiency in these ages. Bournemouth, with its great relative excess of elderly people, and of the women whose business it is to care and provide for them in various ways, provides a striking contrast.

In brief, the result of these comparisons is to show that Southampton is increasing at a decreasing pace, though its growth has slackened less than that of other great ports, that after a period of loss by migration, it is growing by moderate additions from other areas. Its birth-rate has followed closely that of the country generally, and is lower than that of Hull, Cardiff, or Liverpool. In consequence, the proportions of those of the industrially productive ages has increased, a fact so far making for a higher average standard of living; and it is considerably better off in this respect for certain ages, than England and Wales generally.

CHAPTER III
INDUSTRIES

In studying the bearing of Southampton's industrial structure on the standard of life, we have to press beyond the more obvious facts relating to the different classes of skill which these industries require, and ask further what proportions of its population depend on the fluctuations of the international, national, and regional markets, and why this particular distribution of effort between these markets took place. The geographical advantages, such as favourable tides and proximity to London, need no discussion, for the real interest lies not in the simple facts which indicate that there will be a substantial traffic in passenger and certain classes of perishable goods, but in the more detailed differences which determine whether Southampton, London, or Bristol shall be victorious in the struggle for the marginal ten per cent of traffic.[1] It is precisely at this point that detailed information is wanting. In any case something depends on the industrial growth of the vicinity, for the success of its hinterland in attracting industries is another aspect of the same competitive struggle. Similarly, an endeavour ought to be made to determine the boundaries of the markets for its various products and services, and since these boundaries themselves have to be explained, we have to enquire into the relative strength of the "pulls" which the town's various advantages exercise in drawing industries to the area and in retaining them. We are still far off the time when employers are willing to supply in enough detail information relating to their material, labour, and other costs to make an inductive test of any particular theory of the location of industries possible, and for the time being one must rest content with illustrative rather than conclusive statements of the motives and advantages which brought typical businesses to the town.

[1] See Colson, *Transport et Tariffs*, Section on competition between ports.

We may approach the matter by observing the distinction between the town's geographical, administrative, and "economic" areas. Certain of these are clearly defined for obvious technical reasons; three services supplying gas, water, and electricity have the limits of their supply areas outside the borough boundary. The town-planning area, which has to concern itself with traffic and other problems, also protrudes into the surrounding country. Their populations in 1931 were for gas 238,000, water 271,000, electricity 210,000, and for the borough area plus additions for town-planning, 181,000. These technological areas may be compared with that visualized by Professor Rishbeth in the *Southampton Civic Survey*. He points out that a circle of three miles radius, having its centre at Six Dials, would include not only the present town and its northward extensions, but also the area on the other side of the Test, opposite the new dock works. Southampton thus defined includes three land areas separated by two rivers. In one sector, the little peninsula, the historic town developed, and building has pushed northwards to the circumference. In the other sector, Woolston grew into the urban district of Itchen, and was later absorbed by the town. Two of the three sectors are thus partly filled in with population; and if the reclaimed area develops industrially as it is expected to do, a new residential district may arise opposite in the third, Marchwood district, for a ferry service would make it more accessible than the outer portions of the Itchen sector. The gas supply area does, but the electricity area does not include this district. It is included in the regional planning scheme. The "dormitory" area of Southampton is harder to define, but it certainly reaches to Chandlers Ford and for a few persons as far as Compton, on the north side, and across the water to Hythe on the other. In contrast to these fairly definite limits are its curiously equivocal economic affiliations with other regions, arising from the lack of a dense population in its immediate hinterland, and its central position on the south coast. Does it "belong" to the south-west or the south-east of England? For the purpose of electrical development it is included in the south-western area and looks to Bristol. The divisional office of the Ministry of Labour is also at Bristol; and it was organized in the south-west district for the Ministry of Munitions during the war. The head or divisional offices of some businesses and agencies are similarly located. On the other hand, it is included in the traffic area controlled by the Commissioner at Reading. The Ministry of Health, for Poor Law purposes, regards it as a part of the south-eastern area. Certain firms make Southampton itself a divisional centre, and include in the area so controlled a territory which goes east of Chichester, north of Haslemere, Petersfield, and Andover, north-west of Salisbury and of Bridport, and includes the Isle of Wight and the Channel Islands. A much less definite but no less vital region is that which imports freights through Southampton. What proportion of goods traffic passing through the docks consists of industrial materials and consumable products for its immediate region? What proportion of it passes out of the hinterland into another area? In view of the trade disturbances of the last few years, and of the number of transport firms involved, it is not easy to provide any precise normal figure, but from enquiries of various firms, it appears that the following broad statement would give a reasonable picture of the situation. Leaving aside transit goods, rather over 500,000 tons of freight are normally imported through the main docks, and another 99,000 tons through the Town Quay. Of the larger figures some 30,000 tons, or 6 per cent, left by road. What was the radius served by road-borne traffic? A little less than half goes to London, about one-quarter to distances up to twenty miles, and about one-fifth a further twenty miles. Apart from the London area, therefore, the main service area of the docks road traffic is within forty miles radius. If we turn to rail traffic the picture is different in several respects. The main market is again the London area, potatoes and fruit being obvious examples, but many consignments are to more remote places. Thus 25,000 tons to 30,000 tons of wool are imported, and of this Yorkshire takes a share, as well as of hides, skins, and mohair. Timber goes mainly to the surrounding region, but also to Somerset and Birmingham. Of the 30,000 tons of meat imported, two-thirds pass on to London, the great bulk of it by road, but four-fifths of the rail-borne meat goes to such places as Oxford, Banbury, Cheltenham, and Birmingham. Fruit also goes to Manchester, Birmingham, and Newcastle.

In discussing the separate industries we may commence with the group connected with the construction, repair, and furnishing of ships. The number of insured persons engaged in this industry was about 4,000 in 1930, though it was nearer 5,000 in 1928. Briefly, from the present point of view four types of firms may be distinguished—(1) those engaged in the construction of light war vessels, e.g. Messrs. Thornycroft; (2) those engaged in repair and overhaul of liners: Messrs. Harland and Woolf, Thornycroft, J. and S. White; (3) those engaged in the construction and repair of yachts and high-speed motor boats, which include Camper Nicholson, J. and S. White, and others; (4) small boat building. The lines of distinction between some of these types are not hard and fast, but they are of some importance, since the changes of demand for war vessels and new commercial construction are different in origin and kind from those affecting expensive yachts, or repairs to passenger liners. The severity of the depression is due to the coincidence of disarmament, adverse trade conditions affecting the incomes of those whose hobby is yachting, and its spread to the luxury Atlantic passenger traffic. The firms vary in size, as tested by the numbers employed, from depression figures of roughly 2,500 (Harland and Woolf), 1,900 (Thornycroft), to 500 (Camper Nicholson) and 80 (British Power Boat Company).

The history of two firms will suffice to illustrate the development of this industry. In 1860[1] John Isaac Thornycroft, at

[1] This account is based on printed material supplied by the firm, and on information given in interview by Mr. T. Donaldson.

the age of seventeen, constructed a motor launch, four years later started the Chiswick shipyard for building small launches, and in 1873 patented the Thornycroft screw propeller. The firm was strengthened by the partnership with J. Donaldson, an association which lasted until the latter's death in 1899. It did not become a public company until 1901. Speed and light construction were the aim, and the firm was prominent in the development of the torpedo-boat industry. In the first decade of the century competition in naval building between England and Germany became acute; building was increasing and along with the enlarged navy came an increased amount of repairing, so that the firm had opportunities of developing its special class of work. On the other hand, there was a constant tendency on the part of the Admiralty to enlarge the size of torpedo boats, but the firm was building to the capacity that the Chiswick yard would allow; and there was the further difficulty of the "measured mile" for trials. A site near Portsmouth would have obvious advantages. Eventually, the firm purchased the existing yard from a firm which had been engaged in commercial constructing and repairing. The move had many advantages, for besides destroyers and fast river vessels, all classes of moderate-size vessels could be built; and there was extensive repair work. The firm had been appointed by the Admiralty to fit out merchant vessels for transport and other purposes in the event of war; and during the war, some twenty-nine destroyers were built and over 500 war vessels repaired, so that the numbers employed in the Woolston yard and the docks together reached 6,000. Since the war, the firm has naturally suffered from the decline in commercial building and war-vessel construction, and in the last two or three years, from economies which shipping companies have been compelled to make.

In contrast to this, one may take a firm of local origin, that of Day, Summers & Co.,[1] founded in 1834. Mr. Summers

[1] Southampton Harbour Board Commission, Evidence of W. Summers, Proceedings, q. 571–96, 619. Also from information supplied in interview by Mr. Graham Day.

was a Southampton engineer, who, after experimenting with engines for transport on land, turned his attention to marine engines. Mr. Day had been connected with the East India Company, and, after his retirement to Southampton, agreed to assist in financing Summers's enterprise, and works and yard were eventually established at Northam. The firm was in many ways a pioneer one, for not only did it build ships for the P. & O., Royal Mail, and Hamburg-American Lines, but in 1862 took out patents for its traversing tripod sheer legs, and in the following year its patents for slipway machinery. These patents, especially the former, were very popular, and the firm made great progress in these directions. Yacht building was also part of its activities. The number employed in normal times was about 700, though this rose to about 1,000 during the war. The firm had remained a personal one. Latterly the Summers connections with it had ceased, and its management passed from father to sons in the Day family. The continued depression in shipbuilding brought the firm to an end in 1928, and the property and patents were sold.

There is next a group of industries which may be regarded as attendant upon shipping and shipbuilding industries. These include such diverse businesses as Parsons Marine Motors, Southampton Oxygen Company, Allen Liversidge & Co., and the British Oxygen Company; and the Solent Carpet works. The first of these businesses was founded in 1904,[1] its product being marine and stationary oil-engines of various kinds. The head of the business, Mr. H. Parsons, designed a light van with a single valve, and arranged for a Southampton firm to manufacture them. The firm went into liquidation, the present owner took over the business, and started on the present site. The van seems to have been before its time, for it was not taken up, but the engine was adapted for marine work, and is now used for emergency sets on large ships and on fast river boats. The countries supplied include the West Indies, Africa, the Malay States, Siam, and a number of

[1] From information supplied in interview by Mr. H. Parsons.

South American States. The various oxygen firms are, of course, depots or branches of firms having connections in other areas. The Solent Carpet Company manufacture carpets, rugs, and velvet coverings for furniture for use in ships. From the nature of the market, the size of these business units is small, ranging from seventy persons to sufficient to run an easily managed depot. The total numbers employed are about 130 to 140 adults and juveniles. We may also add various firms making and supplying yacht and other ship equipment, as distinct from furnishing. Five firms or sections of firms employ about 60 persons on this work.

Another industry related to the town's transport advantages is the manufacture of aircraft. For seaplane manufacture and testing, the area offers the obvious facilities that the Schneider Cup contests have advertised, though the fact that the water is used by shipping may be some disadvantage. The Super-Marine Aviation[1] works sprang out of the enthusiasm of a small group of sportsmen who turned their attention from yachting to flying, Mr. Pemberton Billing being among them. Eventually the firm was founded at Woolston in 1921. The personal origin of the enterprise is sufficient to account for its location in Southampton, but the fact that the craft were designed not so much as aeroplanes to float, but as flying boats, also gave the town attractions. For the early models were of wooden structure, and there was an ample supply of craftsmen experienced in hull building. Various technical problems, such as the making of the craft seaworthy without endangering air performance, needed solution if the firm were to prosper. The construction of the craft has been changed from wood to metal, but while this adds to the useful load of the craft and saves water soakage, it requires a different labour skill from that initially relied upon. It has also undergone a business revolution, and has been controlled by Vickers (Aviation) Ltd. since 1928. The varied demands of Govern-

[1] From certain printed information and material supplied by various members of the firm.

ments must obviously be of importance in its markets, for it is for coastal defence and accompanying fleets to sea that such craft are adapted. The firm normally employs 600 to 700 workers, but this number naturally varies with the Government demands. The Avro works are outside the borough, and have also been purchased by outside interests. A smaller firm commenced production at Southampton but later removed to the Isle of Wight.

So far we have dealt with the shipbuilding industry and the businesses related to or dependent upon it. Fresh considerations arise when we turn to general manufacturing. The consumers of products include not only those widespread buyers for whose service the work is permanently undertaken, but the producers and their dependents themselves. The mere growth of an area by the addition of more producers thereby adds to its consuming power and makes further growth possible. It is for this reason that, compared with other ports, the comparatively sparse population of much of Southampton's hinterland constitutes an initial difficulty in its powers of attracting miscellaneous industries, against the competitive pull of more populous centres. Granted this limitation, in order to develop it must push out of its market area (the boundary of which is the limit to which the products can be competitively delivered), by advantages in transport, labour, and other costs. Any industry using non-local imported materials which are "weight-losing," or destroyed in the process of manufacture, may save transport costs if it is located at the point of importation, especially if part of its product is locally marketed, or is exported. If a local material forms a main part of the weight of the product, it may be conveniently situated near the source of the material. On the other hand, it may be cheaper to be located at a port if some of the material is imported, and if other bulky material is obtained from the surrounding region. Southampton affords several examples illustrative of these principles. Another important variable affecting the radius of the market is labour costs. Granted

RATES OF WAGES OF CERTAIN CLASSES OF SKILLED AND UNSKILLED LABOUR

		Southampton	*London*	*Bristol*	*Hull*	*Liverpool*	*Newcastle*	*Cardiff*
Engine shop labourers	(per week)	41/–	45/3½	39/6 to 44/–	45/–	41/– to 42/9	42/6 to 43/6	49/6
Electrical installation wire men	(per hour)	18d.	22½d.	19½d.	19½d.	19½d.	19½d.	19½d.
Vehicle building, skilled men	(per hour)	17d.	18½d.	18d.	18d.	18d.	18d.	18d.
Shipbuilding repairing—								
Shipwrights on repair work	(per week)	63/–	69/–	70/–	63/–	64/–	63/–	70/–
Ship joiners on repair work	(per week)	63/–	69/–	70/–	63/–	67/–	63/–	70/–
Labourers	(per week)	41/–	54/–	52/–	42/6	50/6	41/–	54/–
Cabinet makers	(per hour)	18d.	21d.	18d.	19½d.	20½d.	18½d.	—
Upholsterers	(per hour)	17d.	21d.	18d.	19½d.	20½d.	18d.	—
Building—								
Craftsmen	(per hour)	17½d.	20½d.	19d.	19d.	20½d.	19d.	19d.
Labourers	(per hour)	13¼d.	15½d.	14¼d.	14¼d.	14¾d. to 15½d.	14¼d.	14¼d.
Local authorities—								
General yard labourers	(per week)	48/3	60/5	9/11 per day	52/–	51/9	—	54/10
Tram conductors	(per week)	52/6 to 55/6	64/– to 73/–	—	56/6 to 59/6	56/8 to 61/5	56/6 to 62/6	54/6 to 59/6
Printing—								
(General assistants, book jobbing work)	(per week)	49/6	—	55/6	53/6	57/6	55/6	55/6

uniform transport costs, low labour costs will enable one centre to reach farther from its base than another centre with high labour costs. Since Southampton is still a port, and not primarily an industrial centre, the wage level is low rather than high. This constitutes an advantage which "pulls" as against other areas, especially where the proportion of labour to the total cost per ton of the product is relatively high. Wage comparisons between localities are notoriously difficult, but the list of rates on page 42 recognized in different industries, as on December 31, 1930, will be enough to indicate that the prevailing wage levels in Southampton were generally lower than in other ports. A comparison of the various labourers' rates and rates of semi-skilled work will strengthen this view:[1]

With these general considerations in mind we may survey briefly a number of the chief enterprises whose history and activity illustrates the various principles. The enterprise of the British American Tobacco Company is the result of a fusion of interests of several firms. The entire product is for exportation to foreign and colonial markets, mainly Eastern ones, including the Straits Settlements, Java, India, Ceylon, China, and the Persian Gulf; New Zealand, Africa, etc. These places are on the whole well served by the shipping of the port. The material is costly, and in its raw state bulky, requiring a lot of storage. The output of the smaller factory at Millbrook required approximately some four million pounds of tobacco annually, and supplies had at first to be drawn from Bristol, Liverpool, and London, for the firm could only carry small stocks in the town itself. From 1927 onwards, after various changes of premises, large new factories were erected in Millbrook, with a possible output at full capacity involving the use of 15,000,000 lb. of tobacco annually. The factory produces cigarettes only, but there are subsidiary operations of packing-case making and tin-box making. The labour employed is dominantly that of women and girls, who are engaged in

[1] Twentieth Abstract of Labour Statistics, Cmd. 3831. See also Standard Time Rates of Wages and Hours of Labour, 1929. Ministry of Labour.

stemming, working in the cutting and leaf rooms, helping on the cigarette-making machines, packing, soldering, and labelling. The wages of the majority of the female workers are governed by the Tobacco Trades Board, and their rates range from 16s. per week as learners, to an adult rate varying from 25s. to 35s. per week. The male staff consists mainly of mechanics who keep various machines in running order. The firm has been suffering from political disturbances and the decline in the purchasing power of its silver-using Eastern markets. The staff employed before the onset of the depression was about 800, of which 600 were females. The new factory fully running would be able to take up to 2,000 workers.[1]

The firm of August Pellerin[2] had its origin in France, and is distinctive in that its manufacture of margarine was built up on the original processes of preparation from animal fats. M. Edmond Pellerin, who had a refinery in Paris, was early associated with the manufacture of margarine, and until 1891 the firm supplied its British market from Paris, but in that year the firm commenced production in Southampton. It used Pellerin's refined animal fats, which were sent via Le Havre. Of its other materials, certain refined animal fats needed to give smoothness and texture were imported, and the milk necessary in the process was obtained from the surrounding region. Since the firm commenced operations, the marketing situation has altered in two respects—the rise of manufacture on the basis of vegetable oils instead of animal fats, and the creation of a great margarine combine controlling a large number of retail stores. The firm, has, however, made continual progress, in particular by increasing its sales of cake and pastry margarines, and has adapted itself to the changing public taste for vegetable margarines for the table. Through an associated company, also an offshoot of an older French concern, in 1930 the works commenced the production of process packet cheese, for which it finds an enlarging sale. Its staff

[1] From detailed memorandum supplied by Mr. F. Thatcher.
[2] From printed material and information supplied in interview.

has consequently increased in numbers, and is now about 200.

The firm of Dixon and Cardus[1] was founded in 1840 by the two persons who gave the firm its name. It crushes linseed and cotton seed by hydraulic presses, producing feeding cake for cattle, linseed oil, and crude cotton oil, which is refined for margarine manufacture. Since the materials are imported —the cotton seed chiefly from Egypt, and linseed from India and the Argentine—the economy of conducting the crushing at the seaboard is sufficient to explain the location of this, as of practically all British crushing mills, at a port. The crushing capacity is from 18,000 to 20,000 tons per annum, and the firm generally crushes about 16,000 tons and employs between 80 to 100 men. The mills are most active in the winter, and in order to keep the presses warm and maintain a satisfactory flow of oil, the mills run in shifts night and day during this period. The firm's buying and marketing arrangements have been affected by changes in its commercial affiliations. The original firm was in due course turned into a limited company, and in later years the original families had no connection with it. Much of the capital of the company was held locally, but three years ago nearly the whole of it was purchased by the British Oil Cake Mills Ltd., which itself was a year later merged into the Unilever Combine. Several economies arose from this. Competitive buying of seeds, which was always troublesome to independent firms, was replaced by bulk purchasing; and the marketing of oil, for which the local outlets were more limited than in the case of feeding cake, was simplified, for the parent concern can distribute orders amongst its productive units to the best advantage. The market for feeding cake is local, the area included being Hampshire, Dorset, Wiltshire, and the Isle of Wight.

Eucryl Ltd.[2] began as a small private company in Hull to provide an outlet for phenol, a by-product of a tar-distilling

[1] Information supplied in written answers to questionnaire and in interview, by Mr. Walsh.

[2] Information supplied in interview by Colonel Methven.

works. The sales increased, especially in London, and works were consequently started in the London area. During the war the firm made great progress, partly on account of the reduced American competition, though this advantage was only temporary. In consequence the business was turned into a public company in 1920, and the premises in Southampton taken. The products include tooth paste, tooth powders, artificial tooth powder, lysol, etc. It has since added a subsidiary line of business in developing, printing, and enlarging photographs for retailers. From the point of view of location, apart from historical circumstances, the pertinent facts are that for some of its main chemical products much of the basic material is obtained locally; and that its sales are almost entirely outside the area. Fluctuations in Southampton's main employment would thus directly affect this part of the work but little. The photographic work is for obvious reasons drawn from the immediate area. The staff is mainly female, mostly girls of sixteen and upwards, and much of the work is at piece rates.

Electric wire and cable manufacture is concentrated in a single firm, Pirelli General. The business was founded in 1913 by an amalgamation of interests of Pirellis, of Milan, and the General Electric Company. The Southampton works were commenced in 1914, manufacture being started in the same year. At the outset it employed about 100 persons, but naturally grew during the war to nearly 2,000. Electrical development has expanded the firm's market, and it has been very successful in obtaining contracts. Since it was first established, plant has been erected at Eastleigh for heavy work, the lighter work being retained in Southampton. In considering the various items of cost, one may note that copper and rubber are imported, but any advantage so derived is lessened by the fact that some of this now goes to Eastleigh. On the other hand, much of the product goes to the North and the Midlands. The Welsh steam coal is rail-borne. Boiler-water is obtained from an artesian well in the works and from the town supply. The firm has found, as others have done, that the town is a favourable one from the point of view of labour costs and supply. The general workers have little to do but feed the machines and keep them in running order. The lighter work is divided about equally between men and women, the women tending, e.g. coil-winding, braiding and wrapping machines, calendering machines, etc., and the men attending to semi-automatic plants. In the Eastleigh works, on the other hand, the heavier work alters the ratio, the proportions being more like six males to one female. The transfer of work to Eastleigh has restricted the number employed in Southampton, but many whose work is in Eastleigh are resident in Southampton. Before the depression began the firm employed about 900 workers in the town.[1] Other electrical works include the manufacturing of switch gears. One firm removed their heavier export from Brighton, and by the end of 1930 they were employing over 200 men and boys. A wireless small-part manufacturer transferred his works from Cricklewood, as a better site was available here and labour costs were rather lower.

Between 600 and 700 persons are employed in commercial printing and bookbinding firms. These include the Southern Daily Echo Ltd. and its associated publications, and the Camelot Press. Both these firms have been growing, the former by reason of the enlargement of its circulation, the latter by reason of printing for outside firms, including London publishers. These two employ two-thirds of the numbers in this industry. The rest are in the main local printers with a local market. The Ordnance Survey Department with 800 workers is a special case.

The original business of Toogood's was founded in the year 1815 as a nursery for the propagation of trees, plants, etc., the growth and distribution of seeds being added by Mr. William Toogood about the year 1846. The firm was gradually developed into its present size with the help of his sons, and was formed into a company in the year 1919. Most of the

[1] Information supplied in interview.

seeds are grown in the United Kingdom. In the company's main distributing premises approximately 400 people are employed in sorting, cleaning, testing, and distributing the seeds. A large proportion of the products are sold in the home counties, but the firm's business is widely distributed and includes also an export trade.[1]

We now come to those businesses in the town which are engaged in making products and rendering services for the town's population, and that of the immediate neighbourhood. Thus there are about 1,400 insured persons engaged in restaurants, hotels, etc., over 300 in providing entertainment and games, over 800 in laundries, and about 700 in municipal tram and bus services, and 1,100 in other road transport, including bus services. These together show an increase since 1928 of 16 per cent to 18 per cent. Raised standards of consumption and change of habits help to explain part of this as they do similar increases everywhere. The increased numbers in transport are due to the decentralization of the town by building in its outer areas, together with the spread of the "touring" habit. In the case of laundries, the increase represents also the results of pushing out the market area through enlarging the delivery and collection radius by motor transport. This factor, together with the establishment of modern mechanical bakeries, accounts also for the increase of those employed in certain large bakeries, for not only has the home market been enlarged at the expense of the weaker competitors, but more efficient methods of motor delivery have enabled them to penetrate further into the surrounding area at the expense of smaller outlying bakeries.

The final group calling for examination includes the businesses engaged in retailing, and in understanding the structure of retail distributive trades we have to recognize a number of facts: (1) the changes in financial organization and control, i.e. the purchase of local stores by outside holding concerns.

[1] Information from statements supplied in reply to questionnaire, by Mr. T. Toogood.

(2) The division of the market in any one line of goods, e.g. food or drapery, into a number of partly competitive sub-markets. Firms may specialize in one of the several income grades of the consumers of that product and service. Alternatively, these sub-markets may be geographical, in the sense that what the consumer regards as a reasonable walking distance for the product in question may create little areas within which competition is limited. These two aspects are of importance in accounting for the number and size of the business units. (3) In the case of some trades the firms catering for specific income grades, especially the higher ones, may have a market reaching considerable distances into the surrounding countryside. (4) The number of units in any line of trade may rise or fall as compared with the population and numbers of families to be served, i.e. the service rendered may be spread over a larger, or performed by a smaller, total number of business units.

We may commence with the third of these questions. In certain lines of retailing, particularly in drapery and furnishing, the better-class stores have a market reaching some miles outside the town. Where, as in this case, there are two or more towns of considerable size close together (Bournemouth being 29 miles and Portsmouth being 25 miles distant from Southampton by rail), the volume of sales and in part, therefore, the volume of employment in these trades will turn upon the result of the competitive struggle for the custom of the populations lying between them. Where between Bournemouth and Southampton as competing centres is the boundary line drawn? Where between Portsmouth and Southampton? Such a market boundary is a "line of indifference," residence on any point of which implies that for the consumer there is nothing to choose in cost between either centre.[1] In the case of retail distribution, however, transport charges may for some

[1] Assuming simplified conditions, if the sale price is greater at one centre than the other, and if transport costs are on a mileage basis, then the line of indifference is a hyperbola, since this is a line such that the difference of any point on it from two fixed points is constant.

goods be negligible, and for others prohibitive beyond a certain radius. For a high-grade drapery store, the "transport costs" become the cost of the customer's personal visit, and if she be a car owner, the difference between one centre and another may be of little or no account. Difference of sale price, plus "other attractions" becomes the determinant; and these attractions may include other stores suited to the income grade of the customer. These, while partly competing against one another, exercise a pull on the surrounding area in proportion to their numbers by providing a greater range of choice, each firm gaining by the existence of the others. There are advantages in agglomeration for retailers as for manufacturers. The actual plotting of the area would be possible only if we secured from each purchaser, for each line of goods under investigation, a statistical account of his purchases from each centre. Failing this, we are driven back on the firms themselves. The "publicity" address lists represent hopes, not sales; a better test would be the distribution in the surrounding area of those having accounts at the respective stores; though this should in some way be modified by a "weighting" for the average annual purchase. The relative importance of credit and cash sales must also be borne in mind. A comparison of the areas of stores of a like grade in each of the centres would give a real idea of the hold of the respective centres over the surrounding territory. It has not been possible to arrange a full study of this kind, but one drapery store has been kind enough to provide a random sample (1 in 10) of locations in sufficient detail to permit of the data being mapped by parish, for the county of Hampshire, including the Isle of Wight. The result is an extremely interesting one, and illustrates with considerable force (1) the effective radius on the "land side" including the difficulty of making inroads into Portsmouth; (2) the effect of time and distance on the market in the Isle of Wight, those in direct communication with Southampton by water and with an easy additional land journey, i.e. Cowes and Newport, being represented, other parts of the Island obviously being

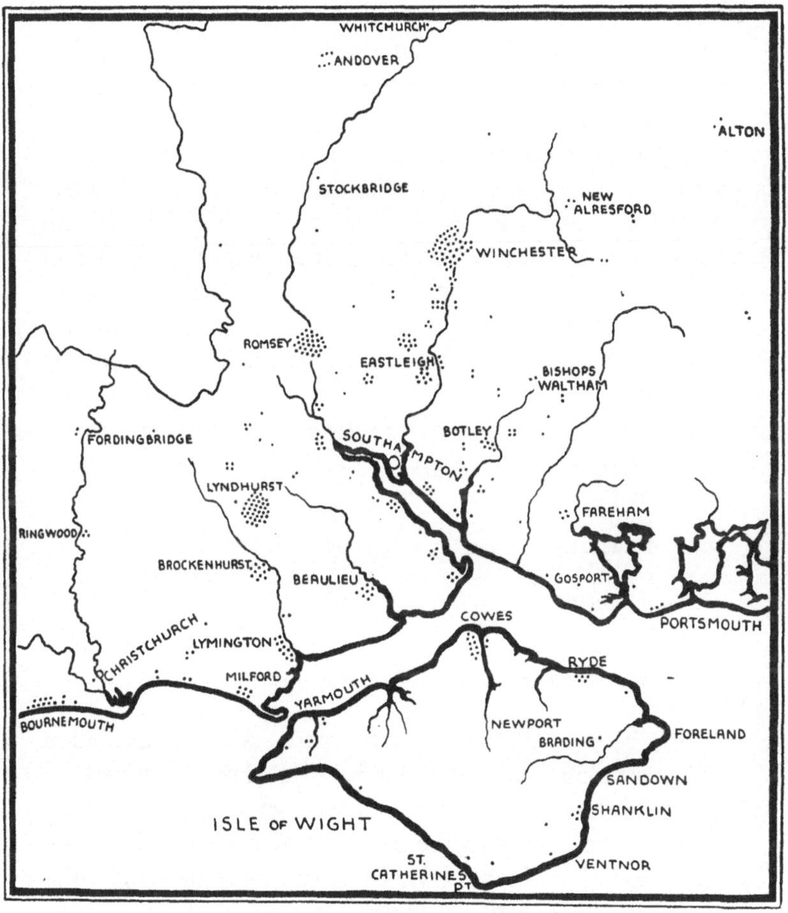

SOUTHAMPTON: A RETAIL MARKET AREA.

Showing the distribution of persons holding accounts at a local store (sample 1 in 10).

affected by the existence of an alternative route to the mainland.[1]

The next question for consideration is the number of shops in relation to the number of families and the size of the population. How far has there been an increase or decrease in the number of shops catering for each thousand families? Has the movement, positive or negative, been uniform as between dealers in different classes of goods? Is the volume of business tending to be spread over a larger, or concentrated in a smaller number of businesses? A preliminary view of the problem may be obtained from the Census of 1921, from which can be obtained the number of shops recorded, the number of private families, etc. Setting forth the ports and other towns with which comparisons have frequently been made in this study, in order of the magnitude of the population, the following facts appear:

	Persons per Shop	*Private Families per Shop*
Liverpool	54	11·6
Bristol	50	12·2
Hull	50	12·2
Newcastle	65	14·7
Cardiff	58	13·1
Southampton	58	13·8
Portsmouth	49	11·5
Bournemouth	55	12·5

It will be seen that amongst the ports, with the exception of Newcastle-on-Tyne, the numbers of shops relatively to families increases as the size of the town increases; though this is not the case with the numbers of persons. Newcastle is an exception in another way. In all the towns in the list, the number of shops with dwellings attached is three or four times greater than the number without dwellings—in Southampton and Liverpool over three and in Bristol over four times, but in Newcastle these proportions are completely reversed, those without dwellings being three times more

[1] For note on other maps relating to retail distribution, see Appendix III, p. 212.

numerous than those with dwellings. The populations living in the dwellings connected with shops is in other towns from five to seven per cent of the total, but in Newcastle it does not reach two per cent.

Some interesting trends are revealed if this comparison is applied to the separate classes of retail trade. The difficulty is that practically the only source of information is the directories, the accuracy of whose classified lists cannot be easily tested. Quite apart from large departmental stores, numerous

NUMBERS OF SHOPS AND FAMILIES

	Numbers of Shops		*Percentage Increase or Decrease*	*Numbers of Families per Shop* 1928
	1901	1928		
Grocers	209	337	+ 61	117
Butchers	90	127	+ 41	309
Confectioners ..	93	205	+120	192
Bakers	106	75	− 29	524
Tobacconists ..	51	117	+129	336
Drapers	87	98	+ 13	401
Chemists	38	50	+ 32	786
Jewellers	13	22	+70	1,786
Watch and clock-makers	44	39	−11	1,008
(Jewellers and Watch and clock-makers together)	57	61	+7	664
"Shopkeepers" ..	311	403	+ 30	98

shops carry on one or more lines of trade, and a decision has to be made whether we mean "shop" or "unit for the distribution of any given line of goods," the latter term making it possible to count a single shop more than once if it dealt in more than one class of goods. The small miscellaneous general shop has obviously to be excluded from any special trade. The above table shows for selected trades the relative growth in the number of shops, numbers of families, and the numbers of persons. By "shops" is here meant the number of distributive units, a number of adjacent shops which have been turned into a single set of premises, however numerous their entrances, were regarded as one shop; but separately located branches under a single business control were each counted separately. The figures therefore show the number of distributive units, irrespective of their size or their financial control.

The increases may be compared with the percentage increase of about 38 per cent in the numbers of persons, and in the numbers of families of about 46 per cent between the same dates.

There is some ambiguity in the term "confectionery" as its use for "sugar confectionery" in the trade board sense and baker and confectioner implies, but the direction of change in each case is in line both with the increased sale of sweets and with the decline in the numbers of bakers arising from the development of mechanical methods of production combined with motor delivery to the home. That the increase in the number of chemists should be smaller than either the growth of population or the number of families is to the outsider not so expected, for it would appear that various circumstances have enlarged the total volume of sales, so that the facts here would presumably represent an increased trade per unit. In the case of drapers the increased demand has everywhere been met partly by the growth in the size of the unit, and not by an increase in their number. The small percentage increase as compared with growth of either population and numbers of families is one indication of the extent to which this has been true of this area. The line of distinction drawn between jewellers and watchmakers is obviously also a very fine one. A variety of factors contribute to these results. A rising standard of life implies that a relatively smaller proportion of consumer's incomes will be spent on immediate necessities and more upon luxuries—witness the growth of sweet and tobacconists' shops. The development of "calling for orders" and of delivery over a wide radius has made it possible for the same number of units to do a greater amount of work than formerly. On the other hand, reasonable walking distance is of importance in certain lines of business where the incomes are low, and the purchases have to be made only at times and in such quantities as occasion may require; hence the decentralization of the population which has marked the town's development since the war gives rise to an increase in the number of units in the outer rim, which, though it may cause a decline in the prosperity of the existing "inner area" establishments, need not cause a corresponding rate of closure.

The number of families per shop, as defined, is also of interest. Any slight error in the estimated number of the families would scarcely affect the general proportions of the figures, an error of 1,000 for example, making a difference only of three in the number of families per grocer's shop. It is, perhaps, the comparatively small number of families per grocer's shop which is most striking, and if we take account of the fact that the small general shop also plays a part in this trade, this certainly represents the maximum number of families. The average grocer's shop thus makes its living on the families of a single lengthy street; and since this represents the average shop, it follows that the smaller concerns deal with a very limited range of families indeed. Mr. Lawrence Neal in his *Retailing and the Public* is inclined to see in the existence of so large a proportion of family shops (two-thirds to three-quarters of the total in some areas), with their many disadvantages in buying and selling, and relatively high levels of costs, one of the obstacles to scientific distribution, and points to the relatively low income earned by many of these. If comparisons are made with larger retail units, it is no doubt true that the earnings must seem meagre; but this comes partly of seeing retail distribution in isolation from other activities. If it is regarded as one of the numerous opportunities of earning a living, it is clear, on the contrary, that the possession of the small capital and perhaps extra keenness has enabled the owners of the small businesses to build up a family income both greater and in many ways more stable, than the pursuit of the manual occupations followed by their friends and relatives. The level of income for these marginal distributors has to be understood in the light of the alternative opportunities available.

A complete account of the business activities of an area should include some measure of the relative success of firms, and the severity of the pressure of adverse trade conditions, as tested by the numbers compelled to cease operations. True "mortality" figures, which would record the proportion of firms compelled to cease operations through losses are naturally difficult to obtain, and it is only of the much less numerous and more extreme examples when withdrawal from business involves bankruptcy also that we have any precise records. Even so, not all the cases come before the County Court, as when an outside firm with a local branch is dealt with elsewhere. Common observation of the numerous openings and closings suggest that the true mortality rate is many times heavier than the bankruptcies, but we have no exact measure of it. The number of residents whose bankruptcy cases came before the Southampton Court from 1928 to 1932 was 73, an average of about 15 cases a year, though the numbers actually rose from 9 cases in the relatively prosperous year of 1928 to 22 in 1932. From so small a number of cases it is not wise to draw too specific conclusions, but it may be observed that of the total number of cases, 28, or over one-third, involved retail distributors, and while these examples were spread widely amongst the various lines of retailing, grocers (5 cases) were the most numerous class. Various building trades, including builders' merchants, contributed 13 cases, but actual builders, 9 cases or 1 in 8 of the total, were the most strongly represented trade of all. Various concerns connected with road transport, including garages, formed 1 in 7 of the number. The aggregate liabilities of the bankruptcies varied between £12,000 and £17,000, except in 1932, when it rose to £38,600, of which £14,000 was accounted for by one firm.[1]

In conclusion, one aspect of the foregoing survey to which

[1] Information courteously supplied by the Official Receiver.

reference was made at the beginning may be reverted to, and this concerns the relative proportions of Southampton's working population which are chiefly dependent on the international, national, and local markets. This division is no doubt artificial, since in fact all the markets are interdependent, in the sense that a depression in the shipping will through unemployment and loss of earnings sooner or later affect employment in the local distributive trades and amongst those rendering personal services. It is true also that some firms work both for export, national, and local consumption, but these difficulties need not prevent us from obtaining a broad impression of the facts. We thus get a rough idea of the numbers exposed to the various types of risk of trade fluctuation. In 1930 there were over 16,000 insured persons engaged in shipping, 4,000 in shipbuilding, 4,200 in dock and port work, and a further 900 in tobacco and other manufacturing for export. The employment of 25,000 insured persons was subject to the fluctuations and risks of the "international" market. About half the seamen were non-resident, and if these are left out of account, this represents between 35 per cent and 36 per cent of the insured population.

Those producing for markets outside the immediate area are limited in number. If we add those engaged in cable making, and such of those employed in chemical making, food manufacture, printing, and certain miscellaneous work whose activity could be regarded as directed mainly to those "national" markets thus defined, the total would be only 2,400 or 2,700 persons, or between 4 per cent and 5 per cent of the insured population. To these there must be added some 800 engaged in the Ordnance Survey Department, who are non-insurable, but came into this category. The remainder, or about three-fifths of the entire number, are more closely related to the regional and purely local markets. Nearly one-fifth are engaged in retail distribution. The remaining two-fifths includes those employed in hotels, restaurants, entertainments, and games on the one hand, and tramways and other Corporation employment and building works construction. It includes certain employees of firms who, by mechanical improvements and motor delivery system, have pushed their market out beyond the town's boundaries, such as laundries, modern bakeries, as well as of sawmills and mineral-water makers whose market also extends beyond the administrative area.

CHAPTER IV

THE LABOUR MARKET

THE effects of the industrial make-up of Southampton, which results from the location of factors examined in the previous chapter, are shown by the census occupation figures. There were in 1921 59,900 males and 64,900 females over 12 years of age, and 51,700 of the former and 16,900 of the latter were returned as "occupied." In what occupations were these engaged? What proportion were in well-paid regular jobs, and what proportion in casual and seasonal occupations?

In the case of males, at the date of the census over one-quarter (27 per cent) were engaged in occupations connected with transport and communications, 14 per cent were metal workers, and 9 per cent were in financial and commercial occupations; 6 per cent were "miscellaneous" general labourers, 4 per cent were engaged in woodworking, furniture making, etc., and about the same proportion were clerks. The characteristic features of employment are clearly seen by comparing Southampton with other ports and neighbouring towns. The table below shows the proportion of every 1,000 males of twelve years and over who were engaged in occupations of local importance.

The table brings into relief very clearly the great dependence of Southampton on seafaring, shipbuilding, repairing, and dock work, and compared with Hull, Cardiff, and Bristol, the relative paucity of other opportunities. Hull has fisheries, and paint and oil manufacture, Cardiff has metal work, and Bristol has bootmaking, printing, and tobacco manufacture, though Liverpool is in this respect much more akin to Southampton. A similar comparison brings out the features of the women's labour market equally clearly. A smaller proportion of its females aged twelve years and upwards were returned as "occupied" than in any of the other towns, the figures of 260 per 1,000 females of those ages being in sharp contrast to

NUMBERS OF MALES EMPLOYED IN LOCALLY IMPORTANT OCCUPATIONS IN SOUTHAMPTON AND OTHER TOWNS, 1921

(*Numbers per 1,000 Males of 12 years and over*)

	Southampton	*Hull*	*Cardiff*	*Bristol*	*Liverpool*	*Bournemouth*
Seamen	102	55	80	15	60	—
Dock labourers	42	69	38	25	61	—
Bargemen	—	12	—	—	—	—
Shipbuilders	25	13	8	—	13	—
Boiler-makers, platers, and their labourers	36	10	12	—	—	—
Fitters	15	15	15	12	—	—
Sheet-metal workers	—	—	105	—	—	—
General undefined labourers ..	76	78	66	67	77	30
Drivers of horses and vans.. ..	10	16	11	19	29	15
Messengers and porters	—	—	—	13	39	—
Fishermen	—	17	—	—	—	—
Paint and oil..	—	26	—	—	—	—
Civil Service officials	14	—	12	22	—	10
Boot and shoe makers	—	—	—	18	—	—
Printers	—	—	—	24	—	—
Coal miners	—	—	—	12	—	—
Makers of tobacco	—	—	—	14	—	—
Salesmen and shop assistants ..	25	21	25	24	27	44
Proprietors, managers of dealing businesses	28	34	34	35	25	60
Retired (not naval and military) ..	28	20	17	29	18	74

(N.B.—No proportion less than 10 per 1,000 is stated.)

356 per 1,000 in Bristol, or 337 per 1,000 in Bournemouth. The relative scarcity of women's industrial employment is emphasized by the distribution of those occupied amongst the various occupations. In Bristol, for example, nearly one-quarter of the women occupied (238 per 1,000) were engaged in the distinctively industrial employments of boot and shoe making, sugar confectionery, and tobacco manufacturing, printing and bookbinding, cardboard box-making, and packing. Dressmaking and tailoring, which always absorbs a proportion of women's labour, are excluded from these figures. In contrast, Southampton's chief industrial employments are tobacco manufacture, printing, packing, and electrical manufacture, which together absorbed but 54 per 1,000 of the occupied women and girls. Hull is better provided with industrial openings, for packing, sugar confectionery making, press work, and tin soldering, oil and paint, etc., manufacture employed 118 per 1,000. In Liverpool the proportion was 81 per 1,000 for sack and tobacco manufacture and packing alone. Cardiff and Newcastle, on the other hand, were in a position rather like that of Southampton. This limitation of the field of employment naturally led to a crowding of domestic and personal service (431 per 1,000), and in work as saleswomen and shop assistants (117 per 1,000), these two together accounting for more than one-half of the occupied women and girls. In no other port are women so dependent on these two groups of occupations. In only one town in the list, Bournemouth, is this proportion exceeded, but this is scarcely an exception, for in this case these two occupations are part of the town's main industry as a pleasure resort; a great part of the domestic work is carried on in businesses conducted for gain, and is thus insurable in the meaning of the Unemployment Insurance Acts. Thus both men and women are concentrated in a very narrow range of employments, there is for both a relative scarcity of industrial openings, and further, as we shall see later, the men's employments are subject to large seasonal fluctuations.

Until the last few months the town's experience in unemployment was relatively favourable. The two exchange areas of Southampton and Woolston together cover a larger territory than that of the county borough, but the numbers on their register may be taken as substantially representing the facts of the town itself. The numbers in recent years are shown on the following page.

In contrast to the relative steadiness of its general unemployment figure, the important feature of the labour market is the seasonal and casual character of the employment provided by the three great trades, shipping, ship-repairing, and port work, on which the town depends. The table shows the number of seamen, ship-repairers, and other casuals on the live register, at quarterly intervals during 1927 and 1932. Ignoring for a moment the upward trend of unemployment, particularly amongst the ship-repairers and other casuals, in the years in which the great depression gathered force, the figures not only give vivid evidence of the great range of seasonal fluctuations between the summer and winter employment of seamen and ship-repairers, but show that the seasonal variation of the one are substantially the reverse of the other. For seamen, the number unemployed reaches the maximum in the winter, and is then three or four times greater than in September. On the other hand, the ship-repairers and other casuals have the minimum unemployment in the winter and their maximum in the summer; and the range of fluctuations, though obscured by the growing pressure of depression on the "other casuals," is still considerable, the maximum unemployment being twice as great as the minimum in 1927, and still 55 per cent greater in 1928. The figures in the third column, those for dockers, are more steady, but in this case the question is one of the degree to which employment is casual, and of the proportion of men having a full working week. From this striking feature of the labour market many problems arise. How does the range of fluctuations compare with that of other ports? What is the character of the demand which produces such a result? Does

UNEMPLOYMENT IN SOUTHAMPTON, 1929–32

(*Numbers of Men, Women, and Juveniles on the Live Register in Southampton and Woolston*)

	1928	1929	1930	1931	1932
January ..	4,641	4,415	5,805	9,591	14,563
July	3,346	3,846	5,812	9,376	12,920

SEASONAL VARIATIONS OF UNEMPLOYMENT AMONGST SEAMEN, SHIP-REPAIRERS AND OTHER CASUALS, AND DOCKERS

(*Numbers on the Live Register at Quarterly Dates, 1927–32*)

	Seamen	*Ship-repairers and other Casuals*	*Dockers*
1927			
March 7	819	1,451	820
June 6	520	1,032	905
September 5	385	1,226	962
December 5	1,270	797	930
1928			
March 5	788	1,188	870
June 4	604	1,148	851
September 3	335	933	778
December 3	1,171	764	643
1929			
March 4	1,049	1,338	925
June 3	828	1,272	883
September 2	380	1,397	1,054
December 2	1,612	1,148	1,090
1930			
March 3	1,331	1,674	1,253
June 2	820	1,464	892
September 6	631	2,336	1,045
December 1	2,551	2,528	1,282
1931			
March 2	1,992	1,823	1,406
June 1	1,630	2,522	1,240
September 7	1,047	2,703	1,293
December 7	2,950	2,728	1,410
1932			
March 4	2,829	2,176	1,525
June 6	1,764	2,498	1,513
September 5	1,269	2,536	1,407

each industry carry a separate pool of labour which remains wholly or partly idle in the off-season? Since the on-season of one trade corresponds roughly with the off-season of the other, is there any transference of labour between them? The variation of employment affects both income levels and the claims for unemployment benefit; what is the effect of the changes on the social services?

(*a*) *The pool of seafarers' labour.*—We may commence with the seafarers. There are some 16,000 of all ratings in the port, but many of them have their homes elsewhere. Those with an intimate knowledge of the trade agree in estimating that about 50 per cent of them live in Southampton, some 10 per cent in Portsmouth, and the rest in London, Liverpool, and elsewhere. In the case of the Union Castle men, Totton was for long a common place of residence. A broad expression is that those from Liverpool are commonly firemen and those from London are often stewards who have come from hotel work. The Atlantic round trip takes seventeen days, followed by four ashore in England without pay. On this basis men expect twelve trips a year, though even in normal times there may be only ten. The South African trips take seven weeks, followed by twelve days ashore, and the number of trips may be five or six a year; but this would involve continuous working. For certain classes of work the field of employment has been rapidly diminishing. A large ship burning coal would need a staff of 120 to 140 firemen; but with oil fuel the number would drop to 40 or 50 men. The change of demand has also affected some shore workers and coal porters.

First as to the range of fluctuations, the figure shows that for seamen, unemployment in December was, in 1927, 1928, and 1929, three to four times greater than for the busiest quarter, September. Taking the quarterly figures uncorrected for trend, the ratio of $\dfrac{\text{maximum unemployment}}{\text{average unemployment}}$ is 1·70, 1·62, and 1·67 in these three years. The excess of the maximum quarterly figures over the average was 521,455 and 645 persons, or approximately 3·3 per cent, 2·8 per cent, and 4·1 per cent of the insured population of the industry. The true maxima and minima do not, of course, coincide with those recorded at the quarterly dates. The lowest and highest weekly figures were:

	1927	1928	1929
Lowest	334	306	380
Highest	1,411	1,513	1,657

Taking the range of fluctuations as between 1,100 and 1,300, this represents between 7 per cent and 8 per cent of the total number of insured persons in the industry. These figures may be taken as indicating the order of magnitude of the labour reserve attached to the industry to provide the personnel for its seasonal variations. Their comparative meaning may be appreciated by the fact that the "typical" trade cycle, up to 1927 showed a fluctuation of employment from minimum to maximum of 5·8 per cent.[1] And in the decade before the war, the trade union percentage of unemployment was 1 per cent greater in December than in May.[2] This range of variation is exceptional even amongst the ports. Thus in 1928, for example, the "surplus" of seamen in Southampton was 2¼ times greater in January than in July, but on the Merseyside, barely 1½ times greater. In Cardiff (Bute Docks), the lowest monthly unemployment figure for 1928 was 827, the highest 1,069; in 1929, the lowest 889, the highest 1,037. In Hull, the range from September 1927 to August 1928 was from a minimum of 312 to a maximum of 503.[3]

(*b*) *The pool of ship-repairers' labour.*—What was the size of the "pool" attached to ship-repairing? Using again the uncorrected quarterly figures, the ratio $\frac{\text{maximum unemployment}}{\text{average unemployment}}$ is 1·29, 1·18, 1·08 in 1927, 1928, and 1929, but this understates the true seasonal fluctuation, as the rising volume of

[1] Pigou, *Industrial Fluctuations*, 1927, p. 15.
[2] Layton, ed. *Is Unemployment Inevitable?* p. 4.
[3] From statistics supplied by the Ministry of Labour.

unemployment amongst unskilled workers obscures its full amplitude. Again using the maximum and minimum weekly figures:

	1927	1928	1929
Lowest	681	404	664
Highest	1,670	1,629	1,807

The definition of "ship-repairing" and "other casuals" makes it difficult to obtain a base on which to calculate a percentage fluctuation. If, however, we add the insured population in the shipbuilding and general engineering industries which includes the bulk of them—a total of about 4,300 males—we shall get an impression of the importance of the variations. It amounts to a maximum variation of over 1,100, or 26 per cent, between the busiest and slackest periods.

In the case of Cardiff in 1928 the maximum monthly figure was 1,743, the minimum 747; in 1929, the maximum 1,348, the minimum 769. In Hull the unemployment amongst other casual workers, including ship-repairers, varied from a minimum of 2,072 to a maximum of 2,927 in 1927–28.[1] We can approach the matter from the side of employment. Counting plumbers, painters, joiners, electricians, and labourers, with a few others—excluding engineers, boilermakers, patternmakers, and foundrymen—at this period the excess of the peak numbers employed in the season, over the average numbers in the other parts of the year was about 2,100 or 2,200; and the range of variation is indicated by the fact that the peak number appears to have been rather more than double this number. About 1,000 of this excess appears to have been labourers, another 800 or 900 the skilled tradesmen named, mainly painters and joiners, while the rest, about 100, were polishers and riggers. This shows a range of variation somewhat higher than the unemployment figures; and raises the issue as to whether some of the excess of the overhaul period is not drawn from outside the shipbuilding industry. The point is discussed later.

[1] Data supplied by the Ministry of Labour.

In the case of this industry there are two other features to be noticed. First, each year contains a major and minor maximum. The numbers on the register at these dates were:

UNEMPLOYMENT AMONGST SHIP-REPAIRERS AND OTHER CASUALS AT VARIOUS DATES, 1927–30

1927		1928	
January 25	681	January 2	404
April 18	1,657	April 10	1,655
July 13	630	May 21	866
October 10	1,670	November 12	1,369

1929		1930	
January 7	664	January 13	942
April 22	1,609	March 31	2,072
June 10	1,075	June 2	1,464
September 30	1,809	December 15	2,887

The second feature is connected with the weekly turn round at the ports. The White Star vessels came in on Saturday and left again on Wednesday; the Cunard vessels came in on Tuesday or Wednesday and left again on Saturday. Any repair work needed was undertaken during the weekly turn round, and often meant overtime. What influence did these arrangements have on employment? One can approach the question thus: if one firm did all the repair work for both companies, the alternation of sailings would make for stability of employment in the shipyards; whereas if two competing firms each received one company's work, then each would need its own reserve of labour for its own season, and each of the staffs would work a part only of the working week. These consequences would be ameliorated as regards actual work if any of the men, with or without their employer's consent, transferred their services from firm to firm so as to secure a share of both seasons. The total variation of employment would then be less than the separate fluctuations summed. It would be modified in its effect on wages if the rush of work at the weekly turn round consistently involved overtime at a rate higher than the standard rate. To the seasonal movement would thus be added the further difficulty of a broken working week in the off season. Reasoning in this theoretical fashion does in fact indicate the difficulties and controversies which arise in practice. The facts are not easy to arrive at, though a proper statistical analysis of the firm's records would make most of the facts plain; and the nature of the work is such that it is bound to produce conflicting statements on many important points, such as the extent to which workmen make up their broken weeks into full ones by going from employer to employer. There is the added difficulty that overtime may be frequently worked, so that a short week counted in "days at work" may not always be so short in wages earned. On the whole, taking overtime into account, the evidence suggests that at least one-sixth of the shipyard men named above were working three days or less, on the average throughout the year. At this point the question whether workmen do or do not move from job to job, making their three days with one up to five days with another firm, is of importance. The employers state that this is done successfully; the unions argue that in fact men "follow" one firm, that foremen would naturally look for a steady gang of men known to them, and that the amount of it, if any, is very small. The actual facts are not easy for an outsider to establish.

So far, then, the precise size of the pool reserve of labour is not easy to establish. Much depends on how far the expansion of the overhaul period is met entirely from the personnel of the industry, and how far it is drawn from adjacent trades and occupations, such as building; and how far seafarers endeavour to steady their own income by work in the yards in winter. This matter may be left aside until we have examined the third trade.

(*c*) *The pool of port labour*.—The third group of workers consists of dockers. The census of 1921 records 2,826 persons as engaged in the docks, wharf, and riverside services, but it is probable that many recorded themselves merely as labourers, of whom there were 4,550. The number of insured persons in the trade was about 4,250 in 1930, but the Employment Exchange definition is known to be a broad one. The name "docker" immediately calls to mind scrambles for work, casual jobs, under-employment and poverty, and so far as the greater part of its modern history is concerned, rightly so. For everywhere the problem of improving these conditions has shown itself to be a very intractable one. The simple expedient of raising the daily rate of wages served only to tempt in more competitors from the ranks of the unskilled in adjacent trades, and left annual earnings disproportionately unaffected. The record of failure of these experiments at least made it clear that the solution could be found only by a definite limitation of the right to work in the trade, and the exclusion of the surplus from the industry altogether. This involves some provision for the peak and variable demands of shipping, the recognition, in fact, of the need for a reserve of men to cope with the maximum demand. As the reserve could not hope to get anything like full employment the year through, limiting it to a reasonable number, and some means of providing these men with maintenance when not employed, were the obvious consequences. These twin principles of proper decasualization stand together Deliberately granting the right to work to a reserve either taught or obliged to look to the industry as their sole employment, implies an endeavour to assist in maintaining them when work is insufficient to provide reasonable earnings, but if in the interests of speedy and efficient handling of ships a very large reserve is allowed, the problem of maintaining them becomes too great to be manageable.

The termination of war presented an exceptional opportunity for limiting the numbers in the ports. Enlistment had reduced the numbers at work, the army had control over the remainder, and a well-organized effort might, in these favourable circumstances, have brought solution much nearer. In some of the ports, the restriction of entry to the occupation by registering habitual dockers was nominal rather than effective, for as in London the numbers registered, so far from being reduced, were not only above any normal requirement, but actually in excess of the probable pre-war numbers.[1]

It is in the light of this trend of events that the organization of dock work in Southampton must be regarded. Is its work more or less casual than in other ports? How far do the seasonal variations of shipping and ship-repairing show themselves also in the demand for dock labour? We may first appeal to the facts relating to the organization of the demand for work. Time is not far distant when posters were to be observed on surrounding railway stations asking for men to unload potatoes during the rush season; and the usual scramble for work at the dock gates is within memory. From this position an immense forward stride has been made. The registration committee has been set up. In the first instance the companies gave estimates of the numbers required and no man was given a tally unless he was recommended by a company as an habitual docker. At present he must bring a note from the company to say that they are willing to accept him. The unions also are said to be strict in the matter also. The numbers of tallies issued rose slowly from 2,500 in 1919 to about 3,000 in 1927. Besides these companies' tallies, with the approval of the committee, temporary registration cards are issued by the union for three or four weeks, the holders of which work for smaller firms who can give them jobs only for a season.

The closure of the industry against an inrush of the unskilled is the first step to decasualization, but there is still the problem of the size of the reserve, and the distribution of work between the registered. In this respect the problem is much simplified by the fact that one firm, the Southern Railway, owns the docks, runs some ships and employs half the registered dockers. The opportunities for the regularization of work are thus more favourable than in a port like Liverpool, where the dock work is undertaken by companies other than dock or railowners, where the firms engaging labour are more numerous and where, in consequence, the promotion of mobility

[1] *Report of Port Labour Enquiry*, p. 30.

between them is more difficult. The existence of a single control over a large proportion of the men is a great advantage. The company has in practice taken further steps. Over one-third of its tally holders are in fact "preference" men, with the first claim to work, and endeavours are made to provide the number on the full weeks' work the year round. The system of using a number of preference men existed before the war, though not under that name. The company then had a number of registered workers to whom they gave cards—at one period three hundred, but the numbers slowly rose to four hundred or more. Secondly, the other "shed call men" are called on a rota system in order of their numbers. Each man has thus a regular opportunity of being called, though the amount of work offered at any moment may be a full shift or a half-shift as the case may be. The purpose of this scheme is to equalize the chances of work. This method is not used by other employers in the port.

The origin of the seasonal variation need not detain us long. It is less marked than in the other two trades, though its influence is exerted in other directions than actual unemployment. The summer demand of the Atlantic traffic and cross-Channel freight traffic is partly offset by the South African traffic in the winter. We ought for full understanding to distinguish between the separate types of labour demand which make up the aggregate demand; for not only does a given change of passenger tonnage mean a smaller variation in the demand for dock labour than a given change of freight tonnage entered, but different classes of freight require different amounts of handling. It is not easy, in post-war years of wide trade dislocation, to set forth a description of "normal" trade behaviour, but in freight traffic certain features may, nevertheless, be noted. Potato imports are at a low level at the first four or five months of the year, rise suddenly to 400,000 tons in June, and drop in July to 10,000 and even 4,000 tons. Fresh fruit, on the other hand, shows a low minor peak of some 6,000–8,000 tons, and rises to its maximum in September and October. Wool imports may be slow in the summer months but rise in October for several months. It is of such variations that the aggregate demand of the freight traffic is compounded.

To what extent do the seasonal changes of demand and the methods of labour engagement together involve a pool of partly employed labour? What kind of reserve does the industry "need"? How much does it actually carry? Such questions are notoriously difficult to answer. How are we to gauge the size of the surplus? By comparing peak employment with average employment? Or is it the excess of the numbers of tally holders over the numbers paid wages? In the latter case, should we not have to consider also whether the earnings of the marginal group were large or very low? In any case a percentage of idle tallies would have to be allowed for sickness.

We may commence with the figures of unemployment. The absolute difference between the highest and lowest weekly figures of unemployed dock workers remains fairly steady, with one exception, despite the disturbed conditions of the trade and the advancing depression:

	1927	1928	1929	1930	1931	1932[1]
Difference between maximum and minimum figure ..	332	557	1,121	583	369	415

Neglecting the exceptional year, the range of variation is thus between 7·8 per cent and 13·7 per cent of the insured population, and the average maximum variation thus 10·6 per cent. If we take not the highest weekly difference in each year, but the difference between the average weekly figure in January and in August, the figures are 1927, 143; 1928, 143; 1929, 47. Thereafter the movement is obscured by the upward movement of unemployment as a result of the world depression.

These figures give us an idea of the range of variation amongst the whole insured population of the industry. What do we know of the smaller groups of tally holders? Unfortunately our information is far from complete. A census or

[1] 9 months.

sample enquiry covering all tally holders, by whomsoever employed, is really required if the situation is to be fully understood, but an investigation of this sort was impossible. For the staff of the predominant employer, the Southern Railway, the amplitude of the seasonal swing—this time tested by the numbers and proportions of the tally holders actually paid wages—would appear to be as follows. In 1927, in the rush month, the number of men employed was 86·7 per cent of the number of tally holders; the average daily number employed was over 65 per cent of the tally holders in six months of the year, and under 65 per cent in the rest. This general average, however, over-simplifies the problem, for it is of its essence that the demands are variable and that the peak demand must somehow be satisfied. In twenty-one days in June, the busy month, the numbers paid wages were over 70 per cent of the total number of tally holders; in four other months in more than one working day in every three the proportion of tally holders paid was over 70 per cent, and there was no month in which the demand on several days did not reach this proportion.

It can be further tested: How frequently did men "miss their calls" for work? We should have to exclude all vacant tallies from such calculation, and remember that some percentage must be allowed for sickness. Excluding all cases of the former, during the first six months of the year there were at least twenty-six days in which the number of men who missed their calls was ninety and upwards. In four rush days of June 178 missed one call or more and 73 missed both morning and midday calls. In another week of the same month 233 men missed one call or more. In the previous week 232 missed one call or more, and on one day in that week 164 non-tally holders were employed. We do not know the reason for the absences, but June is a busy month and whether the men are strictly allowed to do so or not, it is difficult to avoid concluding that some of them must have been due to opportunities of work being taken up elsewhere.

The final test we may use is wages earned. To what extent have the steps taken towards decasualization stabilized the mens' income? How far did the seasonal changes of demand show themselves in pay? Here again our information is far from complete, though it is available for the Southern Railway. As already stated, this company, besides its permanent staff, has 600 "preference" tally holders, a number of stevedores and shed call men engaged on a rotation system. Taking a typical pre-depression year 1927, the total wages paid to the company's tally holders during the last four busy weeks of the half-year ending in June was 75 per cent greater than the amount paid in the first four weeks in the year, and 69 per cent greater than the amount paid in the last four weeks of the year. The seasonal swing is naturally greater than that shown by the numbers employed daily, since the latter figures do not indicate the length of the engagement or the amount of overtime worked. The average weekly wage of all classes of the 1,500 tally holders in this year was £2 13s. 7d., but the range of variation was from an average of £3 1s. 6d. per week in the best months to £2 8s. 7d. in the worst. These figures include the earnings of preference men and shed call men, whose work is rather less regular. For example, the average wage per week of the preference men of various types was £3 9s. 2d., while the figures for the best month were £3 16s., and for the worst £3 4s. 3d. For these men—two-fifths of the total number—the arrangement has secured a substantial stability of employment and income. As regards shed call men, it was possible to obtain information in fifty cases, a sample of one in ten. In the six summer months, April to September, the average weekly earnings were 25 per cent higher than the earnings in the succeeding six winter months. The average for this group was £1 13s. 2d. for the summer months, and £1 6s. 5d. for the winter months. It is important in reading these figures to bear in mind the qualifications as to missed calls noted above.

The median average weekly earnings of the latter group

in the winter half-year (October to March) were 25s., for the summer half-year 32s. The upper quartile was 28s. in the winter months, and 35s. in the summer months, while the lower quartile rose from 24s. in winter to 30s. in summer. The effect of seasonal changes can be seen in a six or seven shillings difference between the summer and winter figures, and of the levelling effect of the rotation system in the range between the upper and lower quartiles, which is 4s. only in the winter and 5s. in the summer. It can be fairly claimed that the rotation system equalized the opportunities.

A consequence of the limitation of entry into the trade is that its members tend to be of a higher average age than in many other occupations in the port. According to the census of 1921, the average age of all occupied males in the town was about thirty-eight, as compared with forty-seven in the case of "other dock labourers." This higher average age is not due simply to methods of registration, for the Port Labour Committee had not been in operation long enough in 1921, if it recruited its original tally holders on any ordinary interpretation of "habitual dockers," to secure so pronounced a skewing of the age distribution. Much of the work is heavy and the opportunities for boys are therefore limited. It is clear that whereas random engagement at the dock gates with a large surplus of labour must have led to older men being gradually shouldered out of employment by younger ones, a restricted and stabilized entry with preferential treatment of registered men must in practice give them a longer life of average earning. The "ageing" of the docker, whether arising from the protection given to older men or otherwise, brings with it the possibility of the declining physical efficiency of the group as a whole, and of the necessity of securing a supply of younger men, or of arranging for the retirement of the older ones.

Much of the success of a scheme of registration of this kind depends on the perfection of the administrative arrangements. Adequate arrangements must be made not only for compiling but for revising the register. It is not only a question of making up wastage, of eliminating unsatisfactory cases, or scrutinizing cases with a poor or unsatisfactory work record in a routine manner, but of taking the opportunity to examine the total numbers of tallies in the light of any change in labour demand, whether due to trade depression or to other causes. A peculiar set of circumstances brought about in London an original registration of 61,000, a much greater number than could possibly find work, and at successive revisions these were reduced to 52,000 in 1925, 40,000 in 1928, and 37,000 in 1930. In Bristol the numbers were similarly reduced from 4,800 in 1921 to 2,800 in 1931; in Liverpool, from 35,000 in 1919 to 21,500 in 1931.[1] As indicated from the number of tallies given above, the total number has not been reduced in Southampton, for until the onset of the depression, its trade was growing. There is, however, a biennial review of the register. The size of the reserve needed is related to the number of separate "call stands," their location and the mobility of labour between them. Southampton is a small port, and although firms have individual call stands, its problem was simplified by the fact that the dock owners were also the largest employers, that the companies interchange information to avoid taking on "outside" men, and that no firm held out from the scheme. Until recently, the geography of the docks made a single call stand for the railway company's men a possibility, but the extension of the docks up the River Test introduces a complication, for old and new docks will be separated by a considerable distance. More stands may be needed, so that there will at once arise the problem of maintaining mobility between them and of preventing the growth of separate reserves.

We have examined the progress and difficulties of decasualization so far as it is affected by the registration system, but the repercussions of the unemployment insurance system cannot be left out of account. The nature of the work, and the existence of an "authorized" labour surplus involves idle days for some of the men. For what proportion of these days can they claim

[1] *Report of Port Labour Enquiry*, p. 30.

benefit? The case is governed by the "continuity rule," which states that once a claimant has completed a waiting period during which no benefit is paid, another waiting period is not required so long as unemployment is continuous. Any three days of unemployment within six consecutive days are regarded as continuous; any two periods of three continuous days are regarded as continuous if they are not separated by more than ten weeks. The interpretation of this rule involves a number of important details, such as: that the six consecutive days do not include Sundays; that the period of consecutive days may be any such period, and is not confined to a given pay week or calendar week; and that the requirement is for any three or more days, irrespective of the sequence of the days of employment and unemployment.[1] It was possible to obtain a full statement for one year (1928) of the complete employment record of nine non-preference tally holders, including their earnings. The following table shows the number of days' benefit which they could claim under the rule and the total earnings. The marital condition, and therefore the extent and amount of dependents' benefit of the men were not certainly known. Two columns are therefore added showing what amount of benefit they would have drawn had they been (1) single and (2) married with two children, at the (unreduced) rates of benefit then in force:

Case	*Wages for the Year* £ s. d.	*Days of Benefit*	*Amount of Benefit if Single* £ s. d.	*Amount of Benefit if Married with two Children* £ s. d.
1	70 0 3	156	22 2 0	39 0 0
2	90 6 6	142	20 2 4	35 10 0
3	68 1 6	168	23 16 0	42 0 0
4	72 11 0	166	23 10 4	41 10 0
5	82 16 8	143	20 5 2	35 15 0
6	106 2 0	113	16 0 2	28 5 0
7	76 3 11	147	20 16 6	36 15 0
8	70 5 0	153	21 13 6	38 5 0
9	68 9 6	168	23 16 0	42 0 0

[1] *Royal Commission on Unemployment Insurance, Evidence,* 21st day, Paper 83; also 1st day, Paper 1.

It is important to notice that these cases were all shed call men, and not preference men, who would naturally have a lower incidence of unemployment and that the preference men are, in the case of the larger employer, a substantial proportion of the total. The figures must not be taken as representative of the average conditions of industry but only as illustrative of the class of workers concerned. Secondly, though the actual cases were not selected because they were exceptional, they seem nevertheless to be cases in which the men received rather more than the average of days of benefit, since three of them, on the present regulation, would be placed on transitional benefit. (Benefit days exceeding 156.) Without pressing the evidence of a small number of cases too far, or claiming them as statistically representative, they illustrate generally the amount of the benefit which *can* be drawn by that class of worker. There is nothing to suggest that the extent to which these Southampton workers drew on the insurance fund is any greater than in ports generally, on the contrary, it is likely to be much less than in some. Glasgow, the Tyne and Wear ports, and the Hartlepools had no registration schemes at all;[1] in the absence of other evidence one may expect the working conditions to be such that the continuity rule was of even greater importance in facilitating claims for benefit than in places where employers and workers have joined their efforts in an endeavour to concentrate work on a smaller body of registered men.

The problem in Southampton is thus bound up with that of the industry as a whole, and a few observations on the general position may not be out of place. The working conditions of the industry in any case make it a difficult one to fit into the insurance system in such a way as to place its workers at no disadvantages as compared with those employed in any other industry, and at the same time to prevent it from permanently and heavily drawing large sums in excess of its joint contributions. The extent of the difficulty varies with

[1] *Report of Port Labour Enquiry*, p. 18.

the success and efficiency of registration in the several ports, and some have been laggards in making serious efforts to decasualize labour. Successive enquiries[1] into the place of the industry in the insurance system have been increasingly pointed and critical in their comments on the general situation. The continuity rule itself was introduced mainly at the instance of those in the industry, who pointed out that otherwise workers who had as heavy an incidence of unemployment as those who were regularly engaged by the week and unemployed for whole pay weeks, were deprived of benefit merely because the methods of engagement scattered the days of unemployment in an irregular fashion between days of employment. All the enquiries have regarded the position as unsatisfactory. The Blanesburgh Committee thought that special arrangements might have to be made for the industry; both employers and workers representatives on the Port Labour Committee agreed that the position was unsatisfactory, although their proposed remedies were different. The Royal Commission summarizing the result of the previous as well as its own enquiries made the following criticisms. First, that during 1921–29 the contributions of the industry to insurance amounted to approximately £6,000,000, while the sums paid in benefit were £22,000,000.[2] Secondly, that the amount of this burden was in part due to the failure of the industry to decasualize, and that the nature of the insurance rules actually tended to encourage continuance of methods which meant irregular work and under-employment. "The dock industry shows a normal percentage of employment of 30."[3] They further quoted with approval the comments of the Port Labour Committee on the anomalies arising from the application of the continuity rule, namely, that where certain classes of port workers earned good wages in two and three days' very strenuous work, they might

[1] See *Report of Blanesburgh Committee, 1927*; *Report of Port Labour Committee, 1931*, and *Final Report of Royal Commission on Unemployment Insurance, 1932*.

[2] *Final Report*, p. 249.

[3] Ibid., pp. 96, 249. See also evidence of Sir W. Beveridge.

be continually placed in a position which leads them to weigh the possibility of a further engagement which may result in only half a day's work, against the risk of breaking continuity, which may lead to the loss of three days' benefit.[1] There is evidence that the nature of the rule is well understood by the workers.[2]

The demand of the critics is not that there should be *no* excess of benefit over contributions in the case of any industry, for that would amount to a demand for insurance by industry, a principle which the original scheme and successive enquiries have repeatedly rejected. Historically the scheme has developed by successive extensions intended to bring in higher income grades of workers with a smaller incidence of unemployment. The criticism is rather that the amount of the excess is far too great, and that the continual provision of it from the general insurance fund encourages slackness in method of labour engagement and organization. The dock employers have suggested various amendments in the insurance rules, such as a differentiation between weekly workers and casual workers, and a restriction of benefit to any day after the second idle day in the case of the latter. To deal with those types of workers where a short but strenuous period of working yields relatively good earnings, and yet admits of benefit being drawn, the Majority Commissioners suggested an earnings test such that, where a claimant for benefit had already earned one pound or more during a specified period, a deduction should be made from the benefit payable, of one-half of any sum earned in excess of one pound. The application of such a rule in the cases quoted above could appear to result in the reduction of benefit of about four to five pounds a case. They urged strongly the desirability of the industry's making special efforts to diminish its surplus of labour, going so far as to recommend, following Sir William Beveridge's suggestion, that in the event of its failing to do this voluntarily, the Ministry of Labour

[1] *Port Labour Committee Report*, pp. 52–3.
[2] Hanham, *Casual Labour on the Merseyside*, p. 95.

should have power to schedule the industry and impose a registration scheme, and to arrange for preference in employment to be given to men who had been definitely following it for a period. It went so far as to suggest that the Ministry should, if necessary, consider special arrangements for the port industry, such as special contributions, an amendment of the continuity rule, and even its exclusion from the scheme altogether.[1]

The alternative to tightening the insurance regulations is the policy put forward by the Transport Workers Union.[2] This started from the position that while a registration scheme can effectively check the inrush of unemployed from other industries, it does not in itself deal with under-employment amongst dockers, or provide for the proper distribution of employment amongst those available. The union proposed to deal with the problem as a whole by the creation of a national authority, to superimpose on registration further arrangements to provide a minimum weekly income from employment and benefit together, and to facilitate the retirement of older workers by a scheme of pensions. The State was to continue to contribute its share of the insurance contributions, and to add also the amount of the present deficit, leaving a balance to be made up by a levy on all goods and passengers entering and leaving the ports. This scheme is full of interest but it failed to commend itself to either the Dock employers, the Government Actuary, or to the Royal Commission. The employers objected to the close national control involved, and to any increase of dock charges at a time when they were already criticized by dock users as excessive. The Actuary was of the view that it would involve a charge on the Exchequer of more than £23 per annum for every man. The Majority Commissioners[3] were not disposed to favour any proposal which involved a continuance of those drawings from the

[1] *Final Report*, pp. 308–9, 351.
[2] *Port Labour Enquiry Report*, pp. 44–5, 65–7, 89–92.
[3] *Final Report, Royal Commission on Unemployment Insurance*, p. 248.

general fund which they had already declared excessive. The scheme proposed a minimum of 50s. per week, and a pension at sixty-five of 25s. per week. The total cost of the scheme, however, arises not only from its principles, but from the rates proposed, and would be less expensive if the minimum wage and the pension were fixed at lower rates.

The Minority Commissioners took a different attitude.[1] They argued generally that there was little reason for supposing that the insurance system tended to encourage casual methods of working, that port employment conditions are better now than in 1909, and that decasualization, however desirable in itself, would not reduce the net volume of unemployment, since this depended on the amount of goods to be landed and not on the way in which work was distributed. They concluded, therefore, that whatever the methods of distribution of work, the total cost of the benefit to the insurance fund would remain the same. No one will deny that the conditions of work have been improved by the establishment of barriers against an influx of large numbers of unemployed from other districts, and by the provision from the insurance fund of benefit which in some measure provides maintenance for the under-employed. As pointed out above, this does represent the achievement of the registration and the insurance systems. But from the proposition that the course of trade determines the volume of employment one cannot conclude that the method of working is one of indifference, even if it has no adverse effect on the insurance fund; for the point of registration schemes is that, given any total demand for labour, it is preferable to distribute the work in the way which will give as many men as possible a full week's employment. There will be general sympathy for the point of view that any change of the insurance system which deprived the labour surplus of such maintenance as is already given without replacing it from some other source, would simply destroy the improvement which has been obtained only at the cost of

[1] *Final Report, Royal Commission on Unemployment Insurance*, p. 486.

years of voluntary and official effort. The Minority Commissioners seem to underrate the importance of the condition that such maintenance can be given on an adequate scale only if the size of the surplus is limited.

The problem of the relation of the insurance system to port workers in Southampton cannot be tackled in isolation from the situation in other areas; and in the meantime, while the port can make sure that its own administrative arrangements for promoting mobility and limiting the surplus are adequate, a settlement of the problem waits partly upon a change in the attitude of those laggard ports which have still refrained from taking the first step.

(*d*) *Mobility between the pools.*—So far we have examined the variations in the demand for labour in each of the three main trades, and found that there exists in each case a reserve of labour designed to meet the peak seasonal and daily demand. There is agreement that the size of such pools ought to be kept as low as circumstances permit in order to minimize under-employment. What is the relationship between them? Does the fact that the peak demand of one trade more or less synchronizes with the slack period of another cause the trade with the excess to spill its surplus into the depleted pool of the other? How far is such transference organized? How far voluntary? Are there any technical difficulties arising out of the nature of the work? Can the amount of dovetailing be increased? These questions are not of local interest only, for one of the proposals which emerged from the campaign for the scientific organization of the labour market which preceded and followed the Royal Commission on the Poor Law in 1905–09, was that the under-employment of the seasonal trades could be remedied in part by the transfer of workers from one industry in its off season to another at its period of peak demand. Yet it is in this part of the scheme for the scientific organization of the labour market (which included employment exchanges, insurance, and decasualization) that least success has been obtained, for "dovetailing" presupposed the existence of trades with complementary seasons; that they were in the same locality, or within reasonable distance of one another; and that they were sufficiently related to permit the less specialized workers to adapt themselves to both jobs. The organization of the transference implied some method of registering workers, and certainly the extrusion of some of the workers made "surplus" by the reduction in the total size of the two pools of reserve labour. In practice the conditions have not been widely satisfied. Geographical difficulties are obvious, and often suitable industries contain numbers of employers not sufficiently organized to undertake the control of their industry which such dovetailing implies. And in some areas, the peak demand of main and subsidiary industries occur together. In the Isle of Wight, for example, the demands for the service of boating, road transport, agriculture, and "pleasure resort" trades occur in the summer months. It will be seen from the foregoing account of the three main trades that in Southampton some of these difficulties are absent, and the situation correspondingly more favourable.

Theoretically, several courses are possible. All the trades could be left unregulated, reliance being placed on the free play of self-interest of men and employers to work out an arrangement which would minimize total numbers of the pools. In practice this is a counsel of despair, and leaves the problem almost untouched. We could limit the entry of men into each of the three trades, and try to minimize the size of the separate pools. In Cardiff the dockers are under a registration scheme, the coal-trimmers form a special pool of labour of their own, and the ship-repairing men are also covered by a special scheme under which the Exchanges stamp both Health and Unemployment Insurance cards. This means that there are, in effect, three separate bodies of workers; and in the normal course of events it appears that it is only rarely that a man changes over from being a docker to being engaged under the ship-repairing scheme. Another course would be to concentrate on the less specialized class of workers in the three trades form a single pool, and employ men where and when demand arose. Alternatively, we could limit the size of the pool in one (or two) and leave the remaining trade or trades unregulated. In Southampton it is this course which is in fact being followed. In the sense stated above, dock labour is a closed trade; the other two are open. What, granted the enormous pressure to which the slack periods subject the workers in these trades, is the extent and nature of any dovetailing by individual initiative?

We may commence with ship-repairing. The magnitude of the seasonal variations have been examined above. From what sources do the extra men engaged in the overhaul season come? How many from other trades, and in particular from the seagoing and dock-side pools, and how many are drawn from a reserve exclusively devoted to work in the yards and otherwise idle? Some are imported either through open advertising in the Press, or through the agency of the Ministry of Labour. For example, from August 1927 to July 1928, 1,378 men were imported by the latter means for at least a month's to six weeks' work. Over two-thirds (941) came during the winter months from October to March. Decoration of the saloons and other highly skilled work is often contracted for by firms like Waring and Gillows and Robson of Liverpool, and these bring with them their own joiners, upholsterers, polishers, etc. (2) Some come from the building trades in the surrounding districts. This is the case with painters, joiners, plumbers, and electricians, and although the shore rates of these trades are often higher than the shipyard rates, the overhaul season is the slack period in their own trade and frequent overtime in the yards is a strong inducement. These two groups are the skilled men. (3) The end of the yachting season releases many men for rigging, sailmaking, and labouring work during the winter overhaul. (4) The unskilled men in the yards are supplemented by seamen, firemen, and stewards. Stewards, both bedroom and kitchen, do light work acting as mates to electricians, joiners, etc., where the work involved is mainly carrying tools, etc. Deck hands work on staging and as members of chain gangs, doing heavy lifting and pulling. The methods by which this interchange goes on are largely personal. Some older seamen have a "nose for shore jobs" and never seem to "go on the Exchange." The yard foremen may themselves be old seamen, or in some of the normal gangs there may be old seamen or relatives, and by these means they secure the jobs available. It has not been possible to obtain precise or substantial figures as to the number of men involved. One guess was that there are always two or three hundred helping during the reconditioning period. The Southern Railway and the Cunard Line do their own outside painting. This is unskilled work, and they are able to use some of their own seagoing staff and thus keep a permanent staff more easily. In the case of the Southern Railway ships, a man with a seagoing rate of 62s. might be employed in the "factory" as a labourer, in which case he would receive the labourers' rate of 45s.; and there is an intermediate shore rate when they are employed about the ships.

Transfer from either ship-repairing or seafaring to dock labour is obviously conditioned by the registration system, which closes entry in the sense of withholding a preferential right to work. Not all the dock labour is pooled, and something depends on how far the separate employers meet a rush by "borrowing" other companies' tally men, and how far they resort to non-tally holders. It is an essential purpose of this scheme of registration that the tally holders should first be called upon, and it appears that this obligation of the companies is carried out. It follows that the chances of work for any man from another trade are practically limited to those which present themselves when the companies' tally men are fully engaged. Thus taking the busy month of June (1928), on six days non-tally holders were taken on, the number being 160, 54, 31, 24, 4, and 2. On the other hand, on each of those days (as well as on others) other companies' men were engaged. It is therefore to the shipyards that seamen must look if they want work in their slack period. The dockers themselves have slack winter months. Do they move to the shipyards? Clearly in the case of tally holders the chances are restricted. They are obliged to present themselves at 7.45 and 11.45, for calls at 8.0 and 12.0, and at 5.45 for 6.0. If the men are not called that day, they have to attend the Employment Exchange and sign on, and failure to do so would involve the loss of a day's unemployment pay. One may presume, however, that in the slack season the companies would be less strict on "missed calls."

The result of this examination, incomplete though the information is, raises the question as to whether these somewhat unorganized arrangements for mobility could be developed into a single pool of general labour for work within the dock area. All, either employers or workmen, who fear that their position might be worsened by any departure from the existing arrangements, will see objections to such a proposal. Employers will feel that they need men accustomed to their own special class of work. Yet the capacity of men to learn new tasks akin to their own trade is often underestimated. The comparative ease with which rising trades get new labour; and war experience in creating new types of semi-skilled work with great rapidity suggest that in this respect the difficulties may seem more formidable than they really are. On the other hand, the creation of such a pool would involve the extrusion of a fringe of underemployed labour in the interest of giving greater stability to those remaining, and the selection of those to be excluded would be an unhappy business. As with dock decasualization schemes, the gains might be worth the effort, and if a scheme were appropriately launched on a rising market, hardships would be minimized. One must confess, however, that these considerations are in the nature of speculation suggested by incomplete data rather than conclusions supported by the full facts. A full study of the present transference is much to be desired, but this will involve some troublesome work and the co-operation of a number of firms.

Reference has already been made to the peculiarities of the age composition of the general body of dock workers, and its relation to the registration system. Here we may note the contrast between seafaring trades and the various classes of dock workers and others. The most striking feature of the table is the sharp contrast between the seafaring trades and the port workers. The maximum number of seafarers is found in an age group twenty years earlier than either class of port worker, and on the other hand the dock workers' age groups 45–65 are heavily weighted as compared with all occupied males. The average age of the latter was in 1921 about 38 years, while that of other dock workers was 47 years, petty officers and seamen 35 years, and of firemen 33 years only. Dock work is for the most part heavy, in any case it appears that few tallies are ever granted to men under 25 years of age. There are more opportunities for boys on the sea, and recruitment at an earlier age is the regular practice. Are we to conclude from this contrast between the port and sea occupations that seamen get tired of being away from home, seek shore work of some kind, and find it in dock work? Or is the recruitment of dockers in practice limited to the sons of dockers? A large number of tally holders have been to sea at some time, though that description would apply to many workers in other trades in Southampton, and apparently 40 to 50 per cent of those who apply for tallies, when asked for recommendations, show a seaman's discharge book. From an employer's point of view the seaman would be a desirable type of applicant, for he would probably be on the average physically fitter than other classes of applicants; and since deck hands must do a certain amount of cargo work on board, such men would have experience of many of the classes of work they would be called upon to do. According to one employer, two-thirds of the applicants —not necessarily successful ones—are over 40 years of age, though it is unlikely that anyone over 35 years would be accepted as a preference man.

In the case of more permanent men in the docks, the previous

AGE DISTRIBUTION OF SEAFARERS AND DOCK LABOURERS, 1921

(Numbers per 1,000 in each Trade)

Occupation	*Age* *Total over 12*	12	14	16	18	20	25	35	45	55	60	65	*70 and over*
Petty officer, seamen, and deck hands ..	1,000	—	18	56	66	163	252	204	137	41	36	19	8
Firemen, trimmers, greasers, donkeymen	1,000	—	1	13	40	232	325	221	121	26	11	6	4
Pursers, stewards, and domestic staff ..	1,000	—	13	39	60	168	320	231	127	26	11	4	1
Stevedores	1,000	—	—	—	2	14	132	250	357	118	74	42	11
Other dock labourers	1,000	—	—	7	14	41	133	198	302	124	93	74	14

occupation of thirty-six men engaged in operating cranes will illustrate the varied sources from which the workers were recruited: Navy, 3; steward, 2; sailor, fitter's labourer, 1; marine fireman, 1; dock labourers, 3; fitter and fitter's labourer, 3; arc lamp trimmer, 2; soldier and lamp trimmer, 3; electrician, electrician's labourer, 2; engine cleaners, 2; farm labourer, builder's labourer, 1; cab driver, 1; cycle fitter, 1; house decorator, 1; shop assistant, 1; others, 4.

CHAPTER V

INCOME AND POVERTY

We have now to study the result of industrial and occupational factors on the standard of life of the population. The nature of the problems of describing the poverty and welfare of a population is now well known. That the term "economic welfare"—especially when associated with the word "poverty" —may to some people have an ethical content doubtfully valid and impossible to measure need not deter us, for institutionalist economists, like Hamilton,[1] and their critics like Benham[2] agree as to the need of "standards of appraisal" or "objective indicia" whereby progress and prosperity can be measured. The construction of arbitrary standards of poverty and "overcrowding" whereby the achievements of the economic process can be assessed, so far at least as the working-class population is concerned, is therefore an essential part of the investigation. We require some knowledge of the general shape of the curve of income distribution, and of the relation between income and needs in the many possible types of families. It is indeed the bewildering variety of family types which causes much of the labour of the investigation. As Professor Bowley has pointed out, even if all the possible variants of age, sex, and earning capacity are grouped into but nine classes, there are still over 350 categories of family type, each needing as many different amounts of income to sustain them in health and efficiency. The conventional family of man, wife, and three children still used even for official purposes[3] is found in but 6 per cent of a representative sample of Southampton's working-class

[1] Hamilton, "Economic Opinion," in *Civilization in the United States,* 1922, pp. 268–69.
[2] Benham, "Economic Welfare," *Economica,* 1930.
[3] For comments on this, see *Southampton Civic Survey,* p. 61. Five per cent in the *Five Towns Enquiry.* See *Has Poverty Diminished?* p. 8.

families. The difficulty of the work lies not so much in the lack of the volume of information, as its insufficiency at critical points. Failing analysis of the wealth of material in the possession of the public authorities dealing with taxes, labour regulation, and the eleemosynary social services, we have to rely upon information voluntarily given. The methods of obtaining it are well established, and only the adjustments necessary for their application to the peculiarities of local circumstance need any detailed description. Three principal sources of information were drawn upon: (1) an assessment of the income of the heads of all families with school children; (2) a representative, or random sample of the town's households, limited to the lower ranges of incomes, i.e. the working-class families; and (3) a detailed examination of various special groups also in the lower range of income, in receipt of voluntary or public assistance, where the problem of insufficiency of income might arise. It is not easy to conduct these diverse enquiries so that each should yield its maximum in correcting, supplementing, and confirming the impressions given by the others. As far as the limitations of the various groups of data would allow, the definitions, rules, and procedure were made uniform, but there was a point beyond which the nature of the information would not permit of this being done. It was also desirable that all the branches of the investigation should take place simultaneously, in order to prevent any injury being done to the comparability of the data by any changes in basic conditions. All of them together, however, presented so formidable a task in collection and tabulation that the resources available were not equal to it. In the circumstances the risk of changing conditions of trade, employment and wages had to be run, a risk which unfortunately materialized. As it turned out, there was some troublesome work in placing some of the results on a comparative basis. Even so, the value of the three kinds of enquiries in their relation to one another was considerable. The first enabled us to define more clearly "working class," or "poor streets," and contributed to the ease of arranging and checking the random sample. The details of the special groups gave indications of certain difficulties in relation to family means for which provision had to be made in the random sample.

1. *The Income Survey*

For securing a broad knowledge of the distribution of income, the method used was that of the mass interview developed by Charles Booth for his *Survey of London*, and consisted of an assessment of the income of the heads of all the families with school children. Booth wished by this method to discover what proportion of the population could be regarded as below a defined poverty standard. Yet path-breaking as this work was both in method and result, Professor Bowley's studies have shown how much the relationship of families to poverty depends on the number of wage earners, and the supplementary private and social service incomes, and how much care has to be taken of the marginal cases. An assessment of such a variety of factors is a hazardous matter, and would give suggestive rather than definite evidence of poverty. In this case the method was used primarily to obtain the picture of the distribution of income, as tested by the assessed earnings or other direct income of the head of the family only. How far we can argue that the scheme of income distribution amongst heads of young families holds for the adult population in its entirety is discussed below.[1] No safe conclusion regarding the distribution of income in two different populations could be drawn from a comparison of the incomes of the parents of school children, for the proportion of such families to total families varies greatly in different areas. The proportion of the population consisting of school children varied (in 1921) from about 28 per cent in Southampton to under 20 per cent in Bournemouth, under 24 per cent in Brighton to 30 per cent in Hull, and 30 per cent in Newcastle.

[1] Bowley, *Measurement of Social Phenomena*, p. 114. Mallet, *Statistical Journal*, 1908, p. 67.

As occupations were known almost without exception every family was separately assessed. Where the natural family had been broken by the death of the father, the income of the person legally responsible for the children was taken. Income was defined neither as "full time earnings" nor "earnings of the previous week," for although these seem precise in meaning, they are not easy to apply by assessment method to such seasonal occupations as seafaring and ship-repairing are in Southampton. Further, for this purpose we want to be sure that in the case of seamen we take into account not only the value of the allotment note, but the balance of pay brought into the home at the end of the voyage. The apparently less precise phrase "average earnings" avoided these difficulties better, and this was the direction given. It will be observed that the rule prevented a low grading on account of unemployment at the date of the enquiry, but did include consideration of seasonal or casual employment. And it was also possible to allow for permanent disability.

The Survey was made at the end of the summer of 1928, information being obtained in respect of 21,538 families and 43,519 children up to school-leaving age. The census appears to have been practically complete. The results of the census taken by the school attendance officers of the local authority in March 1930, gave a total of 40,079 children under 14 years old. A number should be added to this to allow for the children actually fourteen who were staying at school until the close of the term in which they became school-leaving age. The Survey figure then shows a slight excess of children, mainly accounted for by the inclusion of children over school-leaving age but not yet 15 years old. The official number under 15 years of age was 42,962, or 557 less than the Survey numbers.

Not only individual accuracy, but uniformity of grading was essential. One's confidence in the result of the process depends upon three factors. First, the assessors were all men with exceptional knowledge and experience, with intimate acquaintance of their areas; secondly, the wage rates and even earnings of large classes of workers are fixed by collective agreement, and as each man's occupation was known, we had, within limits, the range within which his income from that source might be expected to lie. A number of firms allowed their wage sheets to be inspected, and from these some measure of earnings was obtained in a number of trades where we needed them. Thirdly, the size of the area was an advantage. In a large area such as London, it is impossible for anyone to have even a slight acquaintance with all its districts, but Southampton is still small enough for one person to obtain by inspection some knowledge of nearly every street. This was made part of the method, and it was therefore possible to raise queries as to comparative gradings of streets, any serious discrepancy being dealt with at joint meetings of assessors. At a later stage these facts were compared with the rateable values for each street.

Booth's classification into eight income grades was taken as a basis. The difficulty of any such grading is to avoid basing the distinctions on social characteristics instead of differences of income, and of treating the lower grades of clerical and "white-handed" occupations as in a different grade from a manual worker of equivalent income. The scheme was, therefore, modified to suit the immediate purpose and the conditions of Southampton, and an endeavour was made to work as far as circumstance allowed to specific income limits. On page 96 are the grades showing, (1) the descriptions, mostly derived from Booth, (2) the income limits of the class, and (3) some typical occupations found in that grade. The description enables comparisons to be made with Booth's classes.

It was income limit and not description which was decisive in determining into which income grade a given case should go, for there are certain men who are not skilled in the sense that they are tradesmen who have served an apprenticeship, but earn wages equal to and often greater than a craftsman's. It will be observed that Classes II, III, IV, have income limits which overlap. They are, in effect, one income group 20s. to 42s. subdivided according to the regularity of their earnings. As the examples of typical occupations found within the class show, there are some occupations within this broad range which fit conveniently into these sub-groups. The distinction between Classes VII and VIII is not completely watertight; broadly it was made to turn on whether the occupation yielded £250 per annum or more, but there are two difficulties. First, as we pass into the higher income levels, income from property

INCOME GRADES

	Description	*Income (Shillings)*	*Examples*
I.	Lowest class of occasional labour	—	—
II.	Casual	20 and under 30	Fringe of dock and shipyard labourers
III.	Intermittent and seasonal	20 and under 40	Ice cream vendors
IV.	Small regular earnings	30 and under 42	Labourer
V.	Regular standard earnings	42 and under 50	Blacksmith labourers, riggers, some classes of seamen
VI.	Skilled	50 and under 80	Joiners and other tradesmen, tram motor men
VII.	Supervising and clerical	80 and over	Foremen: some clerical
VIII.	Middle class ..	100 and over	

becomes a steadily more important factor. Secondly, for a number of occupations the distinction can only be rough and ready. There are different grades of retail stores, some owners making substantial incomes, while many small general shops make but meagre earnings. There are equally different grades of lodging and boarding houses, some landladies falling below and some above the limit. The extreme cases are clear, but there is still a large marginal group the exact position of which is a matter of some doubt. For the purpose of classifying the population into broad income classes, Grades VII and VIII were merged into a single class, though it was found possible and useful to preserve the distinction for certain purposes. In the same way Grades I and II were merged.

The tables on pages 98–9 show the number and percentages of the families and children enumerated in the various income classes in each ward.

On the basis of these results it is worth making an attempt to turn the income classification of families with school children into one of the entire population. It can be done only on the assumption that we can argue that the proportions of rich and poor found in this group of persons will hold good of the whole population. We are not here judging similarity in the proportions of the two groups found beneath the poverty line, but the proportions in different income classes. The heads with school children are likely to be in their full earning period, while the population contains younger men not yet at full earning power, as well as a number of single men of low income such as are found in the ranks of unskilled labour in the port. The total population will also contain older persons, some of whom have become old-age pensioners, and others who have reached the difficult gap between industrial old age and pensionable age. Against this must be set the fact that, at any rate in the higher income groups, the older persons are often better off than younger ones, since they have had more time to accumulate savings. Booth thought that the incidence of poverty was probably greater in the total population than in the families with school children. It is possible, therefore, that the application of these results to the entire population will present a picture slightly too favourable.

There are certain other adjustments to make. The Registrar-General's estimated population for 1929 was 169,900, of which, taking the proportions of 1921 as a basis, we may estimate 161,300 as being the population in private families, and the remaining 8,600 as in institutions, barracks, hotels, etc. We may thus divide the former of these figures into the relevant grades, by using the means between the percentage in each

NUMBERS OF FAMILIES IN INCOME CLASSES, 1928

Ward	*Income Class* *I–IV*	*V*	*VI*	*VII–VIII*	*Total*
1. Town	234	407	386	139	1,166
2. St. Mary's	594	233	367	136	1,330
3. Northam	246	634	576	85	1,541
4. Trinity	324	233	433	88	1,078
5. Newtown	14	231	471	148	864
6. All Saints	66	199	499	250	1,014
7. Bevois	17	238	371	236	862
8. Banister	9	60	323	403	795
9. Freemantle	97	173	457	195	922
10. Millbrook	331	305	883	314	1,833
11. Shirley	173	356	933	541	2,003
12. Portswood	39	241	456	667	1,403
13. St. Denys	20	296	724	342	1,382
14. Bitterne and Pear Tree	130	263	551	200	1,144
15. Bitterne and Sholing	157	772	565	116	1,610
16. Woolston	103	217	592	156	1,068
17. St. Nicholas	138	336	769	280	1,523
Total	2,692	5,194	9,356	4,296	21,538

NUMBERS OF CHILDREN IN INCOME CLASSES, 1928

Ward	*Income Class* *I–IV*	*V*	*VI*	*VII–VIII*	*All*
1. Town	536	938	868	268	2,610
2. St. Mary's	1,362	579	852	274	3,067
3. Northam	599	1,527	1,212	168	3,506
4. Trinity	747	447	872	146	2,212
5. Newtown	19	431	884	257	1,591
6. All Saints	147	326	789	461	1,723
7. Bevois	38	502	706	403	1,649
8. Banister	13	95	498	679	1,285
9. Freemantle	191	320	840	357	1,708
10. Millbrook	590	547	1,433	608	3,178
11. Shirley	373	804	1,865	928	3,970
12. Portswood	83	493	806	1,030	2,412
13. St. Denys	44	575	1,334	640	2,593
14. Bitterne and Pear Tree	340	647	1,394	399	2,780
15. Bitterne and Sholing	376	1,872	1,165	209	3,622
16. Woolston	203	402	1,173	302	2,080
17. St. Nicholas	374	849	1,743	567	3,533
Total	6,035	11,354	18,434	7,696	43,519

NUMBERS IN CLASSES I–IV

Class I, 77; Class II, 887; Class III, 876; Class IV, 4,195.

PERCENTAGE OF FAMILIES IN INCOME CLASSES, 1928

Ward	*I–IV*	*V*	*VI*	*VII–VIII*	*Total*
	Income Class				
1. Town	20·1	34·9	33·1	11·9	100·0
2. St. Mary's	44·7	17·5	27·6	10·2	100·0
3. Northam	16·0	41·2	37·4	5·4	100·0
4. Trinity	30·0	21·6	40·2	8·2	100·0
5. Newtown	1·6	26·8	54·5	17·1	100·0
6. All Saints	6·5	19·6	49·2	24·7	100·0
7. Bevois	2·0	27·6	43·0	27·4	100·0
8. Banister	1·1	7·6	40·6	50·7	100·0
9. Freemantle	10·5	18·7	49·6	21·2	100·0
10. Millbrook	18·0	16·7	48·1	17·2	100·0
11. Shirley	8·6	17·8	46·6	27·0	100·0
12. Portswood	2·8	17·2	32·5	47·5	100·0
13. St. Denys	1·4	21·4	52·4	24·8	100·0
14. Bitterne and Pear Tree ..	11·4	23·0	48·2	17·4	100·0
15. Bitterne and Sholing ..	9·8	48·2	35·2	6·8	100·0
16. Woolston	9·7	20·3	55·4	14·6	100·0
17. St. Nicholas	9·0	22·1	50·5	18·4	100·0
Total..	12·5	24·1	43·5	19·9	100·0

PERCENTAGE OF CHILDREN IN INCOME CLASSES, 1928

Ward	*I–IV*	*V*	*VI*	*VII–VIII*	*All*
	Income Class				
1. Town	20·5	35·9	33·3	10·3	100·0
2. St. Mary's	44·4	18·9	27·8	8·9	100·0
3. Northam	17·1	43·5	34·6	4·8	100·0
4. Trinity	33·8	20·2	39·4	6·6	100·0
5. Newtown	1·2	27·1	55·5	16·2	100·0
6. All Saints	8·5	18·9	45·8	26·8	100·0
7. Bevois	2·3	30·5	42·8	24·4	100·0
8. Banister	1·0	7 4	38·8	52·8	100·0
9. Freemantle	11·2	18·7	49·2	20·9	100·0
10. Millbrook	18·6	17·2	45·1	19·1	100·0
11. Shirley	9·4	20·2	47·0	23·4	100·0
12. Portswood	3·4	20·5	33·4	42·7	100·0
13. St. Denys	1·7	22·2	51·5	24·6	100·0
14. Bitterne and Pear Tree ..	12·2	23·3	50·1	14·4	100·0
15. Bitterne and Sholing ..	10·4	51·7	32·1	5·8	100·0
16. Woolston	9·8	19·3	56·4	14·5	100·0
17. St. Nicholas	10·6	24·0	49·4	16·0	100·0
Total..	13·8	26·1	42·4	17·7	100·0

PERCENTAGES IN CLASSES I–IV

Class I, 0·2; Class II, 2·0; Class III, 2·0; Class IV, 9·6.

according to the numbers of families and the percentage found on the basis of the number of children:

POPULATION IN PRIVATE FAMILIES IN INCOME GRADES

Income Class	*Families*	*Children*	*Mean*	*Estimated Number*
VII–VIII	20·0	17·7	18·85	30,400
VI	43·4	42·4	42·9	69,200
V	24·1	26·1	25·10	40,500
I–IV	12·5	13·8	13·15	21,200
	100·0	100·0	100·0	161,300

No special difficulty arises respecting the numbers in the middle-class groups. When Booth made a similar classification of London's population, he found it necessary to make a separate estimate of the numbers of the middle and upper classes, since his information relating to families with school children in that group was known to be incomplete. In this case, as stated above, this gap in knowledge had been successfully closed, and there is no need for such an adjustment. There remain to be allocated the 8,600 persons not in private families. These include those in Poor Law institutions, barns, and sheds, etc.—16·2 per cent of the total number of this non-private family population in 1921. These are all clearly in Classes I–IV, and in consequence 1,400 were added to that group. The remainder included men in barracks, hotels, hospitals, residents in shops and warehouses, ships, etc. It was assumed that these would be in the income grades in the same proportions as the whole population, and they were allocated in accordance with this rule. As a result of these adjustments, we get the following number as representing an approximate population for each income grade:

POPULATION IN INCOME GRADES

Class	*Numbers*	*Percentage*
VII–VIII	31,700	18·7
VI	72,400	42·6
V	42,300	24·9
I–IV	23,500	13·8

Certain aspects of these facts have been represented on a map which shows the local distribution of rich and poor by streets. This map, inspired by Booth's map of London, shows each street coloured according to its predominant income grade. In classifying the streets, it was found that the distinction between Class VII and Class VIII could, despite the margin of uncertainty, be usefully retained. There were no streets dominantly Class I. Classes II and III, which have been merged with IV in classifying the population as a whole, did together represent a group with casual, seasonal, and intermittent earnings distinct from low regular earnings of Class IV. After examination of the records, it was decided for this purpose to preserve them as a single amalgamated group separate from Class IV. There were thus left six grades of streets, II–III, IV, V, VI, VII, and VIII. In certain respects the map differs from Booth's. It is based on information concerning families with dependent children, but some almost purely commercial streets have few such families, occasionally only one, and grading the street on that basis was apt to be fortuitous and occasionally fantastic. The main commercial streets were excluded from the scheme altogether by being given a neutral colour. Secondly, the colour scheme itself was based on the spectrum, commencing with violet for the lowest Grades II and III and passing through the colours of the spectrum to red for the highest income grade. The colour scheme has the advantage that it is both natural and universally known. A discussion of the various problems, cartographical and other, which arise in representing street classification in this manner, together with details as to the actual arrangements made, will be found in an appendix.

2. *The Random Sample Household Enquiry*

The method of mass interview is useful in determining the proportions of the different economic classes in the town, and for throwing some indirect light on the extent of poverty, but more precise measurement of insufficiency of income or housing and similar characteristics requires the inclusion of families without school children and the collection of information respecting the numbers and incomes of subsidiary earners, receipts from social services, etc. Fortunately it is not necessary to add to the scale of the task both as regards the number of cases to be surveyed and the amount of information required, for a satisfactory description of a whole group of families can be given without collecting information of all or even most of them. The method of investigating a random sample, i.e. a group selected by some mechanical rule, such as one in every twenty, which will ensure that every member has an equal chance of being represented in it, has been sufficiently explained by Professor Bowley, who has both developed and popularized its use for this type of investigation. Only details of the size of the sample and certain adaptation of method to the peculiarities of Southampton need description. Two initial difficulties faced the attempt. One relating to the attitude of the public, and the other financial. First, such an enquiry involves detailed questioning of the persons interviewed, and no prominent social worker or trade unionist in the town (and most were consulted) would prophesy anything but complete failure from such an attempt. Nor were these gloomy fears without real basis. A well-known man leaving the town declared in a friendly farewell speech, that it was like a "big village," and although the phrase was used in another context, it sums up aptly the nature of the difficulty. This was a very discouraging start. The enquiry was in fact carried through with complete success, but the unanimity of view was sufficient to suggest the advisability of limiting the objectives of the survey and minimizing the number of questions to be asked.

Secondly, the resources of the survey were not sufficient to make possible a sample of 1 in 20 which had been the aim, and in consequence the method had to be scrutinized to increase the effectiveness of the sample by avoiding any wastage of cards. Random selection will include some middle- and upper-class families, who are notoriously unwilling to answer personal enquiries of the sort, and their cards would have to be excluded, if only on grounds of incompleteness, so that in practice the samples are limited to working-class families. The wastage could be reduced by combining the results of the mass interview, which enabled every street to be given a definite income grade, with that of a random selection. The sample was limited to streets graded in Classes I–VI (working-class streets). There were some risks in this course: but the alternative of a considerably smaller effective sample seemed a greater one. The relation of the sample to the whole group was known in various respects. The number of residences (rated properties other than those classified as commercial) in these streets was 25,693: the number of families investigated was 559 (other than a few spoiled and wasted cards), the ratio being 1 in 46. The total number of residences of all grade streets was 34,024, the residences in the included streets thus being 75 per cent of the whole. There were 348 families with school children in the sample, as compared with 17,242 such families in Classes I–VI in the mass survey, the ratio being 1 in 49½. These 17,242 families were 80 per cent of the total number surveyed. The ratio of children in the sample to children in the mass survey in Classes I–VI was 1 in 47. When supplemented by the larger survey and other investigations, a reasonably trustworthy picture of the major facts can be obtained.

As the sample was a small one, the question of its reliability is of some importance. The census population in 1921 was 160,994, children under the age of fourteen numbering 45,560, or 28·3 per cent of the whole; and since that date there has been a fall in the birth-rate, which would suggest a lower proportion in 1931. In the sample, on the contrary, there were 2,368 persons (excluding boarders), of which 761, or 32·1 per cent, were school children. If boarders were included, it would not reduce the proportion of school children by more than 1 per cent. Was this difference in the proportion of children traceable to the fact that the sample concerned the working-class population only, or the chance inclusion of too many large families, or too many families with children? The close correspondence of the ratios of residences visited (1 to 46) and of school children (1 to 47) will be noted. The average number of children is greater in working-class than in better-off families, and we should on this ground expect a larger proportion of children to be found in the sample. The mass survey gave for all families an unweighted average of 2·0 children for all families, of 2·1 for families in Class VI, and 2·2 for families in Classes I–V. The 761 children in the sample were found in 348 families, the (weighted) average being nearly 2·2 per family. It does not appear likely that much of any apparent excess is due to the inclusion of an undue number of large families. Did the sample contain too few families *without* children? It is possible that the difficulty of securing a card for both families in a shared house led to the omission of a certain number of smaller and no children families. One may conclude that some of the apparent excess was to be expected in a sample concerned with working-class families only; and that part may be traceable to the omission of a certain proportion of small families in shared houses.

The representative character of the sample does not depend on size only. The survey was particularly fortunate in its investigators. The bulk of the work fell on four of them, who worked practically full time; they were all both skilful and experienced. Three had recently been engaged on work for the census and had other experience bringing them in direct contact with working-class houses, while a fourth was an educated man experienced in social investigation. All of them took a great interest in the work and discussed various points connected with it with keenness. It is a tribute to the tact which they exercised that in spite of the secretiveness and apprehensions of so provincial a population there were few refusals, and they were able to get the wages of the subsidiary earners in great detail, in nearly every case where this was known to the parents. One investigator was able to obtain a great deal of additional information not asked for on the card, including the family budgets for the week, as well as to obtain details of voluntary insurances, sick clubs, and other weekly payments for most of the cases.

As already hinted, the comparability of the different enquiries is affected by the fact that the resources available did not make it possible to conduct the several enquiries—together with certain branches of the Civic Survey, which was proceeding over the same period—simultaneously. The mass interview was undertaken in the autumn of 1928, one special group in December 1930, the random sample in November–December 1931. In between the first and last of these dates there was a rapid deterioration of trade conditions. The Board of Trade general commodity index, expressed as a percentage of the 1924 level, fell from 83·1 in the last month of 1928 to 63·7 in the corresponding month of 1931; unemployment in Southampton and Woolston rose from 4,000 in December 1928 to 13,000 in December 1931, although in this case the deterioration occurred in Southampton in the last few months only. While on the income side both employment and earnings, and the amounts received from insurance benefit, were affected, the expenditure side of family accounts was affected by the decline in retail prices, the cost of living index, expressed as a percentage of the 1924 level, falling from 95 to 83. It is no loss to have a measurement of "poverty" in the depths of depression; but since the aim of the enquiries was to get a general impression of the facts by the threefold method of mass interview, random sample working-class households, and a scrutiny of certain dependent and low income groups, the unity of the scheme was adversely affected. The effect in the fall of the cost of purchasing the requisites of the defined poverty standard caused least difficulty, for it involved only the recalculation of the standard at the new prices. The consequences in employment and income were more difficult to handle; estimates of probable effect on various averages are made at the appropriate points below.

(i) THE CONSTITUTION OF THE FAMILY

As a preliminary step to relating income and needs, we have to examine the constitution of the family, the numbers of earners and dependents. When at the outset of the enquiry, various voluntary associations were consulted, two of them advanced views as to the average family: one was the man, wife, and three children of convention; the other, made by more well-to-do persons with modern developments in mind, was man, wife, and two children. The population of the sample surveyed included 2,364 persons, who were distributed amongst 559 families, the average being 4·23 persons per family, or excluding families in which there is no earner, 4·34. This may be compared with 4·36 for the Five Towns.[1] Three hundred and forty-eight families or 62 per cent had dependent children, leaving over one-third, 38 per cent. without.[2] Less than one in ten of the families had three dependent children; the other estimate was nearer the mark, but still was true of less than one in five of the families. Even these proportions must be reduced, for they include all types of families with three and two children, for example, those with grown-up earners. The proportions of families complying strictly with their definitions (i.e. with no other earning adults, etc.) were only 11·1 per cent and 6·4 per cent respectively. That the lower income groups have also a greater average number of dependent children is, of course, well known. The average numbers of children for different grades of income was not worked out for the random sample; but for the Booth Survey the (crude) average numbers of school children per family for the main income classes were:

Class I–IV	*V*	*VI*	*VII*	*VIII*	*All*
2·2	2·2	2·0	1·8	1·7	2·0

[1] *Has Poverty Diminished?* p. 9.

[2] Op. cit. All Five Towns, 46·8 per cent, Reading 48·4 per cent, Warrington 33·2 per cent.

Dependents other than children includes widows, mothers,[1] housekeepers, daughters helping in the home, and adults permanently disabled. Although from the point of the need for care and attention of others, aged persons may also be regarded as dependent, unlike children, they may have, through old-age pensions, an income sufficient to feed and clothe them, if house room is provided. Of the 1,603 persons other than children, 559 were heads of families normally with an income from work or the social services, 434 were normally "other earners," though like the heads of families they may be temporarily unemployed or sick, 63 were old-age pensioners, leaving 547 wives, housekeepers, etc., maintained out of income accruing to heads and other members of the family.

The families in the sample were classified into five types,[2] representing roughly their economic strength as tested by the presence or absence of earners, in particular adult male earners:

Type 1. No one earning. Examples: two old persons living alone; widow or deserted wife with young children; and entirely depending on social service payments.

Type 2. No adult male earner; women, girls, male minors only working. Example: widow with earning daughter or earning son not yet of age.

Type 3. One adult male earner only. The natural family of man, wife, and young children.

Type 4. One adult male earner, and subsidiary earners (i.e. boys, youths, girls, and women).

Type 5. Two or more adult earners, with or without subsidiary earners. Examples: man and wife, with one or more grown-up sons earning, with or without female earners; a less common type, two unmarried brothers living with unmarried or widowed sister.

The scheme has the advantage that each successive grade represents an advance of economic strength, though naturally

[1] Some wives and mothers earned small amounts for service to lodgers.

[2] Following in some measure the classification in *Has Poverty Diminished?* and the Liverpool Survey (*Journal Royal Statistical Society*, 1930, p. 506).

the actual family income of a Type 4 family may be greater than that of a Type 5 family. The Types 3, 4, and 5 in serial order may be said to show the natural evolution of the family as the children grow up. Type 1 is in some cases the position of parents towards the end of their life. Type 2 in most cases represents a family broken by death of the chief male earner.

The table opposite combines the facts as to earning strength with those relating to the number of dependent children.

The table makes it possible to get a preliminary view of the extent to which the children are exposed to the risk of poverty or other effects of economic adversity. Over one-third of the children are in families where the earnings of the chief male earner are supplemented by the earnings of another (Type 5), or by the income of subsidiary earners (Type 4), which may remain unaffected by the unemployment of the chief earner. Less than 3 per cent are in families where there are no earners, e.g. with grandparents in receipt of old-age pensions or in broken families. The remainder (59·7 per cent) are in families almost entirely dependent on the earnings of one adult male only, usually the father; and in these families the average number of dependent children (including the families with none) is 1·9 as compared with 1·22 for the whole sample. Twelve and a half per cent of the families of that type had four or more children, a total of 156, or more than one-fifth of the entire number. It is naturally the position of the one-fifth which may become dangerous if wages are low, or if the head of the family is sick or unemployed. Nearly one-fifth of the children are in a more protected position, being in families where there are subsidiary earners, or two men earning, and in which there are not more than two dependent children.

The average working-class family consisted of 4·23 persons, of which 1·73 persons were earners, and 2·50 persons were non-earners. This proportion of earners is less than was found in Bolton, Warrington, and Northampton in 1924, slightly less than in Reading, but more than in Stanley. The chief source of the difference is the number of women over 16 who

EARNING STRENGTH AND NUMBER OF DEPENDENTS

Number of Dependent Children	*Family Type* 1 *No Earner*	2 *No Adult Male Earner*	3 *Adult Male Earner only*	4 *Adult Male and Subsidiary Earners*	5 *Two Adult Male Earners*	*All*	*Percentage of Total Families*
0	23	12	74	53	49	211	38
1	2	5	67	34	28	136	24
2	—	2	62	30	8	102	18
3	2	—	36	14	1	53	10
4	1	—	22	12	3	38	7
5	—	—	5	4	1	10	2
6	—	—	3	3	—	6	1
7	—	—	2	—	—	2	—
8 or more	—	—	1	—	—	1	—
Total	28	19	272	150	90	559	100
Percentage of total families ..	5	3	49	27	16	100	—
Total with dependent children ..	5	7	198	97	41	348	—
Percentage of all families	1	1	35	17	7	62	—
Total numbers of children ..	12	9	454	222	64	761	—
Percentage of all children ..	2	1	60	29	8	100	—

NOTE.—In this and following tables, the percentages are given to the nearest unit, and the detailed items do not always add up exactly to 100.

were earning; for in Southampton the number in this category of female earners was less than in any of the Five Towns, except Stanley. This is the natural outcome of the relative scarcity of opportunities for women in industrial work to which reference has already been made. The details are as below:

AVERAGE WORKING-CLASS FAMILY

Earners	
Men of 18	1·27
Women over 16	0·29
Boys under 18	0·13
Girls under 16	0·04
	1·73
Non-Earners	
Men over 18	0·08
Women over 16	1·06
Boys under 18	—
Girls under 16	0·01
Children 5–14	0·98
Children under 5	0·37
	2·50
All persons	4·23

(ii) THE DISTRIBUTION OF INCOME

The mass interview provided data on which a broad impression of the curve of income distribution could be obtained. The random sample concerned only the lower and working-class portions of the curve. Here income means not full time or assessed income, but the income of the previous week, and therefore takes account of overtime, short time, unemployment, and includes any payments received from the social services. The figures below show the facts separately for family incomes (both those below and above the poverty datum line), head's incomes, and the income of supplementary earners, adults and juveniles.

If the information had been plotted, in each case the curves

DISTRIBUTION OF INCOME

	Under 15/-	*15/- and under 30/-*	*30/- and under 45/-*	*45/- and under 60/-*	*60/- and under 75/-*	*75/- and under 90/-*	*90/- and under 105/-*	*105/- and under 120/-*	*120/- and over*	*Total*
Family Income—										
Above line cases ..	2	18	79	124	81	58	30	22	25	439
Below line cases ..	7	59	44	9	1	—	—	—	—	120
All families ..	9	77	123	133	82	58	30	22	25	559
Head's Income ..	20	148	164	161	38	21	4	3	—	559
Other Earners' Income—										
Adults	33	92	49	24	3	—	—	—	—	201
Juveniles	146	74	12	1	—	—	—	—	—	233

would have taken the usual polygon shape familiar in income statistics, but with the data grouped into 15s. ranges, some of the facts, in the case of head's income, are concealed. If it had been based on 5s. groups, this curve would show bulges between 10s. and 15s., and between 20s. and 30s., with a depression between 30s. and 60s. The first bulge is due to those old-age and widows' pensioners who happen to be "heads," the second bulge and the depression is the consequence of unemployment removing earned incomes from the upper ranges and concentrating them at the lower and narrower range of income determined by the flat rates of unemployment benefit. The appearance of the curve is thus that of a decapitated polygon. The figures for a portion of the curve will be sufficient to indicate this:

Incomes under..	5/-	10/-	15/-	20/-	25/-	30/-
Numbers ..	2	3	15	22	59	67
Incomes under..	35/-	40/-	45/-	50/-	55/-	60/-
Numbers ..	58	53	53	57	44	60

The figures for supplementary earners show the same influence at the benefit rate for single persons. Family income includes income from all sources. Expressed numerically, the facts for the different categories are:

	Mean	*Lower Quartile*	*Median*	*Upper Quartile*
Heads	41/3	28/9	40/1	53/6
Juveniles	15/3	9/10	13/4	18/2
Family income ..	57/9	36/6	52/8	73/7

(iii) THE POVERTY DATUM LINE

If poverty is to be measured, it must first be defined. Do we mean that a family is in poverty if the head of it has a wage insufficient to enable him to meet his responsibilities? If so, for how many children is he to be regarded as responsible? Enough to maintain the population undiminished? Enough to maintain a steady growth of numbers at some rate suggested by past experience, e.g. 3 per cent per annum? Or do we mean that the family is in poverty unless it has sufficient income to enable it to reach a defined and arbitrary standard of food, clothing, and shelter for all of them, no matter how large the family may be and how many its dependents? It is this third sense with which these studies are concerned. It is customary to distinguish between primary poverty, which is regarded as that which arises when the total family earnings are insufficient to purchase "the minimum necessaries for maintenance at physical efficiency," and "secondary poverty," when the income is sufficient for this limited purpose, but is in fact used for some other purpose, either useful or wasteful. To this practical distinction a third may be added. The definition of primary and secondary poverty both assume that all family income is pooled, the family being regarded as a unit, both in earnings and consumption. It would be useful to know both how far the head of a family with young children is able to support them out of his own income, if he were released from any liability to maintain older children already at work, and they were released from any obligation to contribute to the support of younger brothers and sisters, i.e. ignoring older children both on the income and expenditure side of the family account. Failing any other suitable name, the term "potential" poverty has been given to this. It is on the first and third of these distinctions, "primary" and "potential" poverty, that attention is here concentrated.

The steps in the determination of primary poverty are (1) the selection of some standard of diet, clothing, and house room, etc.; (2) its adjustment to the varying size, age, and sex composition of the individual families by the use of "man values" for women, young persons, and children; (3) its translation into current prices, and (4) the comparison of family incomes with the sums so ascertained. A variety of choices are open to one at each stage, and, in view of certain objections to the procedure recently made, the course actually taken at each step needs some explanation.

First, the minimum need standard as devised by Professor Bowley for the 1924 enquiries has been used, subject to certain modifications. The standard consists of two portions of very different origin. The first, a diet sufficient for health and efficiency, is derived from workers in another branch of science, and is based on calculations of the numbers of calories required to sustain men in full work, etc., as used in war rationing. On this point the economist can only take what appears to be the more or less agreed conclusions of those whose work is in that field, and has merely to satisfy himself that the scale he uses would command their common consent as sufficient for the purpose in hand. On this score the diet seems open to some objection, for it appears to be conceived too much in terms of calories and too little in terms of constituents. There is, for example, a striking absence of green vegetables and of fruit, the importance of which has been emphasized by recent work.[1] The absence of fish is also notable, for poor families rely on getting economical meals when large catches of fish can be bought cheap; and in this southern town, the oatmeal is conspicuous by its absence. The Bowley diet, as set forth in *Has Poverty Diminished?* has nevertheless been accepted without change. There is much to be said for uniformity of practice in studies, part of whose value is their comparability; it can be modified only by those who are expert in this field; and no other authoritative standard seemed available.

The second portion of the standard is both less objective and less precisely measurable than the first, and for it the economist must take sole responsibility. It consists of certain allowances for house room, clothing, heating, cleanliness, etc., and these are obtained by frankly accepting the customary payments made for these by persons of low income. There is nothing approaching such objectivity as the calculation of the calorific requirements of a man in full work. As regards house

[1] E.g. Mottram, *Food and the Family*; Rose, *Foundations of Nutrition*, 1927; Orr and Gilks, *Physique and Health of Two African Tribes*, 1931.

room, for example, one could either take as a basis the amount of rent commonly paid, or try to lay down some physical standard of housing, but both accept convention as a basis, the one of working-class expenditure habits, the other of some arbitrary standard devised in the light of actual practice.[1] In two respects the allowances made in the 1924 enquiries have been revised. A group of working-class men and women, whose activities gave them an intimate personal knowledge of working-class life and standards, were inclined to regard an allowance of 60s. per annum for a man's clothing as likely to be in excess of the facts for low incomes. The poorest sections of the population rarely purchase new clothing, and indeed a donkey and cart can be seen going the rounds with second-hand suits priced at 7s. to 10s. Unredeemed pledges, jumble and Salvation Army sales are other sources of cheap clothing. One estimate placed the expenditure of an adult male, with a meagre income, as unlikely to exceed 30s. per annum. The fuel allowance could be reduced from 3s. to 2s. 6d. per week, if account be taken of the fact that low-grade coal is purchased by the bucket from the wharves at cheap rates.

The man values adopted to convert the full standard diet to suit the needs of varying age and sex were those accepted by Professor Bowley, with one modification.

	Males	*Females*
70 and over	60	60
16–70	100	80
14–16	85	80
5–14	50	50
0–5	33	33

There are a number of alternative scales. The Bowley 1924 scale raises them at the age of 5, 14, and 18 years for males, and 5, 14, and 16 years for females. Attwater's scale raised them at 2, 5, and 10 years, while Lusk's scale, instead of rating a boy of fourteen years at 0·85, gives him the same coefficient as a man—a figure which seems more consistent

[1] Greenwood, *Journal Royal Statistical Society*, 1930, p. 583.

with experience than the lower value. This change was accepted in the more graduated scale adopted by Doctors Cathcart and Murray in the St. Andrews enquiry.[1] In a study of this kind, the breaks at 5 years and 14 years are convenient owing to their importance in the educational system, and they make possible the use of data and methods of verification not otherwise available. The Bowley 1924 scale of values has therefore been used, subject only to the increase of the "value" of youths of 16–18 from 85 to 100. It is perhaps worth observing that the family coefficient method has been questioned, for example, by Professor Greenwood, but it is currently used in nutrition studies, and one outside that field of work must be content to accept the principle of the procedure as it stands.

Three authorities have recently given emphatic warnings against regarding such a standard as measuring poverty in any absolute sense. Sir Josiah Stamp argued that such a standard was relative to one's own ideas, that it changed from time to time, and that, in consequence, there always would be a considerable number below any poverty line likely to be drawn. Professor Greenwood argued that the existence of any such substantial proportion of families below the poverty line should be checked by mortality and morbidity figures, and much evidence ought to be found of chronic under-nutrition; Mr. Clay objected that the procedure was open to doubt since, in practice, all poverty lines worked out approximately to the wage of unskilled labourers in the various countries; that the fact that natives with very low wages produced more than British miners, without apparent harm to themselves, made the diet basis of these studies suspect, and that in any case it would avoid confusion if the term "poverty line," which suggested some absolute measurement, were altered to "poverty datum line."[2]

In emphasizing the relative nature of the standard, and that

[1] Cathcart and Murray, *A Study of Nutrition*, 1931. Medical Research Council.

[2] *Journal Royal Statistical Society*, 1931, pp. 256–58.

its primary purpose is comparing the conditions of populations, not very dissimilar in age composition or customs, or for measuring social progress in a given district between dates not too widely separated, these critics were knocking at the open door.[1] While it may not be possible always to relate the proportions found below any poverty line with mortality and morbidity figures in any given instance, it is the fact that in the earlier part of the nineteenth century, when most of the unskilled and some of the skilled workers were "below" such a standard, the mortality rates were high, and the personal efficiency probably very low also. And, in considering the low wages of natives as compared with their output, we need more evidence on the length of their working life, and their powers of endurance before doubting the validity of diet standards. The enquiries of Doctors Orr and Gilks showed how large a fraction of even selected labour gangs was unhealthy and possessed but a limited power of endurance, and how closely—making every allowance for heredity—the adequacy and appropriateness of the diet appeared to be connected with physical efficiency.[2]

The final step was the comparison of the cost of purchasing the standard at current local prices with the total income of each family. This assumes that the income of every earning member of the family is "pooled," which is probably not very far from the truth if the family is very poor, though habits may be changing in this respect, and more may be withheld for personal use by the younger members of the family than formerly.

Rent and rates are a difficulty. We can incorporate into the standard some arbitrary rent which seems reasonable for each main size of the family, and then compare total family income with this adjusted sum, in which case any actual rent less than the standard amount must be regarded as an undue skimping

[1] Bowley, *Measurement of Social Phenomena*, chap. viii.

[2] See Orr and Gilks, *Physique and Health of Two African Tribes* (Medical Research Council), esp. p. 17 and Graph 6.

on house room, and any higher rent an unnecessary one; or alternatively, we can accept the net sums each family pays as likely to be the best bargain it could make in the circumstances, deduct it from total income, and compare the remainder with the standard for diet, clothing, etc. For the purpose of the random sample, the latter procedure was followed.

(iv) PRIMARY POVERTY

We may first deal with primary poverty and its causes. Counting all sources of known income, including any income from the Public Assistance Committee, 120 of the families or 21 per cent of the total were beneath the minimum standard. Allowing for possible errors due to fluctuations of sampling, we may say that the numbers of working-class families beneath the standard was between 25·8 per cent and 17·2 per cent, and was probably between 22·5 per cent and 20·6 per cent. This is exceptionally heavy. The Survey of Liverpool—an area like Southampton with a large proportion of casual labourers—showed 17·3 per cent, but this was in the autumn of 1929. The Southampton figures refer to the autumn of 1931, when trade conditions were very different. Between these two dates the numbers of unemployed in the town doubled. There were 76 cases recorded as being below the line on account of unemployment, and if we reduced this number by one-half, the percentage of families in poverty would fall to under 15 per cent. Similarly, if unemployment had been at the level of 1928, the proportions in poverty would probably have been about 13 per cent. The heavy load in Southampton does not, therefore, seem so startling, though compared with it the Five Towns of 1924 were enjoying great prosperity. Even Reading, the worst case, showed only 10·3 per cent as probably below the standard, taking the actual income of the week of the investigation.

The table on page 119 shows the incidence of poverty by families and the extent to which their incomes exceeded or fell short of the amount required for the standard. From this

FAMILIES IN RELATION TO THE POVERTY DATUM LINE

(Amount of Excess or Deficiency)

Amount of Excess or Deficiency	*Family Types*					*All*	*Percentage of Total Families*
	1 *No Earner*	2 *No Adult Earner*	3 *Adult Male Earner only*	4 *Adult Male and Subsidiary Earners*	5 *Two Adult Male Earners*		
Families above Line							
20/– and over	2	3	84	75	73	237	42
10/– and under 20/–	4	4	62	33	5	108	19
5/– and under 10/–	4	4	19	11	4	42	8
2/– and under 5/–	3	—	19	7	2	31	6
Under 2/–	4	1	10	4	2	21	4
Total	17	12	194	130	86	439	79
Families below Line							
Under 2/–	5	—	11	3	—	19	3
2/– and under 5/–	2	4	19	7	3	35	6
5/– and under 10/–	2	2	25	6	—	35	6
10/– and under 20/–	2	1	16	4	—	23	4
20/– and over	—	—	7	—	1	8	1
Total	11	7	78	20	4	120	21

it will be seen that if we exclude those cases which fell below the standard by any sum less than 2s. as "marginal," there would still remain a number approaching one-fifth of the families below the line. If we go further and say that those families whose incomes are less than the standard by amounts varying from 2s. to 5s. are only "probably" below the standard, then there are nearly 12 per cent of whom the word "certainly" below could be used.

If we distinguish between the different types of families, the degree of poverty found was heaviest where there were no earners, and decreased as the number of principal and subsidiary earners increased. The total numbers of families in Types 1 and 2 are small, and too much reliance could not be placed on the precise percentage of those two types found beneath the line; but the results run consistently with the increase of the economic strength of Types 1 to 5:

PERCENTAGE OF EACH TYPE OF FAMILY BELOW THE LINE

1	2	3	4	5	*All*
39	37	29	13	4	21

The table on page 121 indicates the sum by which the various classes were below the minimum standard, expressed as percentage of the amount required to enable them to reach the standard; 10 per cent of the families had only three quarters or less of the income required for the standard; 59 per cent had at least half as much again as they needed.[1]

We may now turn to examine the relative numbers of individuals above and below the poverty line. Out of 761 children, 232, or just over 30 per cent, were in families beneath the poverty line; of the 1,603 adults, 278, or 17 per cent, were also below the line. Again, if the tendency shown by the small numbers be really representative, that children found

[1] The figures for Liverpool are: 9 per cent had only two-thirds or less of the income they needed; 70 per cent had at least half as much again as they needed.

RELATION TO POVERTY DATUM LINE

(Families)

(*Percentage Excess and Deficiency*)

Relation to Line	*Family Types* 1 *No Earner*	2 *No Adult Earner*	3 *Adult Male Earner only*	4 *Adult Male and Subsidiary Earners*	5 *Two Adult Male Earners*	*All*	*Percentage of Total Families*
Families above Line							
100 % and over	5	3	84	61	60	213	38
50 % and under 100 %	4	7	59	31	15	116	21
Under 50 %	8	2	51	38	11	110	20
Total	17	12	194	130	86	439	79
Families below Line							
Under 25 %	7	3	38	13	3	64	11
25 % and under 50 %	2	2	21	5	1	31	6
50 % and over	2	2	19	2	—	25	4
Total	11	7	78	20	4	120	21

in Family Types 1 and 2 should tend to fall below the line causes no surprise, nor will the fact that children in Types 4 and 5 are relatively sheltered from danger. Over a third of the children in Type 3 were below the line; one-fifth in Type 4, and only 6 per cent in Type 5.

We may now enquire within what limits the proportion found below the line may be trusted. The scope of the possible errors due to sampling has already been discussed. There are other points of some importance. Difficulties arise in assessing seamen's income. Three figures of income may be offered to an investigator: the Maritime Board agreed rates per month; a statement of actual earnings, taking into account the number of voyages and time ashore for which no pay is received; and the value of the allotment note. The first of these exaggerates the income, the third is the amount which might be volunteered by the wife but is not a full statement, since the balance of pay drawn at the end of the voyage must be taken into account. The general rule for "absent earners" was to include the sum remitted in the family income, and exclude the man from the minimum standard, the scaling down of income being thus partly offset by a reduction of the needs to be met. In some cases, though not all, it was clear that the balance drawn at the close of the voyage was used in part to settle arrears of rent and debts due to retailers. Sometimes definite statements were obtained by the investigators on these points, and the cases were treated accordingly. There remained, however, a residue of cases in which the only information obtainable was the amount of the allotment, and these were treated as absentee earners. The usual rate of allotment is 30s. per week, and assuming a rent of 11s. 5d. (the median rent for the whole sample), the balance would suffice for a wife and three school children, if one were under and two over five years of age, or leave a small margin on the right side if there were two under and one over five years, but it would not maintain the family as the children grew up and came to the stage of three over five years. In short, on this procedure any seaman's family containing four or more children would certainly be below standard, as would the family of three at its later stage before any were earning. Larger families than this are common amongst seamen. It is probable therefore that a number were recorded as below the datum line who would not have been so placed if the full facts were known. In the case of stewards, there is the additional complication of tips. It is difficult to get any correct assessment for these, though sometimes enough information was obtained to enable some figure to be used. Where the absentee earner rule was strictly used, it was obviously more drastic than in the case of the ratings not in contact with the passengers. At the date of the enquiry, however, the income from this source was known to have dropped with the fall in the passenger traffic, and its reduction to have led in some cases to rent arrears and debts to retailers. There were five cases of seafarers who were treated as absentee earners in this way, in which the rule seems to have operated to depress below the line. With this adjustment the volume of "poverty" would be reduced by one per cent. For the purpose of the various tables, the cases were left where the rule placed them.

(v) POTENTIAL POVERTY

We now abandon the assumption that all family income is pooled, and concentrate on the head and the dependent children. A family is regarded as being "potentially" in poverty if its head has insufficient income to enable him to maintain himself (and wife or housekeeper) and his dependent children, above the poverty line.[1] It is of interest to know how far the head of the family can keep his wife and children out of his own earnings and other income, without assistance from or liability to help in supporting any of the older children, or other persons. Stated from the point of view of the older children, we ask what the position of the family would be,

[1] For the adaptation of this definition to broken families, see text and table on page 127.

assuming that the other earners retain their full earnings themselves, not only to prevent themselves falling into poverty at any time in the future, but to enable them to save in order to equip their own households on marriage.

(*a*) We can begin with the special case of the income needed to maintain a constant population on the standard laid down, i.e. the income required by the head to keep that size of family which, taking into account voluntary and involuntary fertility, death before the end of the reproductive period, etc., would provide a constant population. We do not know definitely what the figure is, but we may take the conventional three children, and the now fashionable but inadequate two. Assuming a rent of 11s. 5d., the sum required would be, at the date of the random sample (November–December 1931):

Man, wife, and	s.	d.
two children under 5 years	31	5
one child under 5 and one over.. ..	32	6
two children over 5	34	7
three children—two under, one over ..	36	5
one child under 5, two over	37	4
three children over 5	38	5

(These sums may be set against earnings for various occupation, as a rough-and-ready test of their ability to provide the standard of life defined.)

(*b*) Since in the case of the mass interview we knew the numbers, sex, and age of all dependent children, these considerations suggested that an endeavour should be made to gather from it incidental light on the volume of potential poverty. The difficulties are obvious. We had no information about rents. Instead of deducting net rent from total income and comparing the remaining disposable income with the standard, a reasonable arbitrary rent must be decided upon. Owing to the great inequalities between the rents of controlled and subsidized houses, fixing such a standard rent is not easy, since it is not possible for families to pick and choose in such a way that equal incomes and equal needs pay equal rents, The cheapest Corporation house at the date cost over 9s., but there are low incomes which do not pay this sum, and in the light of this a rent of 8s. was assumed.[1] Secondly, the incomes were assessed by grades and not by specific amounts, and this renders comparison with a minimum need line difficult; but the case is not quite hopeless. The minimum incomes for Classes VII and VIII were in excess of any sum required to maintain above the poverty datum line any family found in practice in those grades. The average number of children in Classes I–IV, V, and VI were respectively 2·2, 2·2, and 2·1. No average family of Class VI would be below the standard whatever the school children's ages, nor would any average family of Class V, even if it received only the minimum income of the grade; on the other hand, all Class II average families would be. In Class IV the average family would be below the standard if it received the minimum, but not if it received the maximum income; a family with three children over five would be. So far, a little useful knowledge on the position of the average family in each class was gained, but any attempt to proceed further, and to derive actual numbers or proportions, meets difficulties. It is possible to work out the kinds of cases which were certainly below the poverty datum lines thus: a family in Class IV, receiving the maximum income of the grade, and *a fortiori* if it were receiving less, would be in potential poverty if it had three children, unless one were an infant; if it had only the income for the lower limit of the group, it would be in potential poverty if there were one child. Similar statements can be made for the other income grades. The doubt comes in those cases where the actual average wage lay not in an upper or lower limit, but somewhere in the centre of the range. It was known in the case of the two grades of most importance in this respect, Classes IV and V, that large bodies of workmen were on standard rates

[1] The median net rent of the random sample would have been suitable, but it was not ascertained until later.

near the upper limit of the two ranges of income. Accordingly if all those cases which did not settle themselves automatically as above were determined on the assumption that the family was at the maximum income of its particular class, we could arrive at the minimum number of families in potential poverty assuming the full average earnings. This worked out at 598 families, or 3 per cent of the total number, and 2,991 children, or 7 per cent of the total number. It is obvious that by assuming the maximum earnings of the grade for all cases not otherwise settled, we must have allowed some poverty cases to slip through the net. We are left with the bare statement that at least 3 per cent of the families and 7 per cent of the children were in potential poverty, even if full average earnings were assumed. If we say that, roughly, the effect of removing other earners in this way—i.e. the abandonment of the assumption of pooling—is to add one-third more cases to those below the line,[1] then the amount of primary poverty amongst all families with school children was, assuming full earnings, over 2 per cent.[2] A little truth is possibly better than none. This calculation was more useful in showing the probable distribution of poverty in wards and streets than for yielding an indication of its absolute amount. Four wards, St. Mary's, Northam, Trinity, and Town contained nearly two-thirds of the entire number of cases. Most of them were families whose heads were widows (a little under one-fifth) and labourers (nearly two-fifths), or families of unusual size. In Appendix III will be found some illustrations from the records of typical streets.

(*c*) Fortunately, when we come to the random sample we are on more solid ground. The net rent expense was deducted from the income of the head of the family, and the residue of

[1] As in random sample below, page 128. For East London about one-third are added to all families. Vol. iii, p. 96.

[2] Compare with primary poverty in the Five Towns, 1924, assuming full-time wages; all towns 3·6 per cent, Reading 8·1 per cent, Northampton 2·0 per cent. This included families without children, but was limited to working-class households.

disposable income[1] compared with the appropriate minimum need standard. There were 348 families with dependent children, and of these 118, or 34 per cent, were below the line. The effect of removing supplementary earners from both sides of the account on the proportions of *all families with children* in poverty was thus to add to the 26 per cent already ascertained a further 8 per cent. If we limit ourselves to the stricter conception of a man maintaining his wife (or housekeeper) and dependent children, i.e. to Family Types 3, 4, and 5 only, the proportion in potential poverty is nearly 33 per cent. If incomes had not been pooled, the numbers of *families in the whole*

NUMBERS OF FAMILIES WITH DEPENDENT CHILDREN IN POTENTIAL POVERTY

	Family Types					All
	1 *No Earner*	2 *No Adult Earner*	3 *Adult Male Earner only*	4 *Adult Male and Subsidiary Earners*	5 *Two Adult Male Earners*	
Families above line ..	1	3	135	62	29	230
Families below line ..	4	4	63	35	12	118
All families with dependent children	5	7	198	97	41	348
Families with unemployed heads below line	—	1	40	22	7	70

NOTE.—Total of families in poverty in this sense differs from total of families with dependent children below line in table showing earning strength and dependence. There are a few cases where the other earner is a liability and not an asset (e.g. a young boy out of work, but not of insurable age). If other earners are neglected, such a family might come above the line.

[1] No earnings of married women, whether derived from industrial work or from sums received on account of work for lodgers, are included in heads' income, but lodger's contribution to rent is deducted from full rent in accordance with the rule.

sample, including those without children, who were beneath the datum line was increased to 146, or 26 per cent of the total. This method of calculation thus adds about one-fifth to the number of all families, and less than one-third to the number of families with dependent children who were beneath the line.

It will be seen from the table that about one-third of the families with dependent children in each type of family where there were one or more male earners were below the line, even where there were supplementary and second adult male earners. The last row of the table shows that the bulk of those in potential poverty—60 per cent of the families, and somewhat similar proportions for each of three principal family types concerned—are beneath the line because the head of the family is unemployed.

It must be remembered that the wide differences between the proportions shown in potential poverty in the mass interview and the random sample is in the main due to (1) the fact that one assumed full-time earnings, the other actual earnings in a bad year; (2) the different method of allowing for rent; (3) the fact that the mass interview included all families with school children, of whatever income grade, while the random sample concerned working-class families only. This can be seen if, as a rough check, we deduct the 70 cases where the heads were unemployed, which leaves 48, or less than 14 per cent, in potential poverty. In the mass survey a rent of 8s. was assumed, whereas in fact net rents were higher than this. If we exclude all those further cases in which the amount by which the family was below the line was less than the difference between 8s. and the actual net rent, this reduces the number of cases below the line to 27, or 7·7 per cent. The mass assessment gave 3 per cent as the minimum.

(vi) THE CAUSES OF PRIMARY POVERTY

The following table, which is based on a well-established model, gives an impression of the relative importance of the various immediate circumstances or "causes" which have thrust the various families beneath the poverty datum line. Death, permanent disability, or unemployment of the chief male earner are obvious factors, but often circumstances seem to have entered into conspiracy to press an unfortunate family simultaneously at a number of points, and the occasion for assigning one cause rather than another is small. Despite the unemployment of the natural head, a poor family might still have been above the datum line, were it not for the fact that the supplementary earner is also unemployed, or sick, and receiving only health benefit. Or a man's full wages may be so low that in any case it would be below the line, yet because he is out of work, the major portion of the amount of the deficiency may be due to unemployment and not lowness of wages. The disparity between actual and standard income may arise from changes in more than one of the variables. Such a tabulation cannot give a complete account of the wide variety of circumstances affecting the cases below the line; each has its own peculiarities, and a full statement really requires the reproduction of all the information on the relevant cards.

APPARENT CAUSES OF POVERTY

	Percentage of Families	*Percentage of Persons*
Natural head—		
Dead	0·5	0·4
Ill	1·0	1·1
Old	2·1	1·2
On short time	0·5	0·5
Unemployed	13·6	13·2
Deserted wife	0·1	0·2
Natural head in full work—		
Second adult dependent	1·0	1·1
Wage insufficient for 3 children—		
3 children or fewer	1·0	1·0
4 or more	1·0	1·7
Wage sufficient for 3 children—		
4 or more	0·5	1·1
	21·3	21·5

The striking feature of the figure is that two-thirds is traceable to unemployment. It is heavy not only compared with the Five Towns in 1924, but also compared with East London in 1929. Twenty-three per cent in Reading and 39 per cent in Bolton are two examples in 1924; while the figures for East London, 1929, were 35 per cent. There were two years of trade deterioration in between the dates of this and the East London survey so that the proportion, though very heavy, was explainable. It is not due to any excessive proportion of unemployed persons in the sample, for the percentage of the insured population of Southampton's unemployed in November–December 1931 was 19 per cent or 20 per cent of the total; and this was the proportion of the adult earners in the sample who were unemployed at the date of the investigation. The heavy figure is a striking comment on the damage likely to be done by prolonged unemployment, since so many are thrust below the severe standard laid down. At the same time, that so many of the families were below the datum line for this reason affords some grounds for hope, since it follows that improvement in trade conditions will automatically remove a large portion of the burden. As stated above, if we assume the volume of unemployment to be at the level of the beginning of 1929, and other circumstances unaltered, the number of families below the line for this reason could be reduced by one-half, and the total volume of poverty would thus fall to between 14 per cent and 15 per cent. An improvement of trade to the conditions of that date would probably decrease the volume of poverty by one-third.

The rest of the families—one-third of those below the poverty line, and 7·2 per cent of the total number—were in distress for reasons unconnected with bad trade. In 3·7 per cent of the sample, poverty was due to the death, illness, or absence of the natural head of the family. Since the date of Booth's study, the social services have been developed to cope with many such cases, but the figures testify to the fact that there are still gaps in the provision made. In the remaining

3·5 per cent of total families, the natural head was in full work, but there was a second adult dependent to maintain, or the children were more numerous than could be supported on the minimum standard out of the wages received, or the wage was unusually low.

(vii) FAMILY MEANS

A description of the economic constitution of the family would not be complete without an analysis of the sources of income. In the comparison of family income with the standard, all income from whatever source has been regarded as a homogeneous quantity, and all of it equally available for the purpose of meeting family needs. This is in some measure artificial. For example, a family with numbers of other earners, particularly adult earners, may seem to be paying less rent and putting up with less accommodation than the gross amount of family income would suggest as possible, but the difficulty before the head of such a family is that some of them may leave or get married, and he would then be faced with a rent beyond the reduced family means; he cannot regard all sources of income as equally permanent and available. Again, throughout these studies, it is the income rather than the capital account of the family which is investigated. We assumed the possession of furniture, etc.; we should therefore be logically bound to allow for some reservation of income by the unmarried other earners, as their weekly saving towards equipping their own homes. The analysis is important from another point of view also. The current discussion of means tests has brought into prominence the question of contributions of other earners and of the social services to the family income. What are the kind of facts which a means test conducted with this purpose would reveal? It is therefore necessary to get some impression of the relative importance of social service payments, head's wages, and other earner's wages, and other receipts in family incomes.

(*a*) *Social Service Income.*—The proportion of families in the sample which contained individuals receiving income from the social services was 47 per cent, but it rose to 81 per cent in the case of the families below, and fell to 38 per cent of the families above the line. This may be compared with the figures for the Merseyside, in which the proportion was 36 per cent. The present enquiry was, however, made at a later date, when unemployment was heavier; if we assume this reduced by one-half, i.e. to a figure similar to that of pre-depression years, the proportion receiving social income would probably have been about 34 per cent.

One in four of the families received at least a half, one in three of them at least a quarter of their income from the social services. There is a marked distinction between the families which are above and those which are below the poverty datum line, for 89 per cent of the former received less than half, and 76 per cent of the latter more than half their income from these sources. Unemployment is the main cause of the difference, and the figures provide a vivid illustration of the extent to which the State replaced the loss of wages.

The relative importance of social income to the different types of families is in accordance with one's general expectation, being highest in the families of least economic strength, those without earners or adult male earners (in which case old-age and widows' pensions are important), and high also in those families where the existence of more than one earner implies greater possibility of unemployment and of the receipt of unemployment benefit. Nine and eight out of every ten families in Types 1 and 2 respectively receive social income of some kind, and one in every two of the families with supplementary earners, as compared with one in three of the families with one adult male earner only. (A reduction in the volume of unemployment by one-half to a less exceptional figure would change these proportions, since its incidence is mainly in Family Types 3, 4, and 5, but it would still be true that a smaller proportion of families with a single male earner

SOCIAL INCOME AS A PERCENTAGE OF FAMILY INCOME

	Nil	*Under* 25 %	25 % *and under* 50 %	50 % *and under* 75 %	75 % *and under* 100 %	100 %	*Total*
All Families—							
Numbers	294	82	42	43	17	81	559
Percentage	53	15	8	8	3	14	101
Families above Line—							
Numbers	271	80	38	27	5	18	439
Percentage	62	18	9	6	1	4	100
Families below Line—							
Numbers	23	2	4	16	12	63	120
Percentage	19	2	4	13	10	53	101
Type 1 families .. .. (numbers)	2	—	2	8	4	12	28
Type 2 families .. .. (numbers)	4	3	4	5	2	1	19
Type 3 families .. .. (numbers)	172	27	7	5	3	58	272
Type 4 families .. .. (numbers)	77	28	15	21	5	4	150
Type 5 families .. .. (numbers)	39	24	14	4	3	6	90

PERCENTAGE OF FAMILIES RECEIVING SOCIAL INCOME

	Family Type					
	1	**2**	**3**	**4**	**5**	*All*
Percentage	93	79	37	49	57	47

only would be receiving social income than the families with other earners.)

The position of the Type 3 families—those with a man only earning—is of some interest. They have the chief burden of dependent children and have no supplementary earners, yet a smaller proportion of them received any aid from the social services than any other type of family. Income was rarely received from more than one social service at a time, a smaller proportion of them received public assistance than of any other class of family except Type 5; and benefit in respect of unemployment was received less frequently than in Types 4 and 5, the other types mainly exposed to this risk. Nearly two-thirds of them received no social income. It is true, no doubt, that they received more assistance in the reduction of rent through tenancy of subsidy houses than the families of Types 1 and 2, though not necessarily than those of Types 4 and 5, who now occupy the earlier housing estates. But when the loss of work puts them on to insurance benefit, they are more entirely dependent upon it than other types of families. It is this type of family which the sponsors of family endowment have in mind; and it is not without interest that a far greater proportion of them than of Types 4 and 5 were below the poverty line.

Some of the social service payments are statutory sums given in return for contributions by the recipient, while others, such as poor relief and school maintenance grants, are made at the discretion of the State after consideration of individual circumstances. The figures on page 135 distinguish the various types of payments.

The results arise partly from the age composition of the population (such as the numbers receiving old-age pensions), partly from local policy (such as the numbers receiving public assistance). The types of payment in order of their importance are unemployment benefit, old-age pensions, widows' pensions, health benefit, with public assistance last. That the latter should be found so infrequently—only two per cent of the families being concerned—causes no surprise in view of the equally small figures found amongst persons disallowed insurance benefit in this area.[1] On the Merseyside public assistance was third on the list and widows' pensions fourth.

TYPES OF SOCIAL INCOME RECEIVED

	Number of Families	*Percentage of all Families*
Unemployment benefit	148	26
Health insurance	24	4
Old-age pensions	76	14
Widows' pensions	30	5
War pensions	9	2
Public assistance	12	2
Miscellaneous	3	1
Total types of income received	302	—
Total number of families receiving payments	265	47

NOTE.—The total types of income exceeds the total number of families with social income, since a family may receive more than one type.

(*b*) *Supplementary Earners' Contributions.*—The central point in the current controversy on the means test concerns the position of the supplementary earners in the family, the real extent of their contribution to family income, and their capacity to maintain and aid unemployed parents, brothers, and sisters. Leaving aside the difference of view on the principle, some of the facts are either disputed or not known precisely. One side argues that the liability of the family to break up makes pooled income unstable, while the other declares that many family incomes are large enough to support unemployed members who have exhausted their actuarial benefit, without undue strain. It is true that as the poverty line allowance (excluding any contribution to rent and fuel) is for a boy of 16–18 years 6s. 1d., and for a girl 5s. 9d., wages at the rates current even in unskilled occupations would give them an income in excess of this amount. But they may be unemployed with benefit, or without benefit because they have been disallowed, or are in non-insurable occupations; they may be

[1] See page below, 169.

under-employed and following inherited casual employment. A subsidiary earner may himself be a liability to his parents, or his full earnings insufficient to make up the deficiency in the income of another who is affected by one of these adverse conditions. It is the peculiar complex arising from the conditions of employment in each case which determines the final result.

Some of the results already arrived at give us a preliminary measure of the importance of other earners in the family economy. In 246 families of the sample, or 44 per cent of the total, there were earners other than the head of the family. The percentage of families in potential poverty, i.e. where the other earners are neglected, was 26 per cent, as compared with 21 per cent of the whole sample in primary poverty, which assumes all income and expenses pooled. Twenty-nine per cent of the families with a man only earning were in primary poverty, as compared with 10 per cent of the families with one or more earners (Family Types 4 and 5).

Any attempt at a more detailed measurement meets with a number of difficulties. In practical life the incomes they pay into the pool are smaller than the full earnings, and it is this "allowance" figure that is badly needed. That there is an element of convention in the sums "allowed," that the amount and proportion reserved by the child will tend to increase as he grows older, that there are "good children," and "bad children" who refuse even to pay for any of their keep, are common knowledge. It is also true that some parents seem to be as ignorant of their children's earnings, if the rates are not well defined, as many wives are of their husbands'. A more complex trouble is that close investigation reveals a great variety of arrangements between children and parents, for some make an allowance but provide their own clothing, while others make an allowance out of which the mother provides all or some part of the clothing. No one has found a means of discovering the full truth of these matters. Public Assistance Committees meet the situation by making an arbitrary, uniform rule respecting the amount a supplementary earner may reasonably reserve for personal expenses—such as one-quarter of the full earnings—and regard the remainder as free for general family expenditure. This practice gets rid of the difficulties by standardizing them, but while it greatly adds to the ease of administration, it is not suitable for our purpose. We wish to know how far the other earners in the family contribute to raise the family above, or help to thrust it beneath the poverty line. Although we cannot discover accurately what proportion of their earnings or other income they actually hand over to parents, we can reach an understanding of this matter by measuring the net "gain" or "loss" to the family as a unit, arising from the excess or deficiency of their full income as compared with the cost of maintaining them on the poverty line.[1] We may then regard any excess of income over the cost of maintaining them as theoretically free to assist the remainder of the family to reach the minimum standard, and similarly, any deficiency as the drain on other family resources which an endeavour to maintain them on the poverty line would entail. If the income of the head of the family is barely sufficient to maintain him and his wife and dependent children on the minimum standard, any considerable deficiency will depress the whole family below the poverty line. Some precision may be imported into the current discussion as to whether earning children are to be regarded as assets or liabilities, by thus giving to these two terms definite and measurable meanings. As will be seen from the table below, in 5 per cent of the families which contained other earners, these persons were a drain on the family income in the sense defined, i.e. required a

[1] Excluding any allowance for rent and fuel. Only by some very arbitrary rule could these items of expense be divided between various members of the family, and they have therefore been treated as the parent's liability. The phrase "cost of maintenance" must be read with this qualification. This use of the poverty line for measuring other earners' surplus income in no way implies that this would be a desirable administrative practice; it is only a device to make possible a numerical answer to the question put in the text.

subsidy from the head to maintain them on the minimum standard.

As a surplus or deficiency of 5s. is of one order of importance when the family income is 120s., and quite another if it is only 40s., the net excess or deficiency has therefore been expressed as *a percentage of the family income from all other sources.* For example: (*a*) The family income is 105s. 6d., the head's being 32s. 6d., partly from wages and partly from benefit; there are four other earners who together receive, again partly from wages and partly from benefit, an income of 73s., while the cost of maintenance on the standard is 28s. 6d., leaving a surplus of 44s. 6d. This is an addition to the income from all other sources (32s. 6d.) of over 100 per cent. (*b*) Head's income, 68s. 8d.; uninsured adult daughter sick, without benefit, no income; cost of maintenance 5s. 11d., the income from all other sources thus being drawn upon by about $8\frac{1}{2}$ per cent.

OTHER EARNERS' NET CONTRIBUTION TO FAMILY INCOME

Numbers of Families in which other Earners contributed more or less than the cost of maintaining them on the poverty line.

	Above Line Families	*Below Line Families*	*All Families*
1. Total families with other earners	220	26	246
2. Number with other earners contributing *more* than cost of maintenance.. ..	213	21	234
Number of families which excess was—			
under 25 % of all other family income ..	44	9	53
25 % and under 50 % of all other family income	54	10	64
50 % and under 75 % of all other family income	34	1	35
75 % and under 100 % of all other family income	28	—	28
100 % and over of all other family income	53	1	54
3. Number with other earners contributing *less* than cost of maintenance	7	5	12
Families in which deficiency was—			
under 25 % of all other family income ..	6	3	9
25 % and under 50 % of all other family income	1	2	3

(c) *Miscellaneous Income.*—Apart from the income of the heads of the families, there remain certain miscellaneous items of income. First, there are certain items of income which accrue to wives. In twenty-one cases there were one or more boarders in the family, and the allowance made for this must be regarded as income arising from the wife's activity and as her "earnings." This occurs in $3\frac{1}{2}$ per cent of the families. Secondly, there are seven cases only of married women (not widows) working full-time, and one part-time, a very low proportion which corresponds to the few cases occurring in the Disallowance Enquiry.[1] The industrial make-up of the area is not such as to offer many opportunities for married women, and a scrutiny of the cases for determining the apparent reasons for their doing so is worth while. Is it "necessary" for them to work? Such questions, though at the bottom of much of the arguments as to "marriage bar" or the payment of insurance benefit to married women, scarcely admits of a very definite answer. The extent of the pressure can perhaps be gauged a little by the relation of the family to the poverty line. One was below it, even with the woman's earnings. Two would have been below it but for the woman's earnings; in the remaining cases the families were well above the poverty line even without the wife's earnings; three of them had no children; in the other there were two over ten years of age.

Briefly the facts are:

(1) Husband, old-age pension. Wife 56, girl of 12 years. Takes in washing and earns an average of 10s. a week. Below poverty line.

(2) Husband a traveller, 47, unemployed on benefit; no benefit for earning wife. Wife 43, canvasser for lingerie, earning 50s. Two dependent children, and one girl of 17 who looks after house. Rent 30s. Takes one boarder. Without wife's earnings would be 6s. 8d. below poverty line.

(3) Husband a marine engineer unemployed and on benefit. Dependent mother aged 50 years. Tenants of a large house, rent 35s. Two rooms let off as a flat, and one single room let off also. There

[1] *Royal Commission on Unemployment Insurance, Evidence,* Appendices III, Reports on Southampton and Manchester Areas.

is a child of two years. Wife earns 15s. less insurance at clerical work. Without her earnings the family would be 9s. below the poverty line.

(4), (5), (6), and (7). Two laundresses and two cleaners. The youngest wife of these cases was aged 38; there were no dependent children in three cases, and the women were obviously freed of the home duties that married women normally have at their age. In one case the husband was earning £3 per week, daughter of 21 kept house to allow her mother to continue her work at office cleaning which she had kept for many years. The earnings were 20s. per week, a sum which is less than the daughter herself would probably have earned considering the income and occupation of the father. In another case there were no children, and the husband was away at sea.

In a further case a wife did cleaning work on two days, earning 3s. 6d. per week. There were three children under ten, but although above the poverty line the husband's earnings were only 46s. 5d.; and the investigator's comment on the family was "hard working." In addition there were nine widows who were working part-time full-time, in every case at charing or domestic work. In three cases the family would have been in poverty without the additional income obtained, and one, a widow, with a young family not living with parents or friends, was in poverty even with the addition. Only a really hardened believer in a work fund theory could possibly doubt that in many of these cases the activity of the married women was a reasonable and often successful endeavour to make up the family income to an adequate amount.

The various items of income above—that from boarders and work of married women—must be regarded as income accruing to the family from the wife's activity. Although important in the individual families, neither the number of cases, nor the amounts involved are great enough to make any difference to the trend of the figures respecting head's income. Where widows were earning the income has been placed under "other earners" unless the widows were themselves the head of the family.

A further item consists of forty cases (7 per cent of the total) in which income was derived from house-ownership.

In most cases it was not possible to find out accurately whether the house was wholly owned, or to what extent it was mortgaged. It is common knowledge that the practice of house purchase through a building society or by "£25 down" arrangement with the builder has spread much during the past few years, and from an inspection of the age, the street, and other facts respecting the owner, it is probable that most of them were subject to mortgage. Nearly all of them were the typical case of the occupier purchasing the house in which he lived, though there was an odd case or two of ownership also of the next-door house or two or three small properties.

(*d*) *The Composition of Family Incomes.*—The facts relating to the separate sources of income may now be gathered together to form a composite picture of the make-up of the family income. For this purpose income is separated into that derived from the social services, that received by other earners as wages, and that received by heads of families as wages, plus miscellaneous income.

The family income was composed of:

Head's wages only, in 180 cases, or 32·2 % of the total.

Other earners' wages only, in 1 case, or 0·2 % of the total.

Social income only, in 81 cases, or 14·5 % of the total.

Head's wages and other earners' wages, in 113 cases, or 20·2 % of the total.

Head's wages and social income, in 73 cases, or 13·1 % of the total.

Other earners' wages and social income, in 57 cases, or 10·2 % of the total.

Head's wages, other earners' wages, and social income, in 54 cases, or 9·7 % of the total.

The figures above show the number of families which received income from each main source, either as its sole means of support, or in conjunction with some other type. We must take account also of the magnitude of the sums received from each source. In the table below an attempt is made to show the importance of the three main kinds of income by stating each as a proportion of the total family income.

RELATIVE IMPORTANCE OF DIFFERENT SOURCES OF FAMILY INCOME

(*Showing the Numbers and Percentage of all Families receiving different Sources of Income*)

Source of Income 1	*Number of Families in which the Source of Income named in Column 1 formed the undermentioned Percentage of Total Family Income:*						
	2 *Nil*	3 *Under* 25 %	4 25 % *and under* 50 %	5 50 % *and under* 75 %	6 75 % *and under* 100 %	7 100 %	8 *Total Families*
Head's wages, etc.	139	21	52	112	55	180	559
Other earners' wages	334	45	115	55	9	1	559
Social income	294	82	42	43	17	81	559

Source of Income	*Percentage of all Families in which the Source of Income named in Column 1 formed the undermentioned Percentage of Total Family Income:*						
	Nil	*Under* 25 %	25 % *and under* 50 %	50 % *and under* 75 %	75 % *and under* 100 %	100 %	*Total*
Head's wages, etc.	24·9	3·8	9·3	20·0	9·8	32·2	100·0
Other earners' wages	59·7	8·1	20·6	9·8	1·6	0·2	100·0
Social income	52·6	14·7	7·5	7·7	3·0	14·5	100·0

The table is of interest in showing the extent to which families are protected against the consequences of a blow at one source of income, by the existence of receipts from others. It has already been pointed out that these sources of income are very different in their permanence and variability, and that the pooling of family income for the purpose of calculating the degree of primary poverty must not lead us to overlook the fact that these items are not homogeneous quantities which can be amalgamated without qualification. Social income is partly the outcome of individual saving, partly the result of a State contribution made to enable standard sums to be paid to all recipients, and partly a discretionary payment made after consideration of individuals' peculiar circumstances. The possibility of changes in the attitude of the State to its social services thus introduces into these payments an element of variation different from that to which wages are subject. Further, as children grow up and marry a considerable fraction of income may be removed—in one-tenth of the cases the other earners' wages were over a half of the family income, and in another one-fifth they were between one-quarter and one-half. As will be shown later, the relative impermanence of this source of income helps us to understand cases of overcrowding of grown-up families with relatively large total incomes.

This study of family income throws some light on the operation of the means test in unemployment insurance payments. The fact that there is sharp disagreement between the political parties on the principle of such tests will mean that the rigour with which they are administered will vary with the political complexion of the local responsible bodies, but differences may also arise from the economic structure of the localities. The composition of family income is affected by the relative number of earners and dependents, and the varied industrial opportunities of the sexes. It has already been pointed out, for example, that in Southampton women have a narrower range of openings than women in textile towns and some other ports. It is worth noting that in Southampton and Sheffield, over a period of seven months, 71·0 per cent and 62·8 per cent of the initial applications were granted benefit at unreduced rates, and in only 6·6 per cent and 6·0 per cent of the cases respectively were no payments ordered. In Liverpool, on the other hand, only 20·2 per cent were given full rates, and 9·9 per cent were disallowed altogether.[1]

(viii) MEANS TESTS

The introduction of a means test into certain classes of insurance benefit is but an enlargement of the field of the social services within which tests are operated, for they have long existed in various branches of the social services. These include the major case of the enquiries into family income by the Public Assistance Committee, the income test in connection with the maintenance grants to secondary scholars, and the grant of the scholarships themselves, the supply of school meals to necessitous children, and the issue of free and cheap milk to nursing mothers and infants. Some consideration of the relation between administrative practices in these cases, to the facts revealed by the foregoing studies of poverty and family income is desirable. Such an examination is the more pertinent, since, while the aim of the authorities is to see that applicants for help are treated on their merits and receive individual consideration, yet in order to clarify practice and preserve unity of treatment between like cases, many of them have drawn up scales of maximum assistance and scales of family income which qualify for different degrees of assistance. Southampton is one of these areas. The importance of the relationship between the scales used in the different branches of administration to one another, and of all of them to any poverty datum line needs no emphasis.

We may consider first the scale used by the Public Assistance Committee in dealing with relief to the able-bodied unem-

[1] *Royal Commission on Unemployment Insurance, Final Report*, p. 62.

ployed, partly because of its primary importance, but partly also because scales for this purpose have raised clear issues of principle. The Poor Law Act of 1930 places no explicit or implied obligation on an authority to draw up such scales, though the practice was widespread amongst the old Board of Guardians and has been continued by many of the authorities which superseded them. In April 1932 there were 68 authorities (mainly rural) without any definite scales, and 87 authorities (mainly urban) which made use of them; and of the latter Southampton was one. Objections have been raised against the use of such scales at all. In 1930, the Minister of Health was disposed to deprecate the general and immediate imposition of scales of relief, and in 1932 the Minister declined to call a conference for the discussion of scales of relief. The objections brought against them are as follows: (1) Their complication. They involve, as does the poverty datum line, the classification of applicants and their families, of allowances for rent, and decision on the extent to which the wages of other earners should be "pooled," etc. (2) A scale so established for any arbitrary period is not so easy to vary with marked or sudden changes in the cost of living, whereas if cases are considered on their individual merits, this can be done more easily. (3) They often come to be looked upon as implying that the applicant has a right to maintenance at the appropriate rates in the scale, and in actual practice, especially where conditions of unemployment lead to large numbers of applicants, they are often applied automatically. (4) Where fixed by directly elected bodies, they are often established at rates, or criticized and varied for reasons unconnected with any scientific or statistical basis. The broad issue of the "right to maintenance" implied in some of these objections lies outside the scope of this book. It is, however, pertinent to press the need of some scientific basis for action, whether scales are used or not, and to point out that if in practice scales have little scientific basis, it is equally true that individual consideration may be often likewise condemned. What individual enquiry can do to establish facts which make it possible to allow for the infinite variety of circumstance which these cases present, but as relief is designed to make up wholly or in part some deficiency of income compared with needs, there must be some standard, however vague, in the minds of those granting the assistance. Standards based on half-realized assumptions may be as devoid of scientific basis as those formulated into explicit scales. Dragging these lurking assumptions and differences into open and formal discussion—which the establishment of a detailed scale involves—is one of the services which the local debates on projected scales have rendered.[1]

Whatever be the merits of the question of "scale" or "no scale," granted the existence of one, as in Southampton's scale for outdoor relief of the able-bodied, the points which need consideration are: (1) its relation to other scales, such as insurance benefit, scales in other areas, the poverty datum line, in terms of amount of payment; (2) the definition of the family whose income is to be tested in any given instance and of persons who are to be reckoned as dependents; (3) the nature of the allowances, and the calculations for different types of expenses.

The changing economic and political conditions during the period of the survey led to a revision of the poverty datum line and of the insurance benefit rates and of the public assistance scales, and the facts made obvious by the table opposite from a striking example of the strains introduced by the instability of prices into the social services making money payments.

The poverty datum line was identical in substance at both periods, being revised only for price changes. The Public Assistance scale was maintained practically unchanged from 1922 to 1932 when the authority became responsible for the

[1] Ministry of Health Circular, L.G.A. 3, 1930, and *London County Council Report to Public Assistance Committee*, April 27, 1932, on "Scales Relief." Also, L.C.C., P.A. 3, "Administration of Relief."

POVERTY, RELIEF, AND BENEFIT SCALES, 1928–32

Size of Family *Man and Wife and—* *Children* 0–5	5–14	*Poverty Datum Line* 1928*	*Poverty Datum Line, November to December,* 1931*	*Unemployment Benefit,* 1928	*Unemployment Benefit reduced,* 1931	*Public Assistance Scale of Outdoor Relief,* 1922, *Unchanged*	*Public Assistance Scale Revised, August* 1932
–	–	26/6	23/6	24/–	23/3	18/6	23/3
1	–	30/–	26/3	26/–	25/3	22/–	25/3
2	–	33/6	29/–	28/–	27/3	24/6	27/3
1	1	34/9	30/1	28/–	27/3	24/6	27/3
2	1	38/2	32/10	30/–	29/3	27/–	29/3
2	2	42/11	36/8	32/–	31/3	29/6	31/3
2	3	47/8	40/6	34/–	33/3	32/–	33/3
–	1	31/3	27/4	26/–	25/3	22/–	25/3
–	3	36/–	32/–	30/–	29/3	27/–	29/3

* The poverty datum line figures here used are those used in the preceding enquiries plus a flat rate of 8/– for rent. The Public Assistance scale of 1922 includes rent, except in very special cases, where allowance up to a maximum of 5/– could be made for rent.

administration of the Means Test to those on Transitional Benefit. It was then adjusted upwards to correspond with the reduced unemployment scale. The alteration in the unemployment benefit scale were matters of central government policy which need not be discussed here. Comparing their general movement, the effect of the various changes was that throughout the period the Public Assistance scale was below the poverty datum line, and in 1928 substantially below it, though the gap was steadily narrowed by the fall of prices, but in 1931, for a man and wife only (though not for large families), they became practically identical. The unemployment scale was not so markedly below the datum line in 1928 for small families, but this difference also had decreased by 1932. The marked contrast is the disparity between the poverty datum line and the other two for large families. These arise from the fact that whereas the children's allowance in the unemployment benefit scale was 2s. per child, and 2s. 6d. per child in the Public Assistance scale, the poverty datum line makes larger allowances for children from five to fourteen, and in any case is more generous than the other two, being 2s. 9d. for children under five years and 3s. 10d. for those between five years and fourteen (1931). This comparison between the scales and the datum line does not necessarily imply that the latter is the desirable figure, and that the others are thereby condemned as inadequate for their purpose. For it is the avowed object of the Public Assistance scale, while making provision against destitution, to avoid making any total payment exceeding or as great as could be obtained by an unskilled man in independent work. In the benefit scale also the original purpose of the scheme was to supplement savings during temporary loss of work and not to provide full maintenance during prolonged and persistent unemployment. Whatever may be the merits and vices of these principles, a comparison with the datum line does reveal the significance of the other scales; and the full meaning of lack of work so prolonged that it involves maintenance at rates below the poverty datum line for long periods—as it has done for thousands—can be more easily appreciated.

The relationship between the three scales which exists in Southampton is not always found elsewhere. The Royal Commission on Unemployment Insurance summarized the position as follows:[1]

	Number of Authorities	
	January 1931	*April* 1932
No. of scales laid down	67	58
Scales below insurance benefit.. ..	36	22
Scales equal to insurance benefit ..	5	20
Scales above insurance benefit ..	9	29
Scales partly above and partly below and partly equal to it	28	16
Total	145	145

It will be observed that Southampton falls into the second of these categories in 1931, and into the third in 1932. The table does, however, exaggerate the differences, for the Commissioners do not point out that despite the maximum scale they may have drafted, in practice many authorities do not grant relief above the benefit rates where the peculiarity of the construction of their scale would in fact permit this. For these areas the benefit rates have in fact come to be regarded as an overriding maximum.

The lack of uniformity between the scales arises not only from differences in the political party control of the various authorities, and from contrast in age, sex, and occupational composition of the populations, but from the detailed construction of the various scales. A few of these taken from

[1] *Final Report*, p. 67.

PUBLIC ASSISTANCE SCALES

	1	2	3	4	5	6
Man and Wife	20/–	18/–, plus rent up to 10/–	18/–, plus rent up to 10/–	23/–	18/–, plus rent up to 10/–	17/6, plus rent up to 10/–
Children	First, 4/–; second, 3/–; others, 2/–	Each child, 2/–	Each child, 4/–	Each child, 5/–	First, 4/6; second, 3/–; third, 2/6; fourth and fifth, 2/–; others 1/6	—
Amount of other earners' income to be regarded as pooled	75 % if all earning, except first 10/– if children 16, 12/6 if children 16–18, and 15/– for children over 18	All except 12/– for first child, 10/– for second child, and 8/– for third child	25% of all income, if it does not exceed £1, and 50% of all income if in excess of £1	75% of earnings of all dependent workers: full earnings of self-supporting workers, less the amount which would be paid in lodgings if away from home	75% of all earnings	—
Maximum relief to any one household	36/–	38/–	—	40/–	35/–	—

areas widely distributed geographically will illustrate this point:[1]

In the case of the other scales and tests in other branches of social services, the publication of the actual figures is deemed inadvisable by the authorities concerned, so that detailed examination is not possible. One may nevertheless make some observations concerning the principle underlying some scales in general use. As regards the scale used to determine the grant of free and cheap school meals, the family whose means are taken into account is not usually defined so widely or loosely as when the amount of outdoor relief to be given to destitute families is being settled, but is generally confined to members of the "natural" family, i.e. to the responsible parent and earning children. The procedure consists in totalling the family income, deducting rent, and dividing the remainder by the total number of persons in the family. The amount arrived at is compared with the scale of maximum income per head. In one scale the maximum qualifying income is, where there are two or three members of the family, 7s. per head, three or four members, 6s. per head. Ease of administration is the advantage of this method of calculation. Scales for this purpose usually approximate to local public assistance scale.

The scales governing the award of scholarships to secondary schools and of maintenance grants for scholars are differently conceived. The principle which runs through the Public Assistance Committee work, and affects the Education and Health Committee grants for food, is the general one that a man in normal regular unskilled work should be expected to make this provision for his family, and that only temporary distress, such as unemployment, or some permanent cause reducing the earning capacity of the family below a low level, justifies the State in providing it. The standard which local

[1] *Royal Commission on Unemployment Insurance*, Appendices to *Evidence*, Part II. See scales for Bristol, Cardiff, and Newcastle-on-Tyne. Other details supplied by local authorities concerned.

authorities thus tend to work to is "one commercially set,"[1] i.e. the wages of the independent unskilled workman. But secondary school fees, the maintenance of an appropriate standard of clothing and equipment, and the loss of earnings of children who would otherwise have been at work in the later years of secondary school life, are regarded differently. There is little question that an unskilled labourer in independent work would be unable to provide these, but the considerations of deterrence which have historically been so important in Poor Law policy are in this branch of administration replaced by the twin principles that, in ideal at least, no child should be deprived of educational opportunities for which he is fitted, by any inability of his parents to pay fees, and that in its own interest the State should make the path clear for personal ability. The service is not in this case working to a commercially set limit, the wage of the low paid labourer. There has, in consequence, been less criticism of the administration of this service, and in many areas the release from that limit has enabled the authority to expand the facilities with great rapidity, and even to provide some of them free. The income limits, where they exist, take into account the income of the family from all sources, but there is no adequate evidence in the scales themselves as to how broadly the family is defined for this purpose, nor to indicate what proportion of the other earner's incomes are reckoned.

In addition to those already examined, there are other services in which some testing of family means takes place, e.g. in assessing the contributions to be made by a family to the support of a blind or other defective child in a home, or to the support of any lunatic and other defective in the appropriate institution.

The frequent use of means tests in local administration and the frequency with which definite scales are used, call to mind the proposals of the Minority Commissioners[2] who reported

[1] Clay in *The Manchester School*, vol. iii, p. 90.
[2] *Minority Report*, p. 406.

on the Poor Law in 1909. Their criticism of the conditions existing at the date of their investigation was the twofold one that development of preventive and ameliorative services was hampered by an association with a " means test," which led to treatment being denied which ought to be given, and that the variety of authorities dealing with the services led to some people receiving services for which they could wholly or partly pay. "If we desire that all those should be treated whom it is important in the public interest not to leave untreated, and that in the interest of public economy and personal independence all those should pay who can afford to do so, we must separate the two processes." Their proposal was that there should be a Registrar of Public Assistance, whose entire function was to keep a register of all cases receiving any form of public aid, and to determine, with the help of a staff of income assessors, the legal liability and economic capacity of the family to pay for the service rendered. He would have nothing to do with the treatment of cases, but only with the determination of the capacity to pay and the recovery of the charges made, if any. The amalgamation of services brought about by the Local Government Act, 1929, has diminished the force of their criticism at one point, and the extension of those services in the development of which the State has not had in mind any "commercially set" limit has also, in some degree, turned the edge of their objection regarding the hampering effect of associating treatment with the test of income. Without, however, discussing these wider issues, their criticism and positive suggestion have some bearing on the question of "scales." It is difficult to perceive any real statistical basis behind many of them, authorities vieing with one another in progressiveness or niggardliness are apt to copy with little change the latest scale of the kind they like. The definition of the "family" to be used in the various tests, and of the allowances to be made to other earners before counting their wages as part of the family income, all need more clarifying, and it would be possible for an officer so functioning to introduce more order into administration. This is no plea for the rigid standardization of such scales between different areas. Just as a uniform rate of unemployment benefit means one thing in an area where wages are high and living dear, and another where wages are low and living cheap, so standard scales would bear unequally on populations of varied age, sex, and occupational constitution. At the same time, if we are to administer services by the use of scales, there is every reason for making them as rational as possible.

CHAPTER VI

DEPRESSED CLASSES

HAVING examined a representative sample, we now proceed to the third part of the enquiry, a scrutiny of selected groups in the lower ranges of income. If we submit the economic order to any criticism at all, our attention must of necessity be given to those individuals and families who do not receive an income sufficient to provide a low real standard, such as that here used, but the problem has a wider significance than just insufficiency of income. Such groups may consist first, simply of persons who in economic adversity, such as unemployment, have been thrust into a position of insufficiency for longer or shorter periods. Or secondly, they may be "depressed classes" who enjoy neither an average share of material comforts and necessities, nor perhaps an average share of the mental and physical attributes possessed by the mass of their fellows. It is characteristic of the second type that the conditions affecting them offer stubborn resistance to tried methods of State and private effort, and they are homogeneous in the sense that children born in such a class tend not to rise out of it. Cairnes's non-competing groups and Cannan's emphasis on the importance of inherited economic advantages in affecting wages point to the broad economic aspects of the problem, just as studies of mental defect and degeneracy call attention to its biological aspects. We are, however, less concerned with the theories which have been devised to account for their persistence in the community than to get some impression of their numbers and condition.

The groups selected for study include examples of both these types; they are (1) the unemployed; (2) a special group of applicants for voluntary assistance; (3) families with mentally deficient members; (4) the legal poor.

(1) *The Unemployed*

In the random sample there were 160 families, or 29 per cent of the total number, with some member unemployed; in 107 families, or 19 per cent of the total, the head only was out of work, and in 30 families, or 5 per cent of the total, the head was in work but one or more other earners were unemployed. There were two or more persons out of work in 30 families. The chief facts relating to their income and relation to the poverty line can be briefly stated. The mean family income of all families with some member unemployed was 47s. 3d., as compared with 57s. 9d. for the entire sample; the median income was 40s. 3d. as compared with 52s. 8d. The proportion of all families in primary poverty was 21 per cent, but only 11 per cent of those whose head was in work were in poverty, as compared with 59 per cent of those whose chief earner was unemployed.

An attempt to answer the question, "How did they live?" would have involved an examination of these persons for their diet and state of nutrition, a task beyond our resources, but if the question be interpreted to mean, "On what sources of income did they rely?" some interesting information can be obtained from the records. The tables below make clear the extent to which these families were supported by unemployment benefit, by other social services, and how far the other earners were a drain on the family income or contributed more than the cost of keeping them on the poverty line standard. It will be seen that in 5 per cent of the 130 families whose head was unemployed, no unemployment benefit was received on his account, in 17 per cent of the families other earners were without work, but that in only 3 per cent did the other earners receive incomes less than the sum needed to maintain them on the poverty standard.

MEANS OF SUBSISTENCE OF FAMILIES WHOSE HEAD WAS UNEMPLOYED

	Families Above Line	*Families Below Line*	*All Families Numbers*	*All Families Percentage*
Families with head unemployed	54	76	130	100
Head without benefit	1	6	7	5
Head with benefit	53	70	123	95
Head with benefit only ..	49	68	117	90
Head with benefit and wages ..	4	2	6	5
Families with other social income	13	6	19	15
With other earners unemployed—				
With benefit	11	5	16	12
Without benefit	3	4	7	5
With other earners contributing more than the cost of maintaining them	43	18	61	47
With other earners contributing less than the cost of maintaining them	—	4	4	3
Actual number of other earners unemployed	54	13	67	—

Their situation can be brought into relief by analysing the family income on the plan used for the whole sample.

COMPOSITION OF THE FAMILY INCOME: ALL FAMILIES WITH MEMBERS UNEMPLOYED

(160 *Families*)

Families in receipt of—	
Head's wages only	3
Other earners' wages only	1
Social income only	64
Head's wages and other earners' wages	1
Head's wages and social income	20
Other earners' wages and social income	44
Head's wages, other earners' wages, and social income	27
	160

These figures may be compared with those for the whole group of families on page 141.

So far, we have dealt with the families of the random

sample, who are nearly all of them in receipt of benefit. How do those fare who are deprived of benefit? The results of the Disallowance Enquiry,[1] which are of interest here, may be briefly quoted. One hundred and thirty-two persons who had been disallowed benefit on one or other of the statutory grounds were visited, information being obtained respecting their source of income, whether they had obtained any employment, etc. All except 24 of them were seen some six weeks after the date of disallowance, over one-half nine or more weeks, and one-quarter twelve or more weeks after the date of the disallowance. Benefit had thus been withheld long enough to make an enquiry as to its success in stimulating work-finding, and the drain on family means, significant; and in view of the circumstances the persons concerned were very willing to answer enquiries. Of the total, which included married women and juveniles, 57·6 per cent failed to obtain work of any kind, 9·1 per cent secured intermittent jobs only, and the remaining one-third obtained work which could be described as regular. There was no recorded case of men taking up subsidiary work or setting up on their own account, a fact which is confirmed by the experience of other areas investigated; the latter implies some savings, and as to the former, the chances are few in a port where there are plenty of casually employed men willing to snatch any opportunity available. In under 3 per cent of the cases was there any poor relief obtained, only in one case was there any known help from charitable organizations. Leaving out of account the juveniles, the disallowed persons received help from relatives (86 cases), parents (43 cases), savings (29 cases), rent arrears (5 cases), selling furniture and debts (5 cases), and landladies (4 cases).[2]

One can obtain a more vivid impression of the adjustment required to meet the drop in income by studying the budgets of unemployed persons. As with all working-class budgets,

[1] *Royal Commission on Unemployment Insurance, Evidence,* Appendix III, pp. 180–89.

[2] Appendices to *Evidence,* Part III, pp. 180–89.

the very fact that detailed records are kept implies that the family is unusually intelligent and that the arrangements made to meet the difficulty are the best and not the average response to the situation. In one such case the husband was a craftsman married and without children. He was out of work for nearly six months—24 weeks—the benefit at that date being 26s. for himself and wife. Of this 12s. 6d. was paid in rent, leaving 14s. for all other expenses. At that date the cost of maintaining the two above the poverty line was, excluding rent, 15s. 6d., so that apart from other resources the family was below the standard by about 1s. 6d. There were, in addition to mere maintenance expenses, standing charges which could not be reduced without consequential loss, namely, premiums on life insurance policy, £5 14s. 3d. for the period; contributions to a sick club at 10d. a week, £1 0s. 4d.; and contributions to a trade union at 1s. per week, £1 4s., a total of £7 18s. 9d. This was the problem for solution. To meet these liabilities a loan of £6 on the insurance policy was obtained, to offset the premiums due, while the friendly society made a grant of £1 to set against the contributions. The union benefit was 6s. for six weeks, and 3s. for six weeks, a total of £2 14s. The total sum available to meet these charges was thus £9 14s., leaving a balance available by these methods, which included borrowing, of £1 15s. 3d.; and this spread over the entire period brought the family practically up to standard. The income was occasionally augmented by 2s. 6d. for assisting friends in domestic work.

The problem was difficult enough, yet easier than in the case of those families with any considerable number of dependent children. How great was the real dependence on social income may be seen from the way in which the savings—the insurance policies—were pledged to relieve the strain.

(2) *A Group of Applicants for Assistance*

There are in every area various groups of families who apply for public and private assistance, and although they are self-selected groups, it should be possible to obtain from them supplementary evidence respecting groups located in a particular range of incomes. The information contained in the records is naturally relevant to the particular task in hand rather than suited to scientific enquiry, but it is often full enough, provided certain adjustments are made, to make possible analysis similar to that applied to the families in the representative sample. The experiment was tried in respect of a group of families who applied for assistance for their children, and who, as a condition of consideration, gave experienced investigators detailed information as to wages, other earners' incomes, various classes of social service payments, and receipts from lodgers; the rent paid, and the age and sex of members of the family. A sample of one-third, or 444 of the total number of cases available, was examined. The poverty datum line was calculated at the prices on the date of the enquiry (December 1930). The two difficulties were that in some cases the precise ages of the children below 14 were not stated; and where the facts were not obvious from inspection, a compromise "man value" of 0·44 was used.

The result of the investigation may be summarized as follows: (i) Of the heads of families, 47 per cent were labourers, 7 per cent were stewards and seamen, and 4 per cent were skilled shipyard workers. (ii) One family in every two had an income of less than 42s. per week, as compared with just over one family in every three in the random sample with income less than 45s. per week. (iii) Nearly three-quarters of them had no supplementary earners. (iv) Where there were supplementary earners they were a liability to the family, i.e. had incomes less than the cost of maintaining them on the poverty line standard—in one family in every five. This arose from the fact that the families were often those in which the supplementary earners were juveniles who had not reached insurable age. (v) Nearly one-third of the heads of families were unemployed; one in every eight had been out of work for more than two months, and one in every six for more than six weeks. (vi) In addition, one-quarter had received both benefit and wages, that is, had had short spells of work and unemployment during the last few weeks before the investigation. (vii) Sixty-nine per cent of the families were below the poverty line. Despite the provisions of the social services, there are enough loopholes in the arrangements for 44 widows, and 18 women who were separated from their husbands, or whose husbands were missing or in prison, to be in poverty. These formed nearly one-fifth of those beneath the poverty line.

These families were a self-selected group of applicants, so that one cannot say what proportion of the working-class population were in this condition, but they were not negligible in absolute numbers. For even assuming that there were no other families in a like condition, the 1,300 cases from which the sample was taken represent over 6 per cent of the total number of families with dependent children; and the proportion in poverty about 4 per cent.

(3) *The Mentally Deficient*

The two special groups already studied may be regarded as primarily "depressed" by economic and social circumstances, such as unemployment and under-employment. This group is subnormal, being handicapped in the struggle to reach or maintain "a minimum of civilized existence," not simply because they are born in a low income class, escape out of which may be difficult for an individual of only average ability, but because they have some inherent personal defect which would make it difficult for them to pursue rational and self-controlled economic effort in any economic grade. In the random sample household enquiry, the investigators had no instructions to look for such cases, but only to account for all persons in the family and secure particulars of work, earnings, etc. Nevertheless, three cases of adult mentally defective persons came to light out of a total of 2,364 adults. What numbers of such person should we expect to find in a population of the size of Southampton? Dr. Lewis, reporting the results of an enquiry into the numbers of defective persons in several areas of different type, thought that the probable incidence of such mental defect was about 8 per 1,000[1] of the population. We do not know to what extent the proportion of such defective persons varies from area to area, except that it is probably higher in the rural than the urban districts, but accepting the figure as a guide, we should then expect to find in Southampton about 1,400 such persons. In a comparatively short period the officers of the Mental Welfare Association have raised the known number of such persons to 5½ per 1,000.

For the purpose of this study a random sample of 50 (about 1 in 20) cases of mentally defective persons was investigated in such detail as circumstances and the available material permitted. The information was not in all cases sufficient to enable us to state with any precision the family earnings, but in all cases the occupation was known, and it was therefore possible to grade the families on the principles of the "Booth" survey. As might be supposed, the cases were dominantly those of the lower income grades, 74 per cent being Classes I–IV and only 26 per cent Classes VI and upwards. The method of selection of the cases was unlikely to cause any appreciable bias. The heads of the families in which the cases occurred were thus mainly in the ranks of the unskilled. Further, if we enquire into how far they were economically self-dependent, the results are not less striking. Twenty-three (46 per cent) of these families were in receipt of social income, a proportion similar to that in the normal sample families (47 per cent); but the form of help from the social services was quite different, for while 27 per cent of the normal families received unemployment benefit, and only 2 per cent obtained public assistance, of these subnormal families only 16 per cent were receiving unemployment benefit, but 24 per cent were obtaining public assistance. The greater resort to public assistance is a natural consequence of the relatively poor economic qualities

[1] *Report of Committee on Mental Deficiency*, Part IV.

of these families in earning constitution or personal qualities. There were more cases of deserted wives, two or three cases of heads who committed, or who attempted to commit suicide, while often there were one, two, or even three defectives of earning age, who, instead of being sources of income were, in fact, either completely or semi-dependent. Thus, in one family in which the head had already reached "industrial old age" and was out of work, there were two defective male adults and one defective daughter with an illegitimate child. Sometimes drink is obviously a factor, but often the other earners, though industrious and respectable, are in the lower paid occupations.

The group also displays the well-known characteristic of such mentally subnormal groups—the sharp contrast between intellectual vigour and reproductive capacity. Its mental vigour can be assessed partly from the records of near relatives with mental defect (as distinguished from illiteracy or mere dullness). In the small group of fifty cases there were only 15 in which the defective person in respect of whom the case arose had no relatives known to be defective. In the other 35 cases there had been 66 known defective near relatives, though not all were still living. If we omit uncles, cousins, and grandparents, there were 54 relatives with known mental defect, and these included 11 parents, 9 sons, 14 daughters, and 16 brothers or sisters. There were numerous cases of physical defect in relatives of the defective person in respect of whom the card was obtained, but as a test of physical vigour we may note the number of non-surviving children. There were 12 families in respect of whom this information was known; and they had 83 children, of whom 31 had died in infancy or at an early age. We may set against these facts those relating to fertility. The average number of school children per family in the mass interview was 2·0 for all families with such children, and 2·2 for families in Income Grades I–V. For the sample enquiry the average number of school children per family (excluding those with none), was

2·2. For this group it was 2·66; and we have already seen that many had died.

The drain on the public funds caused by these families, the least of the evils involved, is not easy to measure. Nearly one-quarter of the families of the sample were receiving public assistance. If this proportion held good in all families where there was a defective person notified or under supervision, this would give a total of about 230 families in receipt of such assistance. If the numbers of mentally defective persons in the area do reach eight per thousand of the population, then 300–350 persons receiving outdoor assistance are of this type. We must not press these ratios too far, but they at least indicate the possible order of magnitude of the problem.

(4) *The Legal Poor*

A fourth group is one in which the existence of poverty is undoubted, since the State through its appropriate machinery has declared the persons concerned, if not absolutely destitute, at least as nearly approaching it as to give them a claim for assistance. From 1924 to 1928 the total number of persons receiving institutional relief in Southampton varied from 1,358 to 1,579; the number of lunatics from 485 to 597, and the number of casuals from 147 to 160 in July, to 283 in December–January. During the same period, the numbers of persons receiving out-relief varied from 2,162 to 2,862 in January, and from 2,179 to 2,659 in July; but in this case the numbers were affected by the seamen's strike of 1925, the General Strike of 1926, and by changes in unemployment insurance law. The total number receiving institutional and domiciliary relief in the few years before the present depression was between 19 and 21 per 1,000 of the population. It is easier to state the numbers of such persons than to determine what that number really signifies, as compared with similar figures for other areas. The burden of pauperism will be less in an area with large numbers of relatively well-to-do people, and with few engaged in fluctuating or casual trades. One area may have good traditions in temperance and licensing, another may have lax ones. Or it may be that one authority follows, as far as central administration allows, a policy of work or maintenance, while another has a long tradition of strict administration. One of the variable factors, especially in respect of outdoor relief, is the policy of the local authority itself. Even the character of local sentiment towards poor relief may have been partly due to a consistently applied and deterrent policy, yet the strain of mass unemployment, or a relatively short period of open-handedness may change dread and reluctance into an attitude which accepts relief as a natural and proper resort in adversity. The degree of pauperism is not just a mechanical consequence of the industrial system. It is thus necessary to scrutinize these factors in Southampton and other towns with a problem of port labour, even although the task of assessing their relative importance is an impossible one.

While the material available is insufficient to enable us to determine whether any of the various ports has persistently followed any particular policy of relief, nevertheless there are certain common features in the history of Poor Law administration in these areas. The Royal Commission in 1834 aimed at creating a tradition of strict administration of outdoor relief, and proposed for this purpose the establishment of unions of parishes, but long before this, even before Gilbert's Act, Southampton had merged its separate parishes into a single area for Poor Law purposes. A special local Act of 1773[1] set up Incorporated Guardians. This body consisted of the Mayor, the Bailiffs, the Recorder, the three Senior Aldermen, and eighteen of the most discreet persons elected by the inhabitant ratepayers. To be qualified for election guardians had to be resident, possess property, or occupy property of the amount of £10 in St. Mary's parish, and £20 in other parishes. The Act also contained the curious provision that no guardian should serve more than two years in succession, a clause not

[1] 13 Geo. III, c. 50.

repealed until 1877. The guardians were given express power to compel "all and every idle and disorderly person who shall neglect or refuse or be unable to maintain himself, herself, or themselves, and also all other people who shall beg, seek or want relief . . . to come into work or dwell" in the said workhouse, and to detain them such time as they thought reasonable (Section 35). The industrious poor, could, however, be relieved outside the workhouse (Section 40). The guardians were to hold monthly meetings for the purpose of granting relief, but in between the meetings the justices might make emergency orders. Both Bristol and Hull unions also had local corporations, Liverpool was a separate parish administered under a local Act, and of the ports with which comparisons have frequently been made in this study, only Newcastle and Cardiff had Boards of Guardians set up under the Act of 1834.[1]

The stormy issue of Poor Law administration has always been that of outdoor relief of the able-bodied. The famous Royal Commission had denounced it, and its various recommendations were designed to build up a tradition of strict administration in this respect. The Poor Law Commissioners established by the Act of 1834, and their successors the Poor Law Board, had in this vital matter developed two separate lines of policy. One was expressed by its Outdoor Relief Prohibition Order, which, being directed to carry out the Act's intention of limiting outdoor relief of the able-bodied as far as possible, prohibited all such relief, with certain specified exceptions, while the other culminated in the Outdoor Relief Regulation Order of 1852. In explaining the latter, the Board said that "looking to the circumstances in most of the unions and Parishes in London, and in other populous places, they have not thought it expedient to prohibit outdoor relief to any class of paupers,"[2] and they proceeded to define the

[1] *Royal Commission on Poor Laws*, Appendix vol. xii, pp. 248–60.

[2] Outdoor Relief Regulation Order, August 1852, covering letter, fourth paragraph. See also revised order and letter, December 1852.

conditions under which it might be given, e.g. half in kind, etc. The emphasis and approach to the problem expressed by this order is different from the other. From this point of view it is worth observing that, in 1847, there were no orders of any kind in force regulating outdoor relief in Southampton, Bristol, Hull, and Liverpool; that it was governed by the Prohibition Order in Cardiff, and a test work order in Newcastle. In 1871 it was controlled by Regulation Order in all the ports except Cardiff, where it was controlled by Prohibition Order, modified by a Test Work Order. The same situation existed in 1906.

We get little help from the statistics of pauperism. In a long memorandum[1] presented to the Royal Commission of the Poor Laws, 1905–09, Charles Booth set forth in great detail the numbers of paupers and the expenditure per pauper on different types of service, at various dates from 1875 to 1905, but a comparison of the figures relating to ports does not yield any conclusive evidence as to the policies pursued by the respective unions. All we can say is that in general the volume of pauperism is rather greater than in "all provincial urban centres," and in some cases the expenditure per pauper is also higher.

When we turn from traditions in administration to contemporary policy we are on somewhat firmer ground. The outstanding fact is naturally unemployment; and its effect in changing the volume of pauperism, both in Southampton and in other ports, is obvious enough. First, the figures below show the downward movement of relief as Southampton recovered from the depression of 1921 to the relatively prosperous year of 1928. The facts for other ports are also given.

The figures show clearly the general rise in the volume of pauperism as trade depression advanced, and the uneven way in which it struck the different ports. Hull, with the heaviest incidence, begins at the top of the list, with Liverpool second;

[1] *Royal Commission of Poor Laws*, Appendix vol. xii, pp. 366–97.

by 1931 the latter had jumped to first place, while a year later Newcastle, whose burden has assumed tremendous proportions, leaped to an unenviable leadership. Meanwhile, though Southampton's burden had increased by one-fifth, it had begun low in the list of ports and feld to the bottom in 1932.

While unemployment is the major factor in recent years, we have still to determine what is the effect, if any, of present

NUMBERS PER 10,000 OF THE POPULATION IN RECEIPT OF INSTITUTIONAL AND DOMICILIARY RELIEF IN CERTAIN PORTS AND OTHER TOWNS, 1930–32

	June 1930	*June* 1931	*June* 1932
Liverpool	429	545	641
Bristol	203	204	398
Hull	500	533	589
Newcastle	404	484	725
Cardiff..	539	418	431
Southampton ..	206	212	249
Bournemouth ..	121	125	148
Portsmouth	141	119	156

NUMBER PER 10,000 OF THE POPULATION IN RECEIPT OF INSTITUTIONAL AND DOMICILIARY RELIEF, SOUTHAMPTON, 1921–29

Year	*June*	*December*	*Year*	*June*	*December*
1921	—	588	1926	214	228
1922	477	328	1927	207	213
1923	297	288	1928	198	201
1924	274	253	1929	197	212
1925	248	268			

local policy regarding the granting of relief. The information is meagre, but something may be gathered from the data in the enquiry as to Persons Disallowed Insurance Benefit, to which reference has already been made. To what extent did the persons disallowed apply for public assistance?

PERCENTAGE OF PERSONS DISALLOWED UNEMPLOYMENT BENEFIT WHO RECEIVED POOR RELIEF, 1930

(Percentage in Sample in receipt of Relief)

	All Cases	*Married and Widowed Men*	*Single Men*
Liverpool	33·0	68·6	38·5
Hull	30·4	68·4	28·0
Tyneside	17·1	51·1	0·5
Southampton.. ..	3·0	7·1	7·1

If the area has suffered for a long period from unemployment—as in the case of the Tyneside—savings will be drained; and other relatives will be less able to contribute. At that date Southampton had a relatively light incidence of unemployment, but the differences were not due to these factors only. For in Liverpool apparently only 10 per cent of the applicants received less than the scale, and relief was not refused without good reasons. In Southampton, on the other hand, the assistance granted was below not only the rates of unemployment benefit, but the authority's own relief scale. If we test the matter by the scales in force in various ports, even allowing for some local differences in the cost of living, the administration of Southampton appears relatively strict:

FROM RELIEF SCALES AS IN MAY 1930

	Southampton	*Liverpool*	*Hull*	*Newcastle*
Man and wife.. ..	18/6	20/–	23/–	22/–
Man, wife, and four children	28/6	33/–	35/–	28/6

We cannot conclude with any numerical statement of the proportions of legal poverty traceable to unemployment, or prolonged unemployment, on the one hand, or to the attitude of the public and the authorities on the other. What has been said will indicate the present tone of local Poor Law administration and the direction, if not the precise extent, of its effects on the statistical volume of those who are "legally poor."

CHAPTER VII

HOUSING

ONE of the interests of the housing problem is its many-sidedness. No one who has observed the differences in type and density of houses on the Tyneside from those in a southern town, like Southampton, whether their origin be taste, cost of land, or local conventions of technique, can doubt their relevance to a study of standards of living or of health. The number of houses built to the acre is now in law, as well as in medical opinion, an important element in health environment. Besides these physical elements of the problem, there is the economic problem of securing an equilibrium between the changing needs of miscellaneous family types and incomes, and durable housing units. And since the disadvantages in health and morals of "overcrowding" are commonly recognized, there is the task of finding a workable definition of "overcrowding" and of determining the extent and causes of the phenomenon. Thus the problem becomes a complex one of tastes, costs, legislation, poverty, and of such human material as the "slummer."

The problem is of further interest, theoretical as well as practical, because any attempt to deal with it implies the definition of standards of desirability. If we are thinking of physical type, there must be an understood, if vague, notion of fitness, for the operation of closing orders; if we are concerned with congestion of buildings to the acre, a standard of desirability underlies both slum clearance schemes and the prescription of maximum density limits in town-planning schemes. If we desire to prevent the "overcrowding" of families in houses, here also a standard must be defined. In what follows, an attempt is made to give a broad impression of some aspects of these problems in Southampton.

We may approach the matter from the physical side of

house type and house density. House types are notoriously difficult to compare quantitatively, unless they are built to prescribed limits, such as Council houses approved and subsidized by the Ministry of Health. The mere quotation of cubic feet and number of rooms leaves vital things unsaid, for a five-roomed house in the North-Eastern counties is one thing, and a five-roomed house in Hampshire and Sussex another; and, even in the same town, a six-roomed house in an old, crowded area represents an entirely different standard in health and amenity and income from a six-roomed house in a more well-to-do area. The consolidation of rating under the Rating and Valuation Act has, however, provided a means of surmounting some of these difficulties within a given area, for a comparison of houses by their rateable values does give us some definite information about them. For the present purpose, all dwelling-houses were classified in five ranges of rateable value, commercial properties being excluded. Generally "commercial" was taken to mean property used for trading and manufacturing purposes, if valued at £40 a year and upwards, all public-houses, and offices; and the whole rule was interpreted with discretion. The table below shows the results by ward for the whole town.[1]

Comparisons with other towns cannot be pushed very far owing to lack of data, but it is worth observing that, in the case of Portsmouth, about 65·5 per cent of the properties were rated under £21 as compared with 60·3 per cent in Southampton: 19·0 per cent at £21–£30, and 5·0 per cent at £31–£40, as compared with 25·8 per cent and 7·7 per cent in Southampton. In the case of Portsmouth, however, commercial properties are included in the figures. As to the difference between the separate wards, little comment is needed. The four town wards—Town, St. Mary's, Northam, and Trinity—may be compared with Banister. Northam is striking by its entire lack of well-to-do houses, and the district is the

[1] The information was also placed upon a six-inch map, the streets being graded and coloured according to the modal range of rateable value.

most homogeneous of all, even although others may have a larger proportion of very small properties. Bitterne and Sholing is noteworthy by reason of the massing of its houses into the two lower ranges of rateable values and the very small proportion in the middle range of £21–£30.

RATEABLE VALUE OF HOUSES, EXCLUDING COMMERCIAL PROPERTIES

(Percentage of Houses in each Class)

Ward	£ 0–13	£ 14–20	£ 21–30	£ 31–40	£ 41 *and over*	*Total Number of Houses*
Town	47·8	26·4	15·5	5·9	4·5	1,499
St. Mary's ..	39·4	44·8	12·9	1·9	1·0	1,630
Northam ..	32·1	57·2	10·2	0·5	—	1,331
Trinity	36·4	24·4	34·9	2·2	2·1	1,518
Newtown ..	15·2	29·6	39·6	10·5	5·0	1,870
All Saints ..	14·6	21·6	38·6	17·3	7·9	1,669
Bevois	11·9	36·0	28·1	12·2	11·8	1,820
Banister.. ..	0·4	9·9	43·9	20·9	24·9	1,974
Freemantle ..	19·4	51·1	15·6	5·7	8·3	1,835
Millbrook ..	16·7	55·4	21·6	2·3	3·9	2,559
Shirley	29·2	21·7	33·2	10·7	5·2	3,340
Portswood ..	11·0	23·8	36·5	16·3	12·4	2,128
St. Denys ..	12·0	53·8	25·9	5·1	3·3	2,239
Bitterne and Pear Tree	11·7	52·0	29·8	5·6	0·9	1,971
Bitterne and Sholing ..	34·5	54·5	8·0	2·1	0·9	2,379
Woolston ..	13·5	60·5	17·7	4·1	4·2	1,688
St. Nicholas ..	12·3	55·2	20·9	5·5	6·1	2,574
Total percentage	20·4	39·9	25·8	7·7	6·1	—
Numbers ..	6,952	13,579	8,787	2,629	2,077	34,024

The figures may be compared with those describing the second important physical aspect of housing—the number of houses built to the acre. No emphasis is needed on the ill consequences of overcrowding houses to the acre, nor upon the expensiveness of the slum clearance operations undertaken by municipalities in their endeavours to get rid of the twin evils of structural unfitness and high density. There is an important difference between what may be termed "gross" and "net" density. Town and St. Mary's wards contain large areas covered with works and businesses as well as open space, and really close packing of houses on the area used for housing could be made to look relatively light if the "works area" and other acreage were thrust into the denominator. It is a great advantage for houses to be adjacent to a large open space, but the houses themselves may be congested and ill-lighted for all that. The results are given in Appendix IV. The figures represent the net density, i.e. the average number of dwelling-houses per acre of land used for housing, including streets. All land used for public buildings of any size, vacant land, foreshore, works areas, etc., was excluded.

In the main, the densities are relatively light, and although the bad lay-out of the land and narrow frontages might seem to suggest the contrary, this is, especially in the older houses in certain parts of the town, offset by the long gardens behind them. The figures are average densities for the whole wards, and therefore conceal the fact that there are individual blocks much more closely built, as in Town Ward, where there are blocks of over 60 to the acre, whilst small congested groups can be found even in the outer districts. The area of the roadways is included in the land used for housing, and this makes some difference where areas were built-up at different dates, under different bye-laws, or where they are only partly built-up. Thus, Northam streets are wider than many of those in Trinity, and the density figure is relatively lightened; whilst the fact that in Bitterne and Sholing there are long roads with vacant plots, increases the proportion of street acreage to the number of houses, and this reduces the density figure.

A comparison of the column representing house density per acre and that representing persons per room in the census figure of 1921 shows vividly the varied nature of the housing problem, even in a town of Southampton's size. Town, St.

Mary's, and Trinity, with high house densities and relatively large numbers of persons per room, may be set against Northam, with a lighter house density per acre but overcrowding per room, and Bevois, which has a density similar to that of Northam, but is less overcrowded per room. To put it more pointedly, the major remedy for Northam is a judicious use of the vacancies in Council houses, but in Trinity, St. Mary's, and Town demolition of some properties will become necessary.

The third aspect of the problem introduces the factors of population and families. In the last thirty years the relation between population and the provision of houses has exhibited the same general characteristics observed in England and Wales as a whole, namely, a fall in the birth-rate and decrease in the size of the family, a long lag between the increase in the number of families and the provision of house room for them, together with a reshuffling of the smaller families amongst houses and tenements designed for larger ones. The boundary change in 1920 unfortunately detracts from the comparability of the various censuses in this important matter, but separate figures are available in 1901 and 1911 for the unenlarged Southampton and for Itchen urban district, which together included in 1921 nearly 95 per cent of the population of the whole borough. For the earlier years we may therefore take the averages, etc., relating to these two areas combined as representing, substantially, the truth for the whole. First, the population of the present area increased between 1901 and 1911 by 17·3 per cent and between 1911 and 1921 by 11·8 per cent, as compared with increases in the number of dwellings of 11·5 per cent and 11·3 per cent. The population for housing purposes does not, however, consist of interchangeable units but of family groups of defined sizes, and provision of houses must be seen in relation to these. The average size of the private family fell from 4·26 in 1911 to 4·11 in 1921, so that the increase in the numbers of families needing separate accommodation was greater than the mere increase of total population would suggest—between 1911 and 1921, for example, over 12 per cent. In consequence, the excess of the number of private families needing accommodation over the number of dwellings available increased from about 4,492 to 6,982. The increased pressure on accommodation can be seen in other ways. The percentage of houses vacant fell from 5·9 per cent in 1901 to 3·9 per cent in 1911 and 1·7 per cent in 1921, a margin barely sufficient for the "normal" vacancies between incoming and outgoing tenancies, much less sufficient to provide any freedom of choice for occupiers. Similarly, the percentage of the population in private families who were living more than two persons per room increased from 1·6 per cent in 1901 to 5·1 per cent in 1911 and 6·7 per cent in 1921. Pressure of this sort naturally led to the increase in the number of "shared" houses, the average number of families per dwelling rising from 1·17 in 1911 to 1·23 in 1921. Further, while the family has proved to be susceptible to rapid reduction in average size, houses are durable, are built in definite sizes, and conversion from one type to another, if it be possible at all, can often be made only at substantial cost. Housing the new smaller family in houses of dominantly older type implies some awkwardness of fit, and for this reason also there is an outcrop of shared and divided houses. In these respects Southampton was influenced by factors which have operated in other areas in varying degrees.

There are also some interesting persistent differences. In 1901, in Southampton and Itchen together, 1·6 per cent of the population were living more than two persons to a room, as compared with 1·0 per cent in Portsmouth; in 1911 the percentage living more than two persons to the room was 5·1 per cent, as compared with 2·3 per cent in Portsmouth and 1·6 per cent in Bournemouth; in 1921 it was 6·7 per cent in Southampton, 3·7 per cent in Portsmouth, and 3·0 per cent in Bournemouth. What accounts for the relative failure of the building industry to adjust itself, more accurately, to the needs of Southampton? Is it land values? A lower range of incomes and so a smaller capacity to pay rents? A relative backwardness in technique? A greater rate of growth of the population and families but the same hindrance to house building? The same differences show themselves in the ratios of persons to rooms. In 1921 the ratio in Southampton was only 1·10 rooms per person as compared with 1·19 in Portsmouth and 1·29 in Bournemouth. One important fact to be noticed is that the size of the family is larger, being only 3·89 in Bournemouth, 3·84 in Portsmouth, as compared with 4·11 in Southampton.

So far our analysis has concerned the whole town, whether the data were drawn from the census or special surveys made for the purpose. The random sample dealt solely with the working-class portion of it, but we have more information about these cases than the census makes available. The relation of the families to house room actually occupied (as distinct from available) can be seen from the figures below, on page 177. They show the percentage of the total families which were of defined number of "equivalent adults," counting all children under ten years of age as a half adult. The half rooms of the table are rooms declared to be "shared" (usually kitchen as distinct from scullery) and therefore not in the sole occupation of any family. No doubt, in practice, such sharing was often implied that one family made more use of the "shared" room than another, but any such right was an important fact in the accommodation of the other family. Dividing the room for this purpose is an awkward compromise, but possibly the best that could be done with an intractable situation.

The detailed analysis of the relation between post-census housing need and the post-census erection of houses, both by private and municipal enterprise, which was made by Mr. F. W. Cuthbertson, M.A., in the *Southampton Civic Survey*, need not be repeated here. It is sufficient to say that, from an analysis of the growth of population of families and house construction since 1921, there appeared a balance of

PERCENTAGE OF FAMILIES OF DIFFERENT SIZES

Size of Families in Equivalent Adults

	1	1½	2	2½	3	3½	4	4½	5	5½	6	6½	7	7½	8	*All*
Percentage of families of different sizes	2·0	—	14·7	8·1	20·2	7·3	14·0	9·5	10·7	2·1	4·3	2·5	1·8	2·9	—	100

PERCENTAGE OF HOUSES OF DIFFERENT SIZES

Number of Rooms

	1	1½	2	2½	3	3½	4	4½	5	5½	6	6½	7	7½	8	*All*
Percentage of families occupying houses of different sizes	0·3	0·7	2·9	6·1	10·4	2·9	21·0	0·3	50·4	—	3·4	—	0·9	—	0·5	100

between three thousand and four thousand houses needed for the working classes in July 1929. The effect of this pressure is shown in the large numbers of shared houses discovered in the sample. It is only to be expected that older and larger houses in the inner districts of the town, and now forsaken by the inhabitants who are building new houses in the outer areas of the town, should be divided into flats and occupied by more than one family, but many post-war houses are also being shared. The pressure of accommodation is such that in Southampton as elsewhere the only satisfactory way for many to secure house room is to buy a house on mortgage and sub-let a portion of it immediately to lighten the burden. Out of five hundred and fifty-nine families in the sample one hundred and five, or nearly 19 per cent of them, were sharing houses. This figure may be compared with the 27 per cent found in the Liverpool survey. And it is significant that, despite denials, Council houses in some districts were found not only with lodgers, but shared by the tenants with a second family.

However inconvenient and undesirable on general grounds, the sharing of houses cannot be treated as synonymous with overcrowding. No doubt Mr. Chesterton would object to the practice for the same reasons that led him to jeer at working-class flats as houses on stilts, and many will sympathize with his robust statement of men's desire on this point; but neither flats nor the sharing of houses need imply the overcrowding of persons per room which is so fruitful a source of ill health and infant mortality. Overcrowding has for long been measured by the Registrar-General's now famous "more than two persons per room," but of late years the exigencies of administration have called forth rivals. It was and is, as the Registrar-General has repeatedly explained, a standard of measurement and not a standard of desirability, a neutral "poverty datum line" applied to one item of the standard of living. In the hands of one able group of administrators, it has evolved into the "Manchester standard" of desirability, for use in deciding on applications for Corporation houses, and has been followed by a third, the Liverpool "capacity standard."[1] The Manchester standard emphasizes bedroom accommodation, provides for sex separation and age difference. It states that:

1. There must not be more than 2½ persons per bedroom, a child under ten being counted as one-half an adult.
2. The sexes should be separated after the age of ten and the parents should be able to occupy one bedroom (with a child under ten if necessary).

As a standard of desirability it has been criticized by Mr. Caradoc Jones, who brought powerful support from psychologists and social workers for a lower age of sex separation. The Manchester standard is, however, spreading in use, it is simple, and is a convenient basis for discussion. It needs, however, clarifying on one point. In counting bedrooms, do we mean those rooms so designed by the builder, or do we permit the use of the parlour as a bedroom, if there is a separate living-room as well? And do we even postulate that there should be at least one living-room? The standard has here been interpreted by the two rules above, plus a stipulation that there should be a living-room. To meet the difficulties of applying such a uniform standard to both non-parlour houses, and those with parlours which could be converted to bedrooms, two calculations of overcrowding have been made, one "actual overcrowding," which counts the parlour as a possible bedroom, and the other, "potential overcrowding" also stipulating the reservation of one living-room, but permitting the parlour to be kept for its original purpose.[2]

[1] *Journal Royal Statistical Society*, 1930, pp. 502–04.

[2] Even this distinction does not surmount every difficulty of classification, e.g. the case of the one-roomed tenement. This has been treated as a bedroom. There is some difficulty in finding suitable terms for these distinctions. The term "potential overcrowding" corresponds to that of "necessary overcrowding" in the new London survey. "Actual overcrowding" is quite different from that of London, in which case it applies to a calculation based on the number of rooms actually used as bedrooms.

The following table sets forth the cases of overcrowding as defined:

NUMBER OF FAMILIES OVERCROWDED

	Family Type					All
	1 *No Earner*	2 *No Adult Male Earner*	3 *Adult Male Earner only*	4 *Adult Male and Subsidiary Earners*	5 *Two Adult Male Earners*	
Families Above Line						
Potential overcrowding ..	—	1	16	25	11	53
Actual overcrowding ..	—	—	10	8	6	24
Families Below Line						
Potential overcrowding ..	1	1	11	2	—	15
Actual overcrowding ..	—	—	3	—	—	3
All Families						
Potential overcrowding ..	1	2	27	27	11	68
Actual overcrowding ..	—	—	13	8	6	27

Potential overcrowding is 12·2 per cent of all families.
Actual overcrowding is 4·8 per cent of all families.

NOTE.—Actual overcrowding—reckoning parlour as possible bedroom.
Potential overcrowding—reckoning parlour as not available for use as a bedroom.

The percentage of actual overcrowding in the sample is 4·8 per cent, and for the whole working-class population would probably be between 5·4 per cent and 4·2 per cent. This does not appear to be heavy as compared with the results arrived at in the Liverpool Survey, and there is little doubt that the percentage of potential overcrowding, 12·2, or between 11·3 and 13·1 per cent for the working-class population, is also much lighter than would be found in many urban areas. But if we remember that the reduction of overcrowding from more than one in ten families (potential overcrowding) to one in twenty (actual overcrowding) is only obtained by assuming the abandonment of the parlour, regarded as necessary by every middle-class family, we can see how much the economic system has yet to achieve. Since most of both the actually and potentially overcrowded families were above the minimum standard, it is pertinent to ask whether they "need" have been overcrowded, or whether, in short, they could afford to pay a higher rent and thus secure more ample accommodation. An arbitrary definition of ability is required, and for this purpose three of the rules devised by Mr. Caradoc Jones as a criterion of ability to pay higher rents were adopted.[1] They are:

1. Neither public assistance nor any recorded charitable assistance is included in arriving at family income for this purpose.
2. There must be a margin of at least 10 per cent between the net income required to reach the minimum standard and the actual net income of the family.
3. If then the net income is 50 per cent or more above the minimum standard, the family is adjudged as probably able to afford a higher rent.

Mr. Jones's criteria contained other rules, but they were refinements which it has not been thought wise to adopt in view of the small number of families affected. Using this standard as a test, we find that (1) none of the below line families, potentially or actually overcrowded, were able to pay a higher rent, (2) that 31 out of 68, or 45 per cent of the potentially overcrowded, and 15 out of 27, or 56 per cent of the actually overcrowded, could afford a higher rent. The reason for this lies mainly in the fact that many of the overcrowded families are Types 4 and 5, that is, those with supplementary earners. The differences between such small total numbers as these overcrowded families are in the sample, scarcely constitute solid and reliable support for any refinement of conclusions, but it is clear that the percentage of overcrowding tends to increase as we pass from Class 3 families to Classes 4 and 5. It is not surprising that these families with the greater earning strength and relatively higher incomes should be overcrowded,

[1] *Journal Royal Statistical Society*, 1933, p. 566.

for they are types which are difficult to house, they contain more persons needing sex separation, and they are also families which may at any time be broken up by marriage. The other earners' contribution to family income is not likely to be permanent, and a head of a family may well pause before enlarging his expenditure on rent in these cases. In this respect the tendency of the figures is to confirm the general conclusions of the Liverpool Survey. In connection with this matter it is worth observing that the full implications of the erection of Council houses of the non-parlour type, and the tendency to select the larger families to live in them, is often overlooked. Whilst the family is young the question of sex separation does not arise, and it is in these years that such families are generally allotted houses, but as they grow older "half" adults become "whole" adults; a family of six children, even if divided equally between the sexes, with the youngest say eleven, and the eldest at twenty-three or twenty-four, will be "actually overcrowded." It is sometimes easy for administrators to forget that children grow up.

Having considered physical types and density, and the adjustment of families to available accommodation, we now turn to the financial aspect—rents. For this purpose "rent" needs defining. Its meaning here is—with an exception which will be noted—not the rent actually paid by the first tenant to the landlord, but the *net rent expense* borne by the family, i.e. full rent and rates, less any rent received from sub-letting or from boarders. It is the expense in rent to the family which is here the centre of interest, and not the return for the house received by the landlord. First, the following table shows the net rent expense of the families in the sample.

NET RENTS PAID BY WORKING-CLASS HOUSEHOLDS

	Lower Quartile	*Median*	*Upper Quartile*	*Q3–Q1*
Families above line ..	8/6	11/-	14/4	5/10
Families below line ..	8/11	11/-	15/4	6/5
All families	8/11	11/-	14/6	5/7

The median rent in the Liverpool Survey was 9s. 5d.

Since families below the poverty line tend to pay higher rents than those above the line, it is worth while enquiring further into the relationships between rents, income, and poverty. The following table compares families by income grades. When the number of families is very small, as in the below line groups for the middle and upper ranges of income, the figures have been omitted. In the lower half of the table the median net rent has been expressed as a percentage of the mid value of the income range (22s. 6d., 37s. 6d., etc.).

MEDIAN NET RENTALS FOR FAMILIES OF DIFFERENT INCOME GRADES

	Upper Limits of Income Grades						
	30/–	45/–	60/–	75/–	90/–	105/–	120/–
	Median Net Rent						
Above line families ..	6/10	10/–	10/6	12/2	12/3	13/11	12/1
Below line families ..	10/6	11/4	—	—	—	—	—
All families	9/–	10/6	12/–	12/–	12/3	13/11	12/1
	Median Rent as Percentage of Income						
Above line families ..	30·1	26·7	20·0	16·5	14·9	14·3	10·7
Below line families ..	46·9	35·7	—	—	—	—	—
All families	41·3	28·0	22·9	17·8	14·9	14·3	10·7

The below line families were paying on the whole higher rent in absolute amounts than those above the line, so that it is no surprise that this item should also be a larger proportion of their income. A larger number of the below line cases are on unemployment benefit, and a rent of the same amount as a similarly situated worker in full work will appear as a more important item in the reduced income. What has been said earlier as to the overcrowding of families with supplementary earners and higher family incomes is pertinent here; the rent paid and the accommodation demanded tends to remain stable as the children grow to full earning age, because the dissolution of the family unit is not far removed. The amount of rent paid therefore tends to hover around a maximum in the middle and higher ranges of income, and the proportion of total income absorbed by it to diminish. In view of the heavy drain which rent makes on the lower incomes, one cannot refrain from observing in passing of a possible consequence of the concurrence of rising rents as more and more houses become decontrolled, with falling money wages and social service payments. Though these events may in the end be counterbalanced by reduced building costs and increased building, there is a real danger of an aggravation of overcrowding.

The relation of rents to the size of the family is to be seen from the table opposite:

As one would expect, the table exhibits a regular reduction in the net rent per persons as the family increases in size, and there is no definite break in the series which would suggest that any particular size of the family experienced a particular difficulty in securing house room. From this point of view the family is a very adjustable unit, in that it can fit into available accommodation by overcrowding. The families below the line tend to pay higher rent per person than those above it; but it must be remembered that the method determining the position of the family in relation to the line is that no rent is deducted from gross income. It follows from this procedure that the high rent cases will tend to be thrust below the line.

We may enquire, finally, as to the net rents paid per room. If we assume, since we are dealing with working-class houses only, that the cost of construction per room would fall as the size of the house and the number of rooms increases, we ought to expect rents per room to lie along a regular descending curve in a similar way. Any considerable irregularity or "notch" in it would raise at once the query as to whether there was not, in fact, an under or over supply of specified size of tenements.

MEAN RENTS FOR FAMILIES OF DIFFERENT SIZES

Number of Equivalent Adults

	1	2	2½	3	3½	4	4½	5	5½	6	6½	7	7½	*All*
Families Above Line														
Rents	6/10	10/3	13/2	12/1	12/11	12/7	13/3	12/5	10/9	13/6	10/8	12/1	10/4	12/–
Numbers	9	62	31	87	34	65	37	50	10	19	12	9	14	439
Families Below Line														
Rents	5/–	10/5	15/–	13/2	14/6	13/9	12/10	13/9	12/6	12/3	10/–	11/3	16/3	12/10
Numbers	2	20	14	26	7	13	16	10	2	5	2	1	2	120
All Families														
Rents	6/6	10/4	13/9	12/4	13/2	12/8	13/1	12/8	11/1	13/2	10/6	12/–	11/10	12/2
Rent per person	6/6	5/2	5/10	4/1	3/9	3/2	2/10	2/5	2/–	2/2	1/7	1/9	1/7	3/10
Numbers	11	82	45	113	41	78	53	60	12	24	14	10	16	559

With this in mind we may compare the figures below showing median rents per room.

RENTS PER ROOM IN SOUTHAMPTON AND OTHER AREAS

	Number of Rooms					
New London Survey	1	2	3	4	5	6
(Eastern Area) ..	5·2	4·25	3·6	3·3	3·1	3·1
Reading, 1924 ..	—	2/3	2/2	1/11	1/11	2/-
Northampton, 1924 ..	—	—	1/11	1/6	1/9	1/8
Southampton, 1931—						
Houses in single occupations ..	—	4/2½	3/4	2/5½	2/7	2/5
All, including shared	—	4/5½	3/-	2/6	2/7	2/4

(London figures in decimals of a shilling, not in pence.)

It may first be observed that this is reasonably true of the London rents. For Reading and Northampton the 1913–14[1] curves would run practically parallel to the base, while that for Warrington would show a regular but gentle declivity, The post-war situation is different. Reading had in 1924 maintained a smooth curve though its slope was altered, the rents for small tenements and larger ones being slightly higher than those for four or five rooms. Northampton shows a marked relative drop in the rents for four-roomed houses. The Southampton figures, if plotted, would show a curve falling rather sharply from relatively high rents for small units of occupation, but with the sharp peak for four or five rooms; and this is true of the rents for all families, whether these were living in shared houses or occupying a whole house. We should expect that the lag of house building, and the larger number of smaller families, would raise relatively the demand for the smaller tenements. The tendency for the figures to rise for five and six rooms, in spite of the fact that these sizes contain not insignificant numbers of Council houses at rents lower than the full commercial prices, may perhaps be read as

[1] *Has Poverty Diminished?* pp. 69, 90, 118.

indicating that there was still an unsatisfied demand for those types. The great disparity between controlled and decontrolled houses must make some difference to the shape of the curve, but the investigators were not able to find out with certainty in all cases whether the houses were decontrolled or not.

Returning to the question of rents paid by the below line families, the query at once arises, in view of the known substantial increases of rent following decontrol, whether any of the families are below the line through having to pay an "excessive" rent. Without endeavouring at the moment to define "excessive," it is worth noting that the below line families pay a larger proportion of their income in rents and larger absolute rents. The former would follow naturally from the facts that the larger proportion of the heads of this group of families are unemployed, and their incomes much smaller than normal full-time income, while the rents are an unaltered charge. The second characteristic would arise from the families being larger, and more accommodation being needed; and it is the case that the mean number of rooms per family is 4·58 as compared with 4·34 for the above line families. On the other hand, they tend to pay more per equivalent adult in the more frequent size of family, and also more per room. For example, the median net rent per "house" (deducting in this case any boarder's contributions to rent) was for five rooms 12s. 11d. in the below line families, as compared with 12s. 6d. in the above line cases; for four rooms, the median is lower, being 9s. as compared with 9s. 6d. for above line families. For the smaller sizes of occupation, the small number of the below line families involved makes the comparison of dubious value, but these are in every case lower. Without being able to clinch the matter quantitatively, we make suspect the anomalies of rent to be the source of disparity of conditions which leaves one family above and thrusts another below the poverty line.

The detailed material collected both in the mass survey and in the random sample suggest some reflections on national and municipal policy which, although they may be pertinent to other towns also, are none the less important for Southampton to consider. The first, concerning the problem of house and estate management, is suggested by a scrutiny of the cases in the different borough housing estates. When a housing estate is opened, usually a considerable number of houses are available for occupation at a given period, and preference is likely to be given to those with families and to those with steady incomes able to pay the rents asked. But the relative uniformity of age constitution raises problems of a varied character. There arises at once an urgent need for school accommodation at a reasonable distance. But the children grow older, pass out to work, and parents pass the reproductive ages, and the passing of time produces a gradual but important change in the family constitution. The Type 3 family becomes Type 4 and Type 5, and the original ground of preference in dependent children passes away also. At this stage the family income is larger; the subsidy to rent is at this stage less necessary, and the school accommodation is less full. There is, however, another side to the problem. New couples marry and need houses. Are we to continue to build for them, leaving the older married folk in the subsidized houses? Or take the view that the housing in total is adequate, and leave the younger ones setting up house to seek accommodation in less congenial and unsubsidized houses in town? Or are we to adopt a combing policy and declare that once the original ground for preference has passed away, the house must be vacated in favour of a family which now satisfies that consideration? The difficulty arises from the fact that hitherto the housing policy has aimed at restricted types of accommodation, five- or six-roomed houses, and provided for a particular type of family typically Class 3. Nor must we omit to look ahead to the time when the Class 4 and Class 5 begin to break up, leaving the need for accommodation smaller and the family income which can be drawn upon to meet rent smaller also. Are we to rely upon them to move out themselves at this stage? Or are they to fill the empty rooms with relations and unrelated lodgers? The management of these estates is a much larger task than collecting rent and keeping down arrears.

A further difficulty is apparent from the information brought back by investigators. They received from the householders they visited expressions of views concerning the general convenience of estates and the effect of removal to them on domestic expenditure. A housing estate, whether the authorities have so envisaged it or not, is more than a mere collection of streets; it is a community which needs all the elements of a full social environment. Sometimes recreation grounds and other amenities are forgotten. No doubt it is wise to rely on private initiative to establish halls, churches, and amusement centres in the outskirts of estates, though reservation of sites within would be wiser. Although the difficulties which face housing authorities if they construct shops on the estate and let them by private tender are obvious enough, the answer that private enterprise soon brings round the periphery a multitude of stores is not adequate. Quite apart from the question of the most suitable walking distances between shops, many of the tenants come from districts where the stores, shops, and general dealers catered for large areas with working-class incomes, where there were often opportunities of picking up cheap lines of food, etc. In numberless small ways which are of importance in the family budget, many of the tenants —certainly those from the "town wards"—had facilities for economical buying which are absent in the new areas, and which the small traders springing into existence around them do not seem able to provide. An endeavour to retain the old facilities of shopping in the old centres means many journeys and expense in fares; and that many nevertheless find it profitable to undertake them, indicates that the new environment created for them is incomplete, in the sense that transfer to an estate involves losses to its tenants.

If we bear in mind the difficulties arising from the selected age group and family type, and from the need of cultural and recreational amenities and shopping centres, it is clear that we have much to learn in the technique of estate management in the larger sense; and that in concentration on house construction and the lay-out, we often forget that we are creating communities, and left out many of the desiderata of communal life. One cannot help speculating whether later generations will not regard us in some respects with the same sort of wonder as we regard our ancestors who multiplied houses in much the same way, if on a lower plane of design. We have done better than they, but we too in our new endeavours have to learn the lessons of inexperience, and to develop a new technique of planning and house management.

Note.—To the figures given on pages 174 and 175, the 1931 census results may now be added. They show that by steady construction the exceptional conditions which existed in 1921 have now been improved upon, but that the situation remains less favourable than before the war. Between 1921 and 1931 the population increased by 9 per cent, the number of families by 22 per cent, and the number of occupied dwellings by 25 per cent, while the average family declined to 3.65 persons. The percentage of vacant dwellings rose to 2 per cent, and the percentage of the population who were living more than two persons per room decreased to 4 per cent, but in both these respects the situation is still not so good as in 1911. The differences between Southampton, Bournemouth, and Portsmouth continue to exist, and Southampton is still the worst placed as to number of families per house, the number of persons per room, and in overcrowding.

CHAPTER VIII

CRIME

FROM the point of view of the present study, the aspects of crime which are of importance are those which concern its relationship to the social and economic environment of the offenders. How far is Southampton "normal" in the number and type of its offenders? Are its economic differences from other ports reflected also in this aspect of social life? What

CRIME IN SOUTHAMPTON AND OTHER PORTS, 1928–30

Numbers per 100,000 of the Population of Indictable Offences known to the Police, and of Persons prosecuted for Non-indictable Offences, for Southampton and several Ports.

(Average, 1928–30, Registrar-General's estimated population, 1929)

	Number per 100,000 of	
	Indictable Offences Known	*Persons Prosecuted for Non-indictable Offences*
Southampton	560	1,225
Newcastle	272	1,458
Cardiff	467	2,388
Bristol	589	1,281
Hull	594	7,951
Liverpool	1,447	2,716
England and Wales	355	1,552

is the occupational and employment experience of the offenders? Has it any bearing on the class of offences? What is the size of the class which give the police the most trouble?

Southampton is as yet free from some of the difficulties of other ports. Its mainstay is the Atlantic passenger traffic and the South Africa service with regular sailings. It has not a great cargo traffic which offers opportunities for petty larcenies; nor has it any considerable number of foreign seamen, either calling at the port or resident in the town, so that it is free from many of the problems which cause special difficulties in, say, Cardiff and Liverpool. The table on page 191 relates the numbers of indictable offences known, and the numbers of persons prosecuted for non-indictable offences, to the Registrar-General's estimate of population for various ports.[1]

Some of the differences are due to police policy or the peculiar local circumstances. Thus the large number relating to non-indictable offences in Hull is due to prosecutions concerning Sunday trading at the rate of 20,000 per annum. In Liverpool there are an unusually large number of indictable offences of one class, namely, "simple and minor larcenies."

We may also compare the main classes of offences. Taking the indictable offences, the average numbers for the year 1928–30, per 100,000 of the estimated population in 1929 were:

INDICTABLE OFFENCES PER 100,000 OF THE POPULATION, 1928–30

Offences against—	*Southampton*	*Newcastle*	*Cardiff*	*Hull*	*Liverpool*
Property, with violence	82	62	138	95	236
Property, without violence	408	178	291	486	1,019
Persons	39	17	24	7	47

Who are the persons concerned in these offences? What is their employment history? Do they belong to a class of labourers who have drifted in from outside and are cut off from the restraining influences and support of family ties? How many are settled residents? What circumstances have led to the breakdown of social constraints in their cases? Have economic conditions played any part? To answer these interesting questions a prolonged and many-sided investigation would be needed; but an endeavour was made to get some measure of the broader facts by a scrutiny of a sample of one in five cases. The sample showed 188 men and 18 women, a total of 206 cases. The figures may be compared with the

[1] Criminal Statistics, 1928–30, Cmd. 3581, 3853, 4036. See also Annual Reports of the Chief Constables of the various towns

proportion of 209 men and 29 women against whom charges were proved in the same year. The age distribution of the cases was as follows:

AGE DISTRIBUTION OF PERSONS CHARGED WITH OFFENCES, 1930

(Numbers in a 1 in 5 Sample of all Persons charged)

	Under 14	14–16	16–21	21–30	30–40	40–50	50–60	60–
Total numbers	1	1	18	59	58	39	26	4

A comparison of birthplaces and residences of those in the sample gave some light on their status as migrant or native born.

PLACE OF BIRTH AND RESIDENCE OF PERSONS CHARGED WITH OFFENCES, 1930

(1 in 5 Sample of all Persons charged)

	Numbers	*Percentage of Total*
Resident and born in Southampton	42	20·5
Resident in Southampton and born outside ..	53	25·7
Resident in Southampton and born outside Great Britain and Ireland	1	0·4
Resident outside and born outside	52	25·2
Resident outside and born in Southampton ..	3	1·5
No fixed abode and born in Southampton ..	6	2·9
No fixed abode and born outside Southampton	46	22·3
Birthplace unknown	3	1·5
	206	100·0

Thus only one-quarter were born in Southampton, and rather less than one-half were residents. This must, however, be set against the proportion of native-born and migrants in the population as a whole. The only comparable figures are those for Liverpool, where the proportion of "native borns" amongst the offenders was larger, the average for 1924–29 being 60·7 per cent and for 1930, 63·1 per cent.

The floating population of offenders consisted largely of

men of no special skill who would fall into the census class of "general and undefined labourers." One would expect their general industrial quality to be low. In the table below, too much precision must not be expected of the occupational description. For this purpose all seagoing occupations—stewards, seamen, firemen, etc.—have been classed together. The class "skilled" includes all those who must have served an apprenticeship and whose work is such that their level of wages would have been appropriate to an artisan (e.g. Class VI of the Income Classification). The "other" occupations include commercial travellers, journalists, salesmen, etc. All women are classed as following "other" occupations. In the year investigated the proportions were:

OCCUPATION OF PERSONS CHARGED WITH OFFENCES, 1930

(*Sample Investigation*)

Labourers	*Skilled*	*Seafarers*	*Others*	*Total*
61	34	49	62	206

The proportion of skilled men is rather higher than expected, but no doubt further light would have been obtained on this matter if resources had permitted the investigation of the offences with which the various classes were charged.

The connection between crime and industrial depression has been commented upon by the Home Office in the *Report on Criminal Statistics for* 1929.[1] It was there shown that, although between 1921 and 1929 the increase of population was rather less in the north than in the south, the increase in all the main classes of crime was markedly greater; and there is little doubt that this increase was one of the sequels of industrial depression. Southampton's employment has been relatively favourable; and the incidence of crime does not show the features common to the northern areas (except in the respect of the increase of the numbers of offences against

[1] Pp. xv–xxi.

property without violence, which show a marked tendency to rise from 1922 to 1929). It would have been of value if the employment records of the convicted persons could be scrutinized, but this was not possible. It appears, however, that about 100 persons had insurance books on them when arrested. If they were unemployed the book should be at the Exchange, if they were in work, with the employers. Some of the books were old ones, and a large proportion of the men possessing them were over forty years of age. One may perhaps hazard that they were men with such poor employment records that they had fallen out of the insurance system altogether and were "not normally insurable."

We must distinguish between the offenders in other ways. The total number of convictions include trivial sins of omission such as over-staying the car-parking time, forgetting the cycle lamp, postponing the dog licence, or trivial sins of commission such as the petty theft of some vain and hard-up adolescent, none of them betokening any serious anti-social habits; and most of them likely to be the only offence in the lives of the prosecuted persons. There are habitual criminals such as thieves, receivers, and keepers of houses of ill repute, but between this small core of evil-doers, and the "one-lapse offenders," are a more vaguely defined class of persons who are neither sincerely forgetful nor maliciously criminal by profession, but whose unsatisfactory tendencies cause them to lead a life in which spells of work are broken by occasional spells of imprisonment. Repeated conviction for drunkenness would place a man in this category. It is difficult to establish the size of such a class, but for the present purpose a note was made of cases with previous convictions, and the result was as follows:

NUMBER OF PERSONS CHARGED WHO HAD BEEN PREVIOUSLY CONVICTED, 1930

Number of previous convictions ..	1	2	3	4	5	6	7	8	9	10	*Over* 10	*Total*
Number of persons	91	57	33	20	18	20	10	10	8	3	52	322

The total represents about 190 per 100,000 of the population. The figures towards the right-hand side of the table include those persons who constitute the "police-court class," though they are not necessarily professional criminals. Some of them are street prostitutes, others habitual drunkards. The number of those with one or two previous convictions will include, for example, persons charged with a second minor motoring offence, but they will also include a certain number of younger persons destined in due course to appear in the "over ten" column, who have really started on a life of crime, and will by stages become habitual criminals.

The organization of the sale of intoxicants is in some of its aspects a problem of retail distribution, the question as to whether there is an "excessive" number of such shops in the purely business sense, being of the same character as a similar question regarding the number of retail dealers in any other commodity. At the same time, both the total number of such business units and their actual location is legally controlled, and the term "excessive" has from this point of view an altogether different meaning. The trade is thus a separate problem in law, and the limit which the control places on competition makes it a distinctive one economically also. From either point of view, the relationship of the number of units to the total number of persons or families to be served is of importance. The total number of licences in 1931, and the number of families per licence,[1] were as follows:

	Number of Licences, 1931	*Number of Families per Licence (Number of Private Families; Census*, 1931)
On	381	108
Off only	95	403
On and off	476	85
Clubs..	55	—

The discussions in licensing sessions as to whether new licences are needed and whether an old one is redundant are not from this point of view very enlightening. The evidence

[1] Licensing Statistics, 1931, and Census of 1931.

and discussions do not reveal the existence of any clear or consistent standard respecting the proper geographical distances between licensed houses (such as that developed in town-planning practice), or of the meaning of "excessive" in the purely economic sense, or from the point of view of the control of vice. And the practice of justices in these matters varies greatly from place to place. Thus, ranging the ports in order of magnitude of their populations, the numbers of licences and of convictions for drunkenness are as follows:[1]

NUMBER OF LICENCES AND OF CONVICTIONS FOR DRUNKENNESS IN SOUTHAMPTON AND OTHER TOWNS, PER 10,000 OF THE POPULATION

	Licences, 1931			*Average Convictions for Drunkenness*	
	On	*Off*	*Clubs*	1926–30	1921–22
Liverpool	15·7	1·7	1·7	35·3	72·9
Bristol	18·4	7·9	1·1	7·0	8·1
Hull	9·6	10·5	4·3	22·0	29·6
Newcastle ..	12·6	5·9	3·7	32·2	51·0
Cardiff	10·2	2·6	3·1	6·3	5·5
Southampton ..	21·6	5·4	2·5	8·7	9·8
Portsmouth ..	23·7	7·6	2·2	15·5	12·6

NOTE.—Licences per 10,000 of the population, 1931.
Convictions. Average for 1926–30, per 10,000 of the population, 1931; average for 1921–22, per 10,000 of the population, 1921.

Police policy as to where the line shall be drawn which divides the degree of drunkenness demanding arrest from that which may be ignored, also varies from town to town. There is some bias in the figures on account of the enlargement of borough boundaries at various dates, which in one or two

[1] Licensing Statistics, 1921–31.

cases would raise the number of convictions in the later years. A comparison of the figures for 1921–22 with those for 1926–30 brings out strikingly the persistence of some of these differences; as well as the great reduction in the number of such convictions in areas where they had previously been heavy.

CHAPTER IX

CONCLUSION

We may now briefly summarize the arguments and numerical results of the survey.

(1) The development in the nineteenth century transformed Southampton from a town owning its docks and foreshore, and controlling its harbour, to a railway-owned port in which the main sources of wealth had passed into private and external control, though the process was accompanied in some stages by local political friction.

(2) After a long period of slow growth, it began to increase at a greater rate after 1890, though that rate had declined to a more modest one by 1921 and 1931.

(3) The effect of varying rates of natural increase and immigration has been to increase the proportion of the population aged 10–70, from less than 3–1 in 1861, to 3½–1 in 1921, so that it was greater than in Hull and Liverpool and less than in Cardiff.

(4) The location of industries has been affected not only by its obvious physical advantages, but by its relatively low labour costs. The lack of a densely peopled hinterland is a hindrance to the initial growth of light industries.

(5) In consequence of the foregoing facts, its men are dependent on three occupations, two of which have wide seasonal fluctuations. For seamen the ratio of the quarterly average unemployment to quarterly maximum unemployment was 1 to 1·6 or 1 to 1·7, and the excess of the highest absolute figure over the lowest absolute unemployment figure represented between 7 per cent and 8 per cent of the insured population. For ship-repairers the range of fluctuations is not easily stated, but the excess of the absolute maximum over the minimum employment may reach 25 per cent of the insured persons, though this figure somewhat magnifies the

variations. The third trade, dock work, is now in process of decasualization.

(6) There are relatively few industrial occupations for women as compared with other ports.

The standards of living which are the expression of the above factors are as follows:

(7) The average working-class family consisted of 1·73 earners and 2·50 non-earners. In 49 per cent of the families, containing 60 per cent of the children, there was only one man earning.

(8) Assessed at the head's full-time earnings, 12 per cent of *all* families with dependent children, 14 per cent of the children, and probably 14 per cent of the population, were in income classes receiving less than 42s. per week; nearly 19 per cent of the population were in grades with incomes from earnings of £4 per week or over (1928).

(9) Primary Poverty. Twenty-one per cent of the families of a random sample of working-class households were below a defined poverty line (1931).

(10) Potential Poverty. In 34 per cent of the working-class families with dependent children the head of the family had insufficient income to maintain his wife and children of school age at this line, without assistance from supplementary earners.

(11) In 5 per cent of the families with "other earners" these earners received less than the cost of maintaining them in food and clothing, etc., on the poverty line standard.

(12) The principal cause of poverty was unemployment, two-thirds of those in poverty, or 14 per cent of all working-class families, being below the line on account of it. If unemployment had been at the level of 1928, the primary poverty would probably have been about 13 per cent, instead of 21 per cent.

(13) The remaining one-third, or 7 per cent of the entire group of working-class families, were below the poverty line either on account of the death, illness, age, or absence of the natural head of the family ($3\frac{1}{2}$ per cent), or because the natural

head, though in full work, was maintaining a second adult dependent, and was earning wages which were insufficient to keep the number of children for whom he had to provide.

(14) Forty-seven per cent of the families were receiving social service income. Twenty-five per cent of them received more than half of their income from this source, 11 per cent received more than half from supplementary earners, and 32 per cent received head's wages only.

(15) The ascertained number of mentally defective persons in the population is about 5½ per 1,000.

(16) The total number receiving public assistance, either indoor or outdoor, was in 1929 between 19 and 21 per 1,000 of the population.

(17) Nearly 5 per cent of the working-class families were overcrowded, if the parlour is counted as a possible bedroom, and 12 per cent if the parlour be used only for the purpose for which it was designed.

(18) The number of indictable offences known is about 560, and the number of persons prosecuted for non-indictable offences is about 1,200 per 100,000 of the population. Only one-quarter of the persons charged with offences were persons born in Southampton, and rather less than one-half were residents. The unskilled were a large proportion of the persons charged, and it is probable that many of them were of the type who are "not normally insurable."

APPENDIX I

DEFINITIONS AND RULES

In obtaining and using the material of the random sample enquiry, a considerable number of definitions and rules are required to impose order on the bewildering variety of families, their methods of earning a living, and on the diverse financial relationships of their members. The importance of some of the rules lies not only in their "reasonableness" for dealing with difficult cases, but also in the service they render in securing uniformity of treatment. In general the rules which have been followed are those of Professor Bowley in the Five Towns Enquiry of 1924, and are set forth in Chapter II of *Has Poverty Diminished?* It is not necessary to repeat in every detail the rules there given, but certain of them, together with various modifications made in the light of Southampton experience, are given below.

Excluded Households.—The enquiry concerned working-class conditions, and the exclusion of the "middle-class" households was necessary. Whether a household was middle class or not depended on the occupation and income of the head of the household. For the purpose of this enquiry, working class does not mean "manual working class," but all persons with incomes below £250 per annum, whether or not on some other ground they may be popularly called "middle class." It will thus include that grade of insurance agents which is engaged on arduous industrial assurance work, if they are within the income limit, and clerks and shop assistants. An exceptional case would be a clerical or business post where the income was known to be a commencing one, or one in the early years of some work which was leading to a higher rank of pay.

Incomes.—The basic fact here is actual earnings during the period of investigation. This was tested by the phrase "previous week"; though this did not suit the case of seamen. For the procedure adopted on this point, see above page 122. All social service payments were included under "social income." "Other income" included income from house property, friendly society benefits, etc. In arriving at net income for calculating the relation to the poverty line in *Has Poverty Diminished?* and in the Liverpool Survey, poor relief is excluded, either because those who received it are presumably in poverty (this is the reason for its being granted) or because it is withdrawable at the discretion of the authority. This practice was not followed in this enquiry. Its purpose was to ascertain what proportion was in poverty, taking all the facts of income, including social services as they are, and not on what it would be if some portions were withdrawn. There are other payments which are at discretion or based on means test, e.g. school maintenance grants and now transitional benefit. Transitional scales of benefit are now sometimes identical with public assistance scales, the grant is discretionary and is periodically reviewed; and the adoption of the rule would logically lead to the exclusion of transitional benefit also. For calculating income in relation to the poverty line, public assistance was therefore included. Any fairly regular gifts from relatives are also reckoned. Where uniforms are provided there is almost always an expressed or tacit understanding as to their weekly value, and these figures were obtained and used. The food given to daily domestic servants was valued at the poverty datum line standard. In practice the standard of food is generally higher than this, and often better than the persons concerned would get at home. When counting up their full weekly wage, the employees themselves value it at a definitely higher figure, but the use of their estimate would sometimes bring the wage above that of older sisters in other classes of work. The effect of this sort of wage contract is that the earners compulsorily spend more on food than they would do if all the wage were received in money which they took home in the ordinary way. Travelling expenses are deducted. Where these consisted not of tram fares but of weekly instalments for the purchase of a cycle, the weekly payment has been treated as the cost of travelling. In the case of men away from home, the sum allowed the family was regarded as income, and the man excluded from the minimum need calculation. The difficulty of seamen is referred to above.

House Ownership.—Where the house was owned by the occupier, its value as income was calculated as equal to the rateable value of the house. Its rent was then taken to be the amount stated as the probable rent to a tenant, unless this seemed from other information relating to similar houses in the same district to be unreasonable; if no statement of probable rent was obtained, it was regarded as the weekly gross rental value. Where the house was mortgaged, if no other information was obtained, it was not treated as income, but the payments were regarded as rent.

Personal Income and Family Income.—For the "Family Means" tables some variations in definitions were needed. In the calculation as to whether another earner contributes more or less than the cost of keeping him on the poverty datum line, the other earner's income was his income irrespective of whether it was wages or a social service payment which he drew himself. There was an example or two where the son and his wife lived in the same house as his parents and did not pay a defined share of the rent for a defined portion of the house, but was in fact pooling a good deal of his income; his contribution was calculated after charging it with the cost of maintaining his wife as well as himself. On the other hand, where the object is to allocate the family income between head's wages and other earners' wages, and social income, other earners' income was then "wages" and did not include income from the social services. In tables referring to potential poverty, head's income included wages, social income drawn by him, income from ownership of house, etc., but where they were designed to show the head's contribution to the family income as distinct from sums received from the social services, the social service payments were not included in his income.

Rent is weekly rent, plus rates. "Net rent" is rent and rates actually paid, less any stated proportion of rent paid by sub-tenants, or less the allocated proportion in the case of lodgers. In an odd case or two this led to zero or negative rents. As in this area it did not prove practicable in many cases to get cards where houses were shared, the rent per room in the appropriate tables is not rent per room received by the owner of the house. The emphasis is on the burden of the rents on incomes, and not on the price per unit received by the suppliers of the article.

Lodgers' Payments.—These have to be divided into rent payments, payment for service, and profits. Lodgers are assumed to contribute one-third of the rent, and net rent expense is calculated accordingly. Where the nature of the contract makes it relevant (there is a difference between male and some female lodgers), 1s. per week was allowed to the housewife as cost of cleaning, lighting, etc. If there were boarders, it was assumed that the housekeeper made a profit on providing food, of 4s. for a single boarder, and 7s. for a man and wife, 1s. 6d. for a child under 14 years of age. The rules are a little rigid, since the character of the food provided obviously varies with the part of the town and the income grade of the family. Where statements were obtained from the housewife, this information was taken as a guide, provided it was adequate.

Furnished Rooms.—Landladies' incomes from furnished rooms were split up between rent, use and depreciation of furniture and service, and light if any, according to information received, if adequate. Otherwise, 10 per cent was allocated to outgoings, 50 per cent to rent, and 40 per cent for any work and as profits (New London Survey Rule).

Description of Houses.—An attempt was made to steer clear of the perennial difficulty of kitchen and scullery by accepting the definition that the former was a room which included the range and could be used as a living-room. At least two-thirds of the visiting was done by investigators who had previously worked on the census, and their previous experience was an asset in this matter. In tabulating rent per room, etc., "half rooms" are often shown (tables on page 177). This arises from the fact that there were houses (without a scullery) being shared, when the use of the kitchen was part of the contract. To omit the kitchen would have overstated the rent paid per room, counting it as a room would have overstated it; the middle course, artificial though it is, seemed the best way out of the unsatisfactory alternatives.

Minimum Need Standard.—This was identical in substance with that in *Has Poverty Diminished?* subject only to the modifications referred to on page 115. Its cost at the dates of the investigation was:

FOOD, CLOTHING, LIGHTING, AND CLEANING

	1928	1930	1931
Man	8/10	7/9	7/1
Woman	7/2	6/5	5/10
Child, 0–5	3/6	3/–	2/9
Child, 5–14	4/10	4/2	3/10
Lad, 14–16	—	6/7	6/–
Girl, 14–16	—	6/3	5/9
Adult over 70 ..	—	—	4/5

Fuel: Unchanged at 2/6

DIET

Bread	5·0	lb.	Cheese	0·75	lb.
Flour	1·1	lb.	Peas	0·2	lb.
Oatmeal	3·6	lb.	Potatoes	2·5	lb.
Bacon	0·75	lb.	Vegetables ..	0·5	lb.
Meat	2·0	lb.	Sugar	0·32	lb.
Lard, dripping, suet	0·3	lb.	Cocoa	0·5	oz.
Margarine ..	0·5	lb.	Tea	2·0	oz.
Milk—New ..	0·8	pint	Coffee	0·5	oz.
Skimmed	4·0	pints	Meat liquor ..	4·5	pints

APPENDIX II

NOTES ON THE GRAPHICAL REPRESENTATION OF INCOME BY STREETS

For the purpose of the survey, two street maps were made, one representing income distribution by street, and the other rateable value of residences by street. The attempt to represent such data by streets presents certain interesting problems of graphical method. Essentially the process is to assign a given tint or shading to a given grade of income or rateable value; if all the units (families or houses) in a given street were in the same grade, the process would be straightforward, and would involve merely the selection of suitable colours for the several grades.

In practice, only rarely, as in the case of the broad income Class VIII, are the families and houses of one grade. The extent of the difficulty naturally depends on the number and width of grades chosen. There were eight grades of income and five grades of rateable value. In the great majority of streets the families or houses were in several of the grades, often indeed concentrated mostly in three groups, but also widely dispersed through many or all of the grades. How are these diversities to be drawn together into a single impression, to which a single colour could be assigned?

Three possibilities were considered.

(*a*) *The Mode.*—The street could be coloured according to its "predominant" income or rateable value grade, in the sense of that grade most frequently occurring. This neglects the extreme ends of any distribution, and is satisfactory on the assumption that the families are of fairly uniform type. To take four actual cases from the income survey:

	I	*II*	*III*	*IV*	*V*	*VI*	*VII*	*Mode*
......Street ..	—	—	—	—	3	15	1	VI
......Road ..	—	—	—	—	8	30	4	VI
......Street ..	4	9	2	16	—	—	—	IV
......Street ..	6	29	10	17	1	—	—	II

In the third, there are as many below the grade as in it—an important fact—and in the fourth, nearly as many are above the modal grade as in it, and in any case the modal class is less numerous than the others. The text of Booth's description of his map uses the phrase "prevailing," but a scrutiny of his records and maps shows that he did not, apparently, use a strict mode.

(*b*) *The Weighted Average.*—The average obtained by weighting the income class number and the rateable value grade by the frequency with which each occurred in the street could be found, and a colour assigned to the numbers so determined. Every family in the street thus assists in determining the grade and colour. The fact that the average so obtained includes fractions presents no difficulty, since they can be neglected. There is, however, an interesting practical result. Since incomes are distributed along a skewed curve, the effect on the colour scheme is to pull the highest grades down to a lower colour grade and some of the lowest grades up to middle colour grades. Streets with a mixture of Class VIII and Class VII families may be reduced to Class VII. There are no streets in Southampton in which all families are entirely Class I; and the mixture with other income classes is always such that under the system they are brought up to a higher colour. The total effect of this system of calculation is thus, in the case of the income map, to alter its physical appearance as compared with a modal map, the "richest" and "poorest" colours being diminished in favour of the middle grades.

(*c*) *An Arbitrary Formula.*—We could devise some quite arbitrary formula for calculating a grade likely to provide a single impression of these mixed streets. On what principle could such a formula be constructed? Much will depend on the purpose of the scheme. If it is to give an impression of "poverty" and not just distribution of income, we could (1) decide that for a "normal" family the poverty line would come between the income limit which divides, for example, Classes V and VI; (2) assign "poor" colours and shades, such as purple and blue, to all streets which work out at Class V and below it, and contrasting "comfortable and rich" colours, such as yellows and reds, for those which work out at dominantly Class VI and above; (3) assign to all the streets which have 50 per cent or more of the families in Classes I to V a "poor" colour; and those with less than 50 per cent of such families as "comfortable" colour; (4) devise supplementary rules, for allocating the exact shades within the two sets of colours. The map would then show at a glance the probable relation of the families in each street taken as a whole to the defined poverty line. This is essentially the London Survey system. For the income map this method of calculation but not of colouring has been closely followed. Two of the lower groups, II and III, were amalgamated, and there was no case of any street which was dominantly Class I, so that a further colour grade was dispensed with, leaving six colours.

The scheme as modified is:[1]

If Grade I is one-fifth or more of the number of families	I	No case
If Grade II is less than one-fifth and—		
(*a*) Grades I–IV are eleven-twentieths of the whole number, or	II and III	Violet
(*b*) If Grades I–IV are only nine-twentieths of the whole number	IV	Blue
If Grades I–V are one-half or more	V	Green
If Grades VI, VII, and VIII are more than one-half	VI	Yellow
Unless Grades VII and VIII are one-half or more	VII	Orange
Or if Grade VIII is one-half or more	VIII	Red

This scheme of calculation was applied in the income distribution map only. In the case of the rateable value map the groups were fewer and wider, and the diversities within the streets correspondingly less. There was also a stronger tendency for the frequencies to be clustered into a single group;

[1] As there are advantages in uniformity of practice, this scheme was adopted as being parallel to that used in the New London Survey. Their scheme was afterwards modified, but the Southampton map had then been completed.

and for this map the mode was used. There were few cases where this gave an unrepresentative impression.

The result of applying these three different methods may be compared. When the families are clustered into one or two adjacent classes, the results are very similar whichever system is used; and all towns have a considerable number of streets of well-defined types. The differences arise where, as in the old town wards, the families are dispersed amongst six and even seven income classes. Taking St. Mary's ward as a test, colouring by the mode would have given a value in 38 streets the same, in 19 above, and in 4 below that of the formula, but seven of those coloured above and one coloured below would have retained this colour under the weighting system. The weighting system gave the same results as the formula in 28 cases, reduced it in 21, and raised it in 12 cases. In other wards, the differences were smaller.

Choice of Colour.—We could either use groups of colours or shades of two colours, one to represent "comfortable" and the other "poor" streets, or we could use varying shades of the same colour. In the present case, since the intention was to show successive income grades rather than poverty, the spectrum colours were used, since they provided a universally known scale. The reasons for excluding certain streets from the scheme have been noted on page 101 above. For the rateable value maps five colours only were needed, and these also were based on the spectrum. In the actual mapping, Booth coloured the area of houses and gardens, but this entails much work for the draughtsmen and is a very expensive method. In the map in this volume plain strips of colour along the roadway were deemed sufficient to convey the correct impression; very little which is essential is sacrificed. It has to be remembered that the colouring is based on families with school children only and not on all families, and that the ratio of the former to the latter is by no means constant throughout the streets; it may be less than half of the total number of families. Colouring the house area is thus a disproportionate attention to detail. It would have been an advantage for reproducing the map on the scale as printed if the colour strips had been widened to broad bands.

Uses of Street Maps in the Study of Retail Distribution.

The uses of street maps of the kind here described in social work needs no emphasis, but there are some commercial uses which are worthy of comment. Subject to the limitations explained in the text and this note, the maps, whether based on assessed income or on rateable value, are a guide to the proportions of different income classes, and thus to the size of the potential market of each type. They should, therefore, be of use to those retailing agencies which are selling an article designed by price or utility to appeal to some specific grades of income and not to others. Canvassers' districts can be organized on the basis of the maps. A retail store catering for specific income classes can test its efficiency in reaching the classes aimed at by finding the proportion of such households to which it is already selling, to the total number in those classes. On to the income and rateable value maps can be superimposed dots showing the distribution in the various streets of a sample of, e.g. account holders, and a clear visual impression obtained of the proportion of customers in each district. This can be made more precise by comparing the number of houses of given grades of rateable value or of families of specific income grades, with the number of customers in each class of street. If the numbers are adjusted by the sampling ratio, an impression of the hold on each of the potential markets can be obtained. The following supposititious figures will illustrate the point.

	Total Number of Houses	*Total Customers*	*Percentage*
Grade V	2,100	350	15
Grade IV	2,600	520	20
Grade III	8,800	440	5

Quite apart from the uses of the map in any given case, useful knowledge respecting the structure of retail distribution in an area can be obtained in this way. Maps of this type have been made for Southampton.

APPENDIX III

STREET RECORDS

THE averages which have been used in various tables and in grading streets for the purpose of colouring are but useful abbreviations for the purpose of describing and comparing diverse quantitative data, and their full meaning can be appreciated only in relation to the raw material out of which they are made. The character of the information available has been explained in the text. The following examples, which summarize some of it, will give an indication of the facts which various street colours represent. The entry, "two families," or "three families" means that the house is shared by families with dependent children. There are houses shared with childless families or single persons, but no record was made of these.

Grade II.—Violet.

.... Street. 59 out of 63 houses, £21 to £31 rateable value. 54 families with children, no skilled worker of Class VI, all the rest being in lower income grades, including 16 of Class II. There were 162 school children in the street, an average of 3·0 per family as compared with 2·0 for the whole town, and 2·2 for the whole of income Classes I to IV. One section of the street reads as follows: Beer house, Class VII, 2 children. Labourer, Class II, 2 children. Stevedore, Class VI, 5 children. Three families with school children: dairyman, Class VI, 3 children; seaman, Class III, 1 child; labourer, Class II, 2 children. Three families: a painter and 2 labourers with 2, 3, and 2 children. Two families: widow, Class I, 3 children; an unmarried person, Class I, 1 child.

.... Street. Houses all under £13 rateable value. Even poorer than the above, there being no case of regular labourers of Class V, all being Classes I–IV, and nearly one-half in Classes I and II. They are hostile or indifferent to suggestions that they should move to better surroundings. There are 13 families, with 39 children. In both streets a considerable proportion of the families are in or on the margin of potential poverty.

Grade IV.—Blue.

.... Street. A portion of the street reads: Labourer, Class IV, 1 child. Two families, both labourers, Class IV, each with 2 children.

Fireman, Class V, 1 child. Widow, Class II, 1 child. Two families, labourer, Class V, 1 child, and vanman, Class V, 1 child. Gasfitter, Class VI, 1 child. Labourer, Class IV, 1 child. Widow, Class II, 1 child. Labourer, Class IV, 1 child. Seaman, Class VI, 3 children.

Grade V.—Green.

.... Street. 14 houses under £13 to £21 rateable value. There are 28 houses, 44 families with school children, 40 children under 5, and a total of 101 children up to school-leaving age. 8 families in potential poverty. One portion of the street reads: Labourer, Class V, 4 children. Three families: invalid, Class III, 1 child; widow, Class II, 1 child; labourer, Class V, 1 child. Widow, Class III, 1 child. Small shop, Class VI, 3 children. Three families: seaman, Class V, 3 children; labourer, Class V, 1 child; widow, Class II, 2 children. Two families: both labourers, with 4 and 3 children. Two families: pensioner, Class V, 4 children; labourer, Class V, 2 children.

.... Street. Houses £13 to £21 rateable value. 74 families, of whom 59 are in Classes II to V. There are 193 children, of whom 78 are in Classes II to IV. Probably 14 families are in potential poverty. Examples from this street: Two families: labourer, Class V, 3 children, and labourer, Class VI, 1 child. Widow, Class II, with 1 dependent child. Two families: labourer, Class IV, 2 dependent children; and a steward, Class VI, with 1 child. Three families: widow, Class III, and labourer, Class VI, with 1 child each; and a bill-poster, Class V, with 2 children. Two families: labourer, Class V, 6 children; ship-fireman, Class V, 1 child. In successive houses there were 5 families, 1 Class III, 1 Class IV, and 3 Class V, with 10 children.

.... Street. All houses with rateable value £13 to £21. All built since 1919. Many are shared by 2 families. A portion of the street reads as follows: Two families, labourers, Class V, 1 child; charge-hand, Class V, 1 child. Two families, Class VI, 1 child. Labourer, Class V, 1 child. Two families, labourer, Class V, 2 children; carpenter, Class VI, 1 child.

APPENDIX IV

HOUSE DENSITY AND OVERCROWDING PER HOUSE

THE following table, referred to on page 173, shows for each ward the number of houses per acre of land used for housing purposes, the number of persons per room in 1931, and the estimated population per acre of housing land.

Ward	*Persons per Room*, 1931	*House Density per Acre of Housing Land*, 1928	*Population per Acre of Housing Land*, 1928
Town	1·04	16·3	99
St. Mary	1·04	21·9	169
Northam	0·97	9·8	58
Trinity	0·92	20·9	112
Newtown	0·77	19·6	94
All Saints	0·73	10·5	48
Bevois	0·68	10·7	47
Banister..	0·60	7·4	32
Freemantle	0·76	9·2	45
Millbrook	0·82	8·3	39
Shirley	0·79	6·5	26
Portswood	0·67	6·9	26
St. Denys	0·75	5·4	23
Bitterne and Pear Tree	0·83	7·1	37
Bitterne and Sholing ..	0·89	3·5	18
Woolston	0·75	6·3	29
St. Nicholas	0·86	5·9	20
Totals	0·80	7·5	38

The figures of population per acre of housing land were arrived at by combining the estimated population with the area of land used for housing. For certain purposes its superiority over the "population per acre" figure of the census is evident. The latter may be reduced by the existence in a ward of a large works area, but the index would then conceal the true state of congestion in the district, thus:

Ward	*Population per Acre*	*Population per Acre of Housing Land*
Town	89	99
St. Mary's	80	169
St. Nicholas	5	20

INDEX

Accuracy of sample, 103
Actuary, Government, 81
Admiralty, 38
Adults, equivalent, 176, 177
Agglomeration, economies of, 50
Allen, Liversidge and Company, 49
Andover, 36
Argentine, 45
Aronovici, Mr., 26
Attwater, 114
Avro, 41

Bakers, 53, 58
Banbury, 37
Bankruptcies, 56
Benham, Mr., 91
Berkshire, 28
Beveridge, William, Sir, 79, 80
Billing, Pemberton, Mr., 40
Birmingham, 37
Birthplaces, 28
Birth-rates, 26, 27, 28
Blanesburgh Committee, 79
Bolton, 103, 108
Booth, Charles, 93, 95, 97, 100, 101, 167, 211
Boundary, 24, 27
Bournemouth, 30, 49, 52, 60, 61, 93, 175, 176
Bowley, Professor, 91, 93, 114, 117, 203
Brady, Mr., 14–15
Bridport, 36
Brighton, 29, 47, 93
British American Tobacco Company, 43
British Oxygen Company, 39
Bristol, 34, 36, 43, 52, 59–61, 76, 166–8, 191, 197.
Brookes, D., 14, 15
Burghclere, 20
Butchers, 53

Cairnes, J. E., 155
Calls missed, 73
Camelot Press, 47
Camper Nicholson, 37
Cannan, Professor, 155
Cardiff, 28, 30–3, 52, 59–61, 65, 66, 84, 166–8, 191, 192, 197, 199
Casuals, 62, 63, 67
Cathcart, Dr., 116
Census, 25, 27–9, 31–2, 52–3, 59, 60–1, 89, 174–5, 196–7
Ceylon, 43
Chandler's Ford, 35
Channel Islands, 36
Cheltenham, 37
Chemists, 53
Chesterton, Mr., 178
Chichester, 36
Children—
  allowances for, 115, 148, 149, 207
  number below standard, 120
  number in income classes, 98, 99, 200
  number per family, 106, 109, 110, 127, 162
  poverty and, 108, 120, 124, 161
China, 43
Clay, H., 116, 152
Clothing, in poverty line, 115, 207
Clubs, 196, 197
Coal, 115
Coal trimmers, 84
Colson, M., 34
Commercial Steam Packet Company, 26
Commons, House of, 18
Confectioners, 53, 54
Continuity Rule, 77–81
Convictions, 195
Cowes, 50

Cunard Company, 67
Cuthbertson, F. W., Mr., 176

Day, Graham, Mr., 38
Day, Summers and Company, 38
Death-rates, 26, 27
Decasualization, 70, 74, 83
Decentralization, 48, 54
Diet, 114, 207
Disallowance Inquiry, 139, 158
Disarmament, 37
Dixon and Cardus, 45
Dock workers, 62, 63, 70, 72, 75, 79, 80, 89
Donaldson, J., Mr., 38
Donaldson, T., Mr., 37
Dorset, 28
Drapers, 49, 53, 54
Drunkenness, 197

Earners, supplementary, 135–8, 157, 160, 200
East India Company, 39
Eastleigh, 46, 47
Echo, Southern Daily, 47
Economica, 91
Egypt, 45
Eucryl, 45

Family—
  average size of, 110
  number of earners, 107, 110
  size of, 91, 106, 177, 200
Firemen, 64
France, 44
Fruit, imports of, 71

General Electric Company, 47
Germany, 38
Gilbert's Act, 165
Gilks, Dr., 114, 117
Glasgow, 78
Graphic, 22
Great Western Railway Company, 21
Greenwood, Professor, 116
Grocers, 53, 54

Hamilton, W. H., 91
Hampshire, 28, 30, 45, 50
Hanham, Mr., 80
Harbour Board, 17–20
Harbour dues, 18, 19
Harland and Woolf, 37
Hartlepool, 78
Haslemere, 36
Has Poverty Diminished? 91–106, 186, 203, 207
Havre, 44
Health, Ministry of, 145
Hearnshaw, Professor, 26
Hill, J., 14–15
House—
  density, 216
  management, 188, 190
  ownership, 140–1, 205
Household inquiry, accuracy of sample, 103, 104
Houses—
  increase of, 174
  rateable value of, 172
  shared, 175–6
  vacant, 175
Hull, 28, 30, 31, 33, 45, 52, 59, 61, 65, 66, 93, 166–8, 169, 191, 192, 197, 199
Hythe, 35

Immigration, 26
Income—
  distribution of, 111, 112
  from social services, 131–5, 157, 161, 162, 200–1
  grades, 95, 96
  map, colouring of, 101, 208–12
  sources of family, 141–4, 157
  types of, 135, 137
Income, pooling of—
  effect on poverty, 113, 123, 128, 143
  effect on overcrowding, 162, 182

India, 33, 45
Indifference, line of, 49
Industries, location of, 199

Java, 43
Jewellers, 53, 54
Joliff, T., 14, 15
Jones, Caradoc, Mr., 179, 181

Kent, 28

Labour market, organisation of, 83
Labour, Ministry of, 65, 80, 85
Labour, mobility of, 83, 87
Labour, pools of, 64, 65, 83
Lancaster, J., 14, 15
Laundries, 58
Layton, W., 65
Lewis, Dr., 162
Licences, 196–7
Liverpool, 31, 33, 43, 52, 60, 61, 64, 70, 76, 118, 120, 144, 166–8, 169, 178, 179, 180, 191, 192, 193, 197, 199
Location of industries, 34
Lodgers, 206
London, 24, 36, 37, 43, 46, 47, 64, 76, 95, 126, 130, 186
London County Council, 146
Lords, House of, 19
Lusk, 114

Mallet, 93
Manchester, 20, 37
Man values, 113, 115
Maps, colouring of street, 208–12
Market, 34
  boundary, 36, 49, 50
  international, 57
  national, 57
  regional, 57
Married women earners, 139
Marsh, 11
Means Tests, 144–54
Mental defectives, fertility of, 163
Mental Deficiency, Committee on, 162
Mental Welfare Association, 162
Mentally deficient, numbers of, 161–4, 201
Methven, Col., 45
Migration, 24, 26, 28, 30, 33
Minimum need standard, 114, 207
Mobility of labour, 83, 87
Mottram, 114
Mudlands, sale of, 11, 13, 15, 17
Murray, Dr., 116

Neal, Lawrence, Mr., 55
Newcastle, 52, 61, 93, 116, 166–8, 191, 192, 197
Newport, 50
Northampton, 108, 126, 186

Occupations, 59, 61
Offender's age, 193
  birthplace, 193
  residence, 193
Official Receiver, 56
Ordnance Survey Department, 47, 57
Orr, Dr., 114, 117
Overcrowding, 178, 182, 201, 216
  actual, 179, 180, 182
  potential, 179, 182
  Manchester standard, 179
  Liverpool capacity standard, 179
Overton, 26
Oxford, 37

Parsons, H., Mr., 39
Parsons Marine Motor Company, 39
Pellerin, A., 44
Petersfield, 36
Pigou, Professor, 65
Pirelli, 46

Poor Law—
  Act, 1930, 145
  area, 36
  Royal Commission on, 1834, 165
  Royal Commission on, 1909, 83, 153, 166–7
Population, 174
  income classification of, 100, 200
  migration of, 24, 27–30, 33
Port Labour Committee, 75
  inquiry, 70, 78, 81
Portsmouth, 49, 52, 64, 171, 175, 176, 197
Potatoes, imports of, 71
Poverty, 118
  causes of, 129
  line, 112, 146, 160, 207
  potential, 113, 123–8, 200
  primary, 113, 118–23, 200
  secondary, 113
Preference dockers, 71
Public assistance—
  numbers receiving, 135, 162, 169, 201
  Relief scales, 144–5

Ranger, W., 18
Reading, 36, 106, 108, 118, 126, 130, 186
Registration, 78, 84
  of dock workers, 75, 76
Relief, scales of, 145–52
Retail distribution, 48–56, 196
  maps of, 212
Retailing and the Public, 55
Rents, 117, 124, 181, 182–7, 206
Rishbeth, Professor, 35
River Test, 76
Robson, 85
Rooms furnished, 206
Rose, 114
Rubie, J., 14, 15

St. Andrews nutrition inquiry, 116
Salisbury, 36
Schneider Cup, 40
Seamen, 57, 62, 64, 89, 112, 123, 199
Sheffield, 144
Shipping, 57, 62
Ship-repairers, 62, 63, 67, 199
Ship-repairing, 65, 85
Shops, number of, 52, 53
Solent Carpet Company, 29, 40
Somerset, 37
Southampton Civic Survey, 91, 176
Southampton Oxygen Company, 39
Southern Railway Company, 70, 73, 74, 86
Stamp, Josiah, Sir, 116
Stanley, 108
Street records, 214
Subsistance, means of, 157
Supermarine Aviation Company, 40
Surrey, 28
Sussex, 28

Tallies, 70, 71, 72, 73, 86
Thatcher, F., Mr., 44
Thornycroft, 37
Thornycroft, J. I., 37
Tinling, Admiral, 14, 15
Tobacconists, 53
Toogood, T., Mr., 48
Toogood, W., Mr., 47
Totton, 64
Town planning, 25, 35, 197
Trade fluctuations, 57
Trade, seasonal, 62, 63
Transport Workers Union, 80, 81
Treasury, 15, 16
Tyne, 78

Unemployment, 62, 63, 72, 105, 200
  seasonal, 63, 64, 73, 199

Unemployment insurance, 76, 78, 79
benefit, 77, 135, 156–7, 161–2
Blanesburgh Committee on, 79
Royal Commission on, 77, 81, 82, 144, 149, 151, 158
Union Castle, 64

Vickers (Aviation) Ltd., 40

Wages, 42, 74, 76, 141, 142, 157
Walsh, Mr., 45
Waring and Gillows, 85
Warrington, 106, 108, 186
Watchmakers, 53, 54
Wear, 78
Welfare and poverty, 91
Whitchurch, 14, 15
White, J. and S., 37
White Star Line, 67
Wight, Isle of, 36, 50, 84
Women, work of married, 139
Woolston, 62
Wool trade, 26

Young, R., 14, 15

GEORGE ALLEN & UNWIN LTD
London: 40 Museum Street, W.C.1
Cape Town: 73 St. George's Street
Sydney, N.S.W.: Wynyard Square
Toronto: 91 Wellington Street, West
Wellington, N.Z.: 8 Kings Crescent, Lower Hutt

APPENDICES

Appendix 1

P. Ford, 'Employment and Income' and 'Population, House Density, and Health', from P. Ford, ed., *Southampton: A Civic Survey*, Oxford University Press, 1931, pp. 45-50, 55-60.

CHAPTER V

EMPLOYMENT AND INCOME

By P. FORD, B.SC. (ECON.)

THE Census of 1921 records that in Southampton there were nearly 60,000 males and 65,000 females over twelve years of age; and that of these, nearly 52,000 males and 17,000 females were gainfully occupied. For the purpose of town planning we need to know (1) where they worked, the relation of their workplaces to their homes, and the volume of passenger and freight traffic created; (2) the nature of the industries, the types of general and skilled labour they employ, and their probable expansion and contraction; and (3) the proportion of the different grades of working-class income, as indicating the character of the house-room demanded, and of the need for the social services of the town.

Maps 1 to 3, showing the utilization of the surface, indicate the localities of the heavy and light industries, while the traffic diagrams show the volume and direction of the road traffic which arises in consequence. The other factor, the numbers employed at the different works, has not been easy to arrive at. The Industries Volume of the Census gives figures for the county, but not for the separate county boroughs; while in any case the seasonal nature of several large trades makes it difficult to give figures at any one date which will not be misrepresentative. These difficulties have been in part surmounted by the goodwill of employers, who gave in interview information relating to their own businesses. It has not been practicable, in the time available, to cover the smaller works. These, together with offices and the distributive trades, have mostly been excluded. The definition of 'works' adopted is thus 'considerable centres of manual employment'.

Taking the Dock area first, in this group has been included the Southern Railway staff of dockers, labourers, and artisans, the shipyard workers in Harland and Woolfs, Thornycrofts, and the Isle of Wight Steamship Company, &c.; Terminus Station and goods sidings, Parson's Motor Works, the Town Quay, &c. In this area the clerical staffs, by reason of their concentration, are important from the point of view of traffic, and the larger groups have been included. The total number of workers in this area is about 8,000 to 8,500, although the fall of shipyard activity in the summer makes the total vary considerably.

Next, there is a belt of employment centres along the west bank of the Itchen, a strip which bulges out at Northam to include the Gas Works; the various yards and wharfs, Camper Nicholsons, Dibles, Auguste Pellerin's Margarine Works being amongst them. The works in this area account for about 2,000 workers, although here again some of the employment is seasonal.

The third group lies west of the Town Quay and includes Pirelli's, the Electricity Works, and West Station. About 1,500 persons are employed in this area.

The fourth group is in Shirley, and includes enterprises as diverse in character as the British American Tobacco Company's factory, Eucryl Ltd., the Camelot Press, and the Co-operative Bakery. This group accounts for about 1,100 workers, though the rapid expansion of the tobacco factory will probably soon raise this figure to 2,000.

On the other side of the Itchen the river-side belt includes Thornycrofts and Supermarine. From 4,000 to 4,500 workers are engaged in this area.

Standing outside these groups is the Ordnance Survey Office, which employs about 750 persons. Tramway employment is non-localized, about 800 men being employed. The various classes of seafarers number from 14,000 to 16,000, but some of these are not permanently resident, their homes being in Liverpool and London.

As regards the occupations of Southampton's workers, as distinct from the industries in which they are employed, the Census is more helpful. Over one-quarter (twenty-seven per cent.) of the occupied males were engaged in occupations connected with transport and communications, fourteen per cent. were metal-workers of one kind or another, and nine per cent. were in financial and commercial callings. Six per cent. were 'miscellaneous' general labourers, slightly over four per cent. were connected with woodworking, furniture-making, &c., and the same proportion were clerks and typists. The narrow opportunities for factory work for women is made clear by the fact that in 1921 eighty-five per cent. of them were found in five groups of occupations not typically 'industrial'. Forty-three per cent. were engaged in personal service and domestic work, and fifteen per cent. in commercial occupations, e.g., shop assistants. Just over ten per cent. were clerks and typists, nine per cent. were in professional callings such as teaching, and eight per cent. in occupations connected with dress and textiles. The development of the tobacco factory since that date is increasing the openings for factory work for women, but they are still scanty as compared with many other towns of like size.

The peculiar industrial complexion of Southampton is made plain by setting these facts against those for other towns. The figures below show for 1921 the proportion of every thousand occupied males of twelve years and over, who were engaged in 'locally important' occupations, the Southampton figures being compared with those for the neighbouring county boroughs and for the ports of Liverpool, Hull, and Cardiff.

Numbers in locally important occupations per 1,000 occupied males of 12 years and over.

	Southampton.	*Hull.*	*Liverpool.*	*Cardiff.*	*Bournemouth.*	*Portsmouth.*
Seamen	102	55	60	80	—	13
Dock labourers	42	69	61	38	—	3
Bargemen	—	12	—	—	—	—
Shipbuilders	25	13	13	8	—	12
Boilermakers, platers, and labourers	26	10	—	12	—	34
Fitters	15	15	—	15	—	24
General and undefined labourers	76	78	77	66	30	57
Drivers of horse vans and lorries	10	16	29	11	15	8
Salesmen and shop assistants	25	24	30	38	44	21
Proprietors, managers of dealing businesses	28	38	29	28	60	29
Retired (not naval or military)	28	22	20	19	74	34

The probable expansion and contraction of Southampton's industries is not an easy matter to discuss, for many elements of prophecy are involved. Acquisition by or amalgamation with outside firms may turn a firm from productive work into a mere distributive agency employing

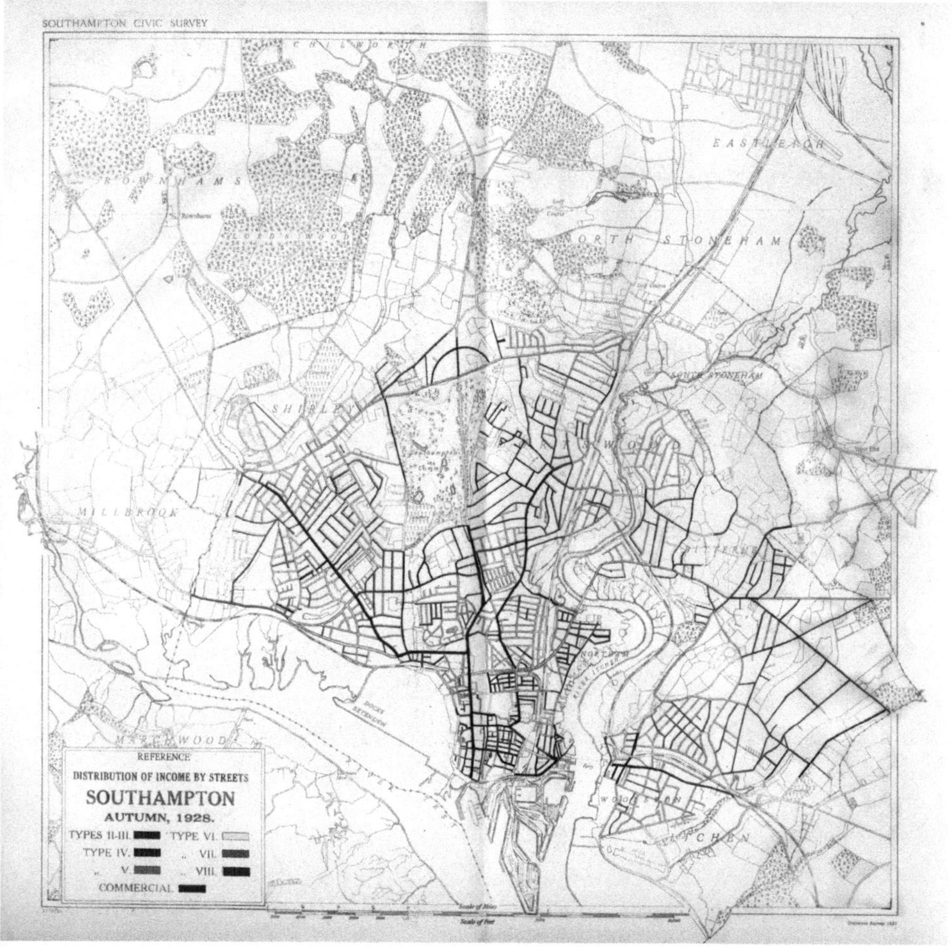
SOUTHAMPTON CIVIC SURVEY
CHILWORTH
NORTH STONEHAM
SOUTH STONEHAM
MILLBROOK
ITCHEN
REFERENCE
DISTRIBUTION OF INCOME BY STREETS
SOUTHAMPTON
AUTUMN, 1928.
TYPES II-III.
TYPE VI.
TYPE IV.
VII.
V.
VIII.
COMMERCIAL

less labour, or it may close down a works altogether. Even in stating increase or decrease of numbers employed between two dates it is necessary to distinguish between temporary expansions and contractions and the more permanent trends of growth and decay. Southampton affords examples of each of these possibilities, and though in this matter the detailed facts are important, they cannot be entered into here. With these qualifications, stated briefly, the chief employment tendencies in 1928–9 and 1930 were as follows.

There is a group of industries providing for the local market which are enlarging their employment along with the growth of population and its spread within the area and beyond its borders. This applies to passenger transport (tramways, and omnibus services feeding the little 'dormitories' outside the boundary, or touring its population), laundries, entertainments, and restaurants, &c. This type of growth is common to other towns. There is also an increase where the introduction of machinery or of modern delivery methods extends the local markets, as in baking and in laundries. Secondly, there are manufacturing firms dependent on the national or international market. Expansion of employment and increased activity are obvious in tobacco and electrical cable manufacture, both meeting modern needs of different kinds. This is also true of food manufacturing. Thirdly, there are trades new to the area. This includes heavy and light electrical manufacture. Fourthly, there are the main occupations of the town, shipping, shipbuilding, and dock work. The extension of the Docks implies an eventual increase of employment in all three, while the number of ships using the port is increasing and the personnel involved growing. Dock employment is not expanding so rapidly, partly because of the introduction of mechanical methods, e.g., electrical trolleys. In shipbuilding and repairing the prospects of the local industry are, like those of the national industry, overcast by immediate difficulties. The shipping companies' difficulties have affected ship-repairing, while firms dependent on the 'luxury' construction and repair of yachts are naturally suffering in the depression. The decline of employment here naturally, at the moment, offsets much of the expansion of other trades. Finally, there has been a great increase of employment on various public and private works of construction. The dock scheme has naturally contributed largely to this, and so have public works in the form of the building of the Civic Centre, sewage works and road construction. In so far as the labour consists of the various firms' nucleus of skilled and other key men, the expansion is temporary; in any case, local unskilled labour employed will have to find other work as the contracts are completed.

The possible growth of industry and employment in the next twenty or thirty years is a matter of some speculation. The great extension of the Docks may be expected to lead to a corresponding growth of passenger traffic, and of certain classes of cargo traffic. Some play may be made with the idea of the 'southward trend of industry', but it is necessary to be clear in what sense this movement, if it continues, is likely to affect Southampton. First, there is an indirect gain. The port is admirably placed for dealing with imported perishable goods, e.g., fruit, which demand speedy transport, and every shift of industrial activity which brings consuming populations nearer to it should augment the traffic it will handle. What are the chances of direct gain by the migration of industries into the town? Here one must draw distinctions, for industries are not all equally 'transferable' from one area to another. The metallurgical industries, which need to be in places giving the cheapest access to raw materials, &c., and heavily capitalized industries are likely to migrate only when the advantages in costs from so doing are substantial, but there is a range of light industries whose location is really determined by modest and even trifling differences of cost. The difference may be due to a low general level of wages, transport costs of product or raw materials, &c. In some of these matters Southampton is relatively attractive, but for those light industries making for home consumption it is under the disadvantage that its immediate hinterland is rather thinly peopled.

A large proportion of the town's population is dependent upon the first five trades in the list above, and it is precisely these which show seasonal or casual characteristics in marked degree. The summer passenger traffic rush implies months of activity followed by a lean winter of unemployment, while the winter ship and yacht repairing season implies reduced staffs in the summer. The numbers of unemployed registered at the Southampton Exchange in 1927–30 were as follows:

	Seamen.	*Ship Repairers and other Casuals.*
1927		
7 March	819	1,451
6 June	520	1,032
5 Sept.	385	1,226
5 Dec.	1,270	763
1928		
5 March	788	1,188
4 June	604	1,148
3 Sept.	335	933
3 Dec.	1,171	764
1929		
4 March	1,049	1,338
3 June	828	127
2 Sept.	380	1,397
2 Dec.	1,612	1,148
1930		
3 March	1,331	1,674
2 June	820	1,464

In 1927–8 the figures for seamen rose from 425 in the second week of September 1927 to a maximum of 1,482 in January 1928, and fell to a minimum of 335 in the following August. Amongst ship-repairers the figures moved in a reverse direction, falling from a maximum of 1,670 in the middle of October 1927 to a minimum of 404 in January 1928. In both cases the highest unemployment figure was more than four times greater than the lowest; but the incidence of unemployment is in different seasons, and two groups of workers are involved. The arrangements of the shipping firms include the use of some of their sea-going staff on shore work at certain times, but the main difficulty is not eliminated. The ship-repairing activity is such that it is found necessary, during the winter rush, to draw in many men, mainly of the skilled artisan class, to do special jobs for longer or shorter periods. As far as can be traced, nearly 1,000 such men came to the town in the last five months of 1927 and the first month of 1928.

The problem of the dock worker is different in character. A great advance has been made by the establishment of the tally system, which has reduced the size of the floating margin and eliminated the grosser evils, but the comparatively steady unemployment figures conceal the fact that the problem of providing regularly a full week's work still awaits solution.

The lack of regularity and stability in these three principal trades is the central feature of Southampton's employment problem. Its significance for housing and town-planning is that it is the most important single factor affecting the amount and regularity of wage-income, and so the capacity to pay rents; and it clearly has an important bearing on the possibilities of improving the housing condition of those now living in congested slum areas. A complete answer to the two questions, 'What are the incomes of the main classes of the population?', and 'What rents are they able and willing to pay?', involves detailed investigation and an elaborate procedure, the stages of which cannot be described here. It must suffice to give briefly the results of inquiries made to throw light on these problems.

An attempt has been made to answer the first question by classifying those of Southampton's families which have dependent children into eight income classes, in accordance with an assessment of the income of the head of the family. The method used was that of the 'mass-interview' developed by Charles Booth in his great Survey of London; but the details as to the steps taken to give precision and uniformity to the work of the investigators cannot be entered into here. It should be observed that the basis of the assessment was the earnings or other income of the head of the family, and does not include the net contribution made by older children to the family income. The broad results of surveying 21,538 families are given in the following table, and some of them are shown in graphic form in the diagram on page 59. The figures represent the facts averaged for each of the respective wards, and they conceal important differences within them; for the ward boundaries are often highly artificial ones made for the purpose of equalizing representation, and they frequently include sections of population of very diverse social and income type. In this sense Northam, which is fairly homogeneous, may be contrasted with St. Denys, which contains two quite different types of population separated by the river. Portswood includes a section of well-to-do and comfortable classes as well as an area of moderate working-class incomes. Further, the facts measured concern income, and although low incomes and bad housing are associated, the two should not be confused. In Town Ward, for example, there are men earning relatively good wages who are living in bad houses on overcrowded sites, because they desire to live near their work.

The significance of the table can be grasped by concentrating attention on classes IV, V, and VI. Class VI represents skilled earnings from about 55*s*. to 80*s*. per week; class V includes those with regular semi-skilled or unskilled earnings from 42*s*. to 54*s*. per week, while class IV consists of those receiving from 30*s*. to 41*s*. per week. The other classes consist of persons with higher or lower incomes. The large number of families in St. Marys, Town, and Trinity Wards, in which the head of the family is placed in or below class IV, i.e., receives less than 42*s*. per week, is worthy of special note. The percentages are 55·5 per cent., 22·1 per cent., and 35·6 per cent. respectively. Where these families contain many dependent children their social condition is one calling for serious public concern. The diagram illustrating Income conditions should be compared with those illustrating Housing and Infant Mortality.

Secondly, a small sample inquiry was made in order to discover what proportion of the various grades of income is absorbed by rent. This showed that of incomes ranging from 35*s*. to 50*s*. per week rather more than one-fifth was spent in rent; of incomes from 50*s*. to 60*s*. per week, about one-fifth, and of incomes from 60*s*. to 70*s*. per week about one-sixth. There is some reason for supposing the sample was not completely unbiased in the technical sense, and the figures are quoted with this reservation.

Percentage of families with dependent children in income classes

(Total families surveyed—21,538)

	Income Class.				
	I–IV	V	VI	VII	VIII
1. Town . . .	20·1	34·9	33·1	10·1	1·8
2. St. Mary's . .	44·7	17·5	27·6	9·4	0·8
3. Northam. . .	16·0	41·2	37·4	4·3	1·1
4. Trinity . . .	30·0	21·6	40·2	6·7	1·5
5. Newtown . .	1·6	26·8	54·5	13·3	3·8
6. All Saints . .	6·5	19·6	49·2	22·0	2·7
7. Bevois . . .	2·0	27·6	43·0	14·9	12·5
8. Banister . . .	1·1	7·6	40·6	34·7	16·0
9. Freemantle . .	10·5	18·7	49·6	18·6	2·6
10. Millbrook . .	18·0	16·7	48·1	16·0	1·2
11. Shirley . . .	8·6	17·8	46·6	22·1	4·9
12. Portswood . .	2·8	17·2	32·5	28·9	18·6
13. St. Denys . .	1·4	21·4	52·4	23·1	1·7
14. Bitterne and Pear Tree	11·4	23·0	48·2	14·5	2·9
15. Bitterne and Sholing .	9·8	48·2	35·2	5·7	1·1
16. Woolston . .	9·7	20·3	55·4	12·5	2·1
17. St. Nicholas . .	9·0	22·1	50·5	15·3	3·1
Totals	12·5	24·1	43·5	15·7	4·2

Note to Map XI on Distribution of Income by Street

This map shows the results of the income inquiry by streets. On the basis of the information obtained, streets were graded to show the dominant income type. Where all the families were of one income class, this was simple. Thus, if all of them were Class VIII, the street was type VIII, and coloured red; Class VII, type VII, and coloured orange; if Class V, type V, and coloured green. Where there was a variety of income grades in a street, a general impression was obtained by the use of a formula, though naturally any formula is bound to lead to a certain number of anomalies. It should be observed that the map illustrates the distribution of income by whole streets, as tested by families with dependent children, and gives no information as to any particular family or person, or as to the character of the houses. The map is easily read, if it be noted that the colour scheme is based on the spectrum, which provides a natural scale. The lower income grades are coloured violet, and the highest red, the intermediate grades being represented by the appropriate colour in the scale.

CHAPTER VII

POPULATION, HOUSING, AND HEALTH

POPULATION AND HOUSE DENSITY

By P. FORD, B.SC. (ECON.)

FOR the purpose of deciding the principles on which the town should be planned, and the public services and amenities it will require, we need to know the rate at which the population has grown in the past and the present tendencies of growth, its distribution amongst the various areas of the town, and its age composition.

The increase of the population of Southampton as recorded at the Census dates since 1801 is as follows:

1801	1811	1821	1831	1841	1851	1861
7,913	9,617	13,353	19,324	27,744	35,305	46,960
1871	1881	1891	1901	1911	1921	
53,741	60,051	65,325	104,344	119,012	162,200	

These figures tend to exaggerate the rate at which the town has been growing during the last forty years. The large increases shown in 1901 and 1921 are due to the extension of the Borough boundary, and not merely to the true growth by excess of births over deaths and the addition of newcomers. By recalculating, as far as the Census information allows, the population of the *present* Borough area at the earlier dates, a different impression is obtained:

		1891	1901	1911	1921
Numbers		94,338	123,346	145,096	162,200
Increase	Numbers		29,008	21,750	15,898
	Per cent.		30·7	17·3	11·8

It is noteworthy that the rate of growth is less rapid in each of the ten-year periods. Up to 1921 this was true even of the 'added areas'. The figures for the Town Planning area, the approximate population of which has been calculated for the four dates, exhibits the same tendency. These facts are made clear in the following table:

			1891	1901	1911	1921
Added Areas.	Numbers		29,013	44,069	59,245	26,926
	Increase	Numbers		15,056	15,176	10,681
		Per cent.		52·0	34·5	18·1
Town Planning Area.[1]	Numbers		97,444	125,937	148,250	164,358
	Increase	Numbers		28,493	22,313	16,018
		Per cent.		29·2	17·7	10·9

It is interesting to compare the growth of Southampton with that of other ports. The percentage increases in the last three decades, 30·7 per cent., 17·3 per cent., and 11·8 per cent., show a rate of growth faster than that of Great Britain as a whole, for which the corresponding figures are 12·1 per cent., 10·4 per cent., and 4·7 per cent. Comparison of the populations within a radius of fifteen miles of the twelve great ports shows that the Southampton area, for

[1] i.e. the whole Borough area plus the additional areas outside the Borough included in scheme No. 1.

which the percentage increases for the last three census decades are 16·9 per cent., 16·8 per cent., and 7·6 per cent., has been growing at a greater pace than most of the others; faster than Hull, for example, on the whole faster than Liverpool, but not so fast as Cardiff.

The growth since the last census can only be estimated. The two sources of increase are the balance of births over deaths, and the balance of those leaving over those coming to take up residence in the area. On the second of these we have practically no information. The first we know accurately. The table below, showing the numbers of births and deaths since 1921, indicates how a fall of the birth-rate from 22·4 in 1921, to 18·0 in 1928, while the death-rate has remained fairly steady, has diminished the natural increase of the population.

Births, deaths, and natural increase

Year.	*Birth-rate.*	*Births.*	*Death-rate.*	*Deaths.*	*Natural Increase.*
1921	22·4	3,621	10·8	1,749	1,872
1922	20·3	3,318	12·1	1,975	1,342
1923	19·4	3,205	11·0	1,817	1,391
1924	18·9	3,204	11·4	1,938	1,266
1925	19·3	3,250	11·6	1,956	1,294
1926	18·6	3,141	11·1	1,880	1,261
1927	17·4	2,958	12·9	2,183	775
1928	18·0	3,047	12·0	2,025	1,022

The Registrar-General's estimate for the year 1928 was 169,900, an increase of only 7,200 over the corrected census figures for 1921. As the natural increase since that date is 10,224 this implies that so far from growing rapidly by the addition of families from Liverpool and other places, the town is not retaining its own excess of births over deaths. The estimate for 1929 is 172,300, which brings the estimated increase up 10,100, but this is still below the natural increase. The Borough Health Department estimated that, in addition to retaining the equivalent of the whole natural increase, the population has been augmented by new-comers at the rate of 1,500 per annum. This seems to be too high, but it may be that the Registrar-General's estimate is too low. It is possible that the small increase is explainable by the growth of 'dormitories' outside the borough. The 'Work-places' census of 1921 shows a small excess of people who worked in Southampton and lived outside the borough, over those who lived in the borough and worked elsewhere. Since then the development of road transport has made it convenient for many employed in Southampton to live in Millbrook, Chandlersford, and other places.

While it is not easy to make a precise estimate of the probable population thirty or forty years hence, it is nevertheless important to avoid the cruder errors, and to keep within probable limits. If the population is likely to grow with great rapidity, town-planning schemes must—if the increase is to be housed within the boundary—reserve considerable areas for house-building, and may be compelled to allow development at a relatively high density per acre; while if the increase is likely to be only moderate, lighter densities can be safely insisted upon. It has been a common vice of many towns to over-estimate their future growth. Beginning with the number of people at some early century, curves are drawn showing a slow rise to the nineteenth and then, under the combined influence of true increase and extensions of boundary, the curves shoot upwards with great speed; and if these are projected for fifty years they give impressive figures of future magnitude. Such calculations overlook the fact that the English birth-rate, and the natural increase are falling, and that if these tendencies continue the country as a whole will shortly have a stationary population. The aggregate total given by these exaggerated estimates is inconsistent with the facts. The confusion has arisen from a failure to distinguish between the true growth of population in a given area, and the increase of numbers due to the enlargement of the area itself by boundary extensions. Yet it would be possible to have an increase of population by the process of boundary extension alone, without a single addition by true increase; and no more houses would be needed in the second period than in the first. It would be unnecessary to labour this point were it not the case that Civic pride predisposes to the error, that there are numerous examples of it, and that the matter has an important bearing on permitted house density. Bearing these cautions in mind, an increase of population in the present area similar to that of the thirty years before 1921 would not raise Southampton's population to 230,000 until 1961 or 1971; while an increase to 280,000 by the later date would suppose an increase of about 2,500 per annum. It would require striking advantages for the Town to add to its numbers at this pace when the country's total population was stationary, for it implies an actual depletion of other areas.

If these estimates are correct the significance of the building development in Shirley, St. Nicholas, and Millbrook wards is that it implies a considerable redistribution of the town's population, and presumably some relief in the more congested areas. The figures below show the numbers residing in each ward in 1921 and, as far as can be estimated, in 1928.

Ward populations

Ward.	1921	1928 *Estimated.*	*Population per Acre.* 1921	1928
Town	11,733	11,100	94	89
St. Mary's	12,989	12,800	81	80
Northam	11,594	11,000	44	41
Trinity	9,065	8,600	113	108
New Town	8,759	8,700	89	88
All Saints	9,706	8,700	38	34
[1]Bevois	8,331	7,700	42	39
Banister	8,318	8,400	14	14
Freemantle	8,239	7,900	44	42
Millbrook	10,843	12,100	21	23
Shirley	11,182	13,900	11	14
Portswood	9,771	10,700	18	20
St. Denys	9,095	9,900	17	18
Bitterne and Pear Tree	8,960	10,000	17	19
Bitterne and Sholing	9,882	11,200	7	8
Woolston	8,187	8,100	12	12
St. Nicholas	4,340	9,100	2	5

The figures for 1928 were obtained by multiplying the numbers of persons on the Parliamentary Register of each ward by the ratio which the total number of such voters in England and Wales bore to the total population of the country, and by adjusting the figure so obtained in the light of the age composition of the population of each ward in 1921. Too much reliance should not be placed on the results so obtained; they are useful only as a rough guide. The

[1] Another estimate: 8,300.

striking growth in St. Nicholas ward can be confirmed in another way. The number of residences enumerated in the ward was 2,688, and allowing for 4·11 persons per house, the population would be 11,050. This is larger than the figure obtained by the first method and is probably excessive, but as parts of the ward are being rapidly built upon it may soon prove to be the more correct figure. The table may therefore slightly under-estimate the extent to which redistribution of population has taken place.

Town-planning clauses were first introduced into English legislation as an after-thought on housing policy, and although the purpose of planning has widened and deepened since 1909 it is rightly regarded as a principal weapon for use in the war on bad housing and disease. A preliminary understanding of Southampton's problem in this respect can be obtained by comparing (1) house density per acre, (2) numbers of rooms per person, and (3) the infant mortality rate.

WARD REFERENCE

1 *Town*	9 *Freemantle*
2 *St. Mary's*	10 *Millbrook*
3 *Northam*	11 *Shirley*
4 *Trinity*	12 *Portswood*
5 *Newtown*	13 *St. Denys*
6 *All Saints*	14 *Bitterne & Pear Tree*
7 *Bevois*	15 *Bitterne & Sholing*
8 *Banister*	16 *Woolston*
17 *St. Nicholas*	

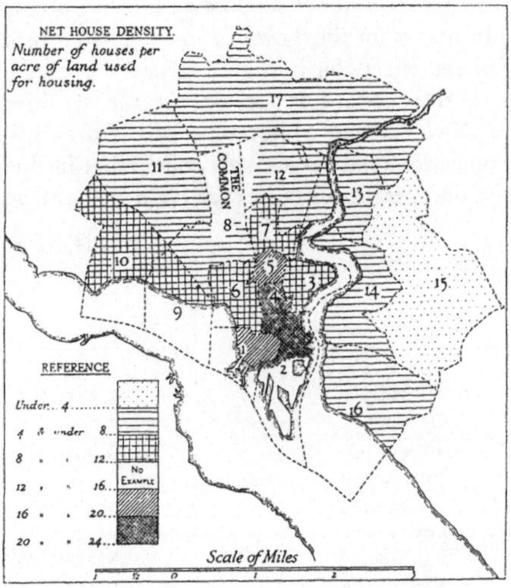

The following figures of net house density, i.e. the number of houses per acre of land used for housing, have been obtained for each ward. As far as possible, all works, offices, and the major business premises have been excluded, except where the building, for example a small shop, is also a family residence. The area used for residential purposes has been arrived at by deducting the acreage occupied by public and private open spaces, works, public buildings, &c., from the total area of each ward. The result is necessarily approximate, as demolition, alteration, and construction is continually taking place, but errors from this cause are not important in the built-up wards. In Town ward, for example, an error of 115 houses would make a difference of 1·3 per acre.

In reading these figures several points should be noticed. First, the figures are the *averages* for the ward, and in some cases cover considerable diversity of density, of small areas within them. Thus, Town ward has blocks with over 60 houses to the acre, and those who assisted in checking this part of the Survey discovered a number of small pockets of bad housing in various parts of the ward. Secondly, the net area of land used for housing includes the acreage

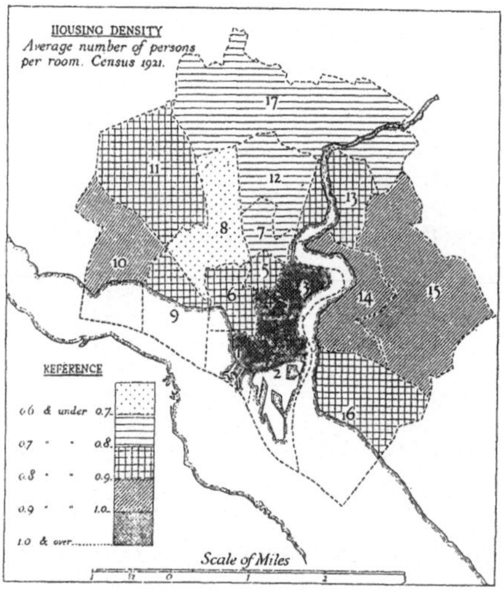
HOUSING DENSITY
Average number of persons per room. Census 1921.
REFERENCE
0.6 & under 0.7
0.7 " " 0.8
0.8 " " 0.9
0.9 " " 1.0
1.0 & over
Scale of Miles

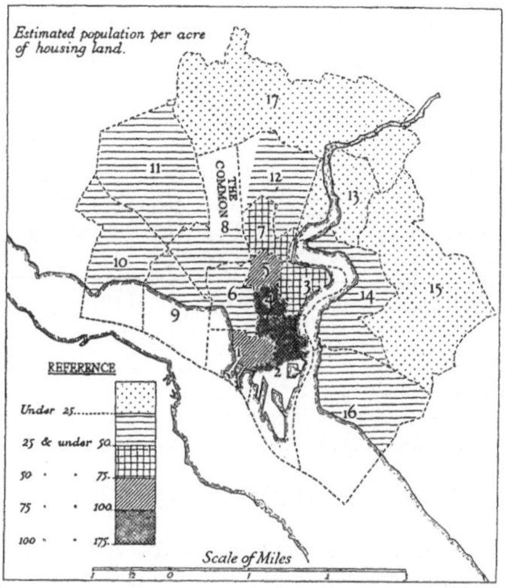
Estimated population per acre of housing land.
THE COMMON
REFERENCE
Under 25
25 & under 50
50 " " 75
75 " " 100
100 " " 175
Scale of Miles

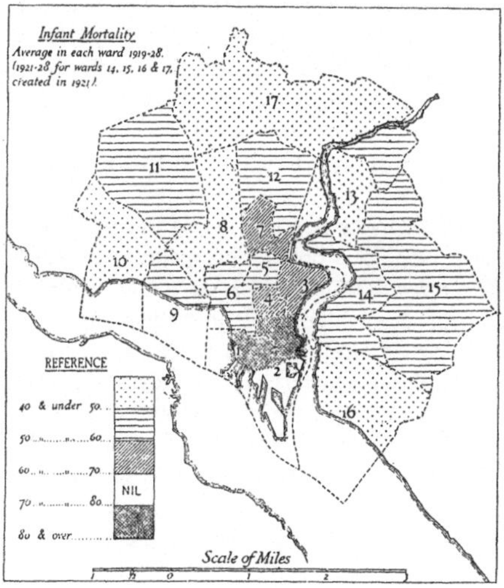
Infant Mortality
Average in each ward 1919-28.
(1921-28 for wards 14, 15, 16 & 17, created in 1921).
REFERENCE
40 & under 50
50 " " 60
60 " " 70
NIL
70 " " 80
80 & over
Scale of Miles

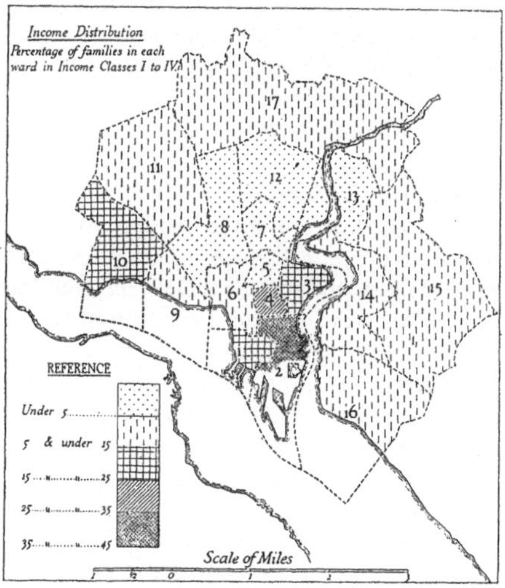
Income Distribution
Percentage of families in each ward in Income Classes I to IV.
REFERENCE
Under 5
5 & under 15
15 " " 25
25 " " 35
35 " " 45
Scale of Miles

House density per acre

	Census Acreage.	*Net Area used for Housing.*	*No. of Houses.*	*House Density per Acre.*	*Persons per room 1921.*
Town . . .	125	115	1,873	16·3	1·11
St. Mary's . .	161	76	1,666	21·9	1·13
Northam . . .	267	188	1,918	10·2	1·11
Trinity . . .	80	77	1,614	20·9	1·00
Newtown . . .	99	92	1,801	19.6	0·82
All Saints . . .	259	182	1,917	10·5	0·85
Bevois . . .	197	165	1,759	10·7	0·75
Banister . . .	604	257	1,906	7·4	0·63
Freemantle . .	188	177	1,620	9·2	0·83
Millbrook . .	524	310	2,582	8·3	0·91
Shirley . . .	1,010	536	3,510	6·5	0·88
Portswood . .	542	405	2,803	6·9	0·77
St. Denys . . .	548	420	2,271	5·4	0·84
Bitterne and Pear Tree	520	273	1,945	7·1	0·96
Bitterne and Sholing .	1,484	635	2,230	3·5	0·98
Woolston . .	700	279	1,747	6·3	0·86
St. Nicholas . .	1,884	456	2,688	5·9	0·79

taken up by the roadways, the resources of the Survey being insufficient to enable it to make the detailed calculation necessary for its exclusion. In the comparisons of wards built up at different dates and under different by-laws this may be a matter of some importance. For example, Northam streets are on the whole wider than the close and narrow streets of Trinity, and the density figures for the former would have been comparatively much heavier if this allowance could have been made. Thirdly, in some wards a very undesirable feature of some of Southampton's building—the construction of houses with very narrow frontages—gives the streets a physical appearance of greater density than the facts warrant, since the gardens behind the houses are often long.

The varied nature of the housing problem can be seen by comparing the figures relating to density per acre, and those showing the number of persons per room. This makes it clear, for example, that the major problem for Northam is overcrowding of families in houses, while for some other areas it is the overcrowding of houses to the acre which needs immediate attention.

The general relationship of income conditions, housing, and health is well known and need not be enlarged upon; their association in Southampton can be seen from diagram facing pages 57, 58. As an index of health conditions the infant mortality rate has been chosen as representative. Other factors besides housing, such as ignorance, poverty, and unskilful attention, affect this rate, but the close connexion of the three factors is obvious. Leaving aside the wider question of poverty, the vicious circle of bad housing and ill-health can be broken into in three ways, one preventive and two remedial. First, by limiting the number of houses which can be built to the acre in new areas in course of development; secondly, by the provision of more house room at rents suitable for the working classes, thus relieving overcrowding per house; thirdly, by clearing slum areas. An examination of the facts relating to the second and third of these lines of policy follows.

Appendix 2

P. Ford, 'Indices of Social Conditions in Southampton', *The Sociological Review*, vol. 23, January-April 1931, pp. 22-33.

INDICES OF SOCIAL CONDITIONS IN SOUTHAMPTON: by P. Ford, B.Sc., Head of the Department of Economics and Commerce, University College, Southampton.

MUCH of the work now done in voluntary surveys ought to be part of the normal process of government. In the records of municipal offices lies buried much vital information which could be made continuously available to illumine both the immediate and underlying problems of administration, if appropriate steps were taken to make use of it. Data from different branches of the service are never seen in their mutual relationship. That is partly due to reasons of administrative convenience; for wards, rate collector's districts, and school attendance districts (for example) are quite different units, and no one is charged with the duty of bringing information together in comparable form. One imagines that if the Town Clerk were replaced by Mr. E. D. Simon's administrative officer or burgomaster, the latter would find this necessary for framing his policies. If the records were kept in an appropriate manner, a well-equipped central statistical office could without difficulty organise the facts on a common basis, and throw new light on problems and policy by showing old facts in new relations. It is as a supplement to, and not a substitute for, this work that the voluntary survey would be needed for the detailed study of particular problems.

THESE considerations must occur to everyone who is engaged on a survey, and they are particularly pertinent to the Southampton Survey. This had in view (I) the construction of a series of indices of social conditions for the various districts of the Town, and (II) the measurement of the distribution of income by classifying the population into income grades. The second of these is related to the first in that from it can be derived a figure, such as the proportion of families below a certain level of income, which would be useful as one of the general indices. The construction of this particular index was the largest of the tasks, and the method used to arrive at it will be described in some detail.

I. INDICES OF SOCIAL CONDITIONS.

SOME of these such as

(1), the infant mortality rate per ward, and

(2) the census figures of persons per room, were already in existence. Others were made from data collected for the Southampton Civic Survey, by whose permission they are here reproduced. These include,

(3) house density per acre of housing land. For this index, only residences and shops with residences above them were counted, while all acreage not used for this purpose, whether utilised for works, open spaces, and public buildings, or consisting of foreshore and unbuilt-on land, was deducted from the total ward acreage. The figure is approximate, for occasionally a single building contains a residence, with a shop or a small meeting hall; many houses built for a single family have been turned into flats, and would be counted as "structurally separate" by the census, although the division would not be apparent from the outside. The biggest difficulty was street acreage, the resources of the Survey being insufficient for the task of measuring this separately, though it is important in comparing a pre-by-law area having narrow streets with one possessing the wider roads required by modern standards, or with an undeveloped ward in which the roads have much frontage not yet built upon.

(4) Population per acre of housing land. This index was used in addition to the more usual one of population per acre. It is known that overcrowding per room is more pernicious in its effects on health than overcrowding of houses per acre, (though the latter is far from negligible): the figure for the former is based on the census of 1921. The population for each ward was estimated from the Registrar General's returns, the Parliamentary Register, &c., and related to the acreage of land used for housing. This index would be raised both by overcrowding per room and by high densities of houses to the acre, but would not be reduced by the existence of a large works area in the same ward—which is the weakness of simple population per acre. The difference between the two figures may be seen from these examples:—

Ward.	Population per acre.	Population per acre of Housing Land.
Town	89	99
St. Mary's	80	169
St. Nicholas	5	20

(5) Public open space per person. Two indices were made, the acreage of public open space in each ward per person, and the public open space accessible within a quarter of a mile of the ward.

(6) The percentage of families in which the direct income of the head of the family was less than £2 2s. per week. This is described later.

A common area was required, and for this the wards were selected. Their boundaries are often very artificial, being drawn for the purpose of equalising political representation, and more suitable areas could have been selected for the several indices, but the labour of classifying the population street by street into wards for the income index, was sufficient to deter one from choosing a unit which would involve similar labour for the other measurements as well. In consequence, since the figures represent the average for the wards, they sometimes conceal great diversities of house density, overcrowding, infant death rate and income conditions within them.

IT would be tempting to endeavour to combine numbers (2) to (5) into a composite index for each ward, and to compare them with the infant death rate, but, as Sir Arthur Newsholme remarks, "There can be no short cut to the satisfactory relegation of a community to its due place in the sanitary heirarchy."*

II. DISTRIBUTION OF INCOME. (A) METHODS OF ENQUIRY.

THE method used for ascertaining this was that of the mass interview developed by Booth for his London survey. He hoped, by securing an assessment of the income of the heads of families with school children, to discover what proportion of the population were beneath the poverty line. Yet, path breaking as his work was in method and in uncovering social evils, the use of the same method to-day must be regarded as yielding suggestive rather than definitive evidence of poverty. Professor Bowley's enquiries have shown how much the relation of a family to poverty depends on the number of its wage earners and how many households are receiving supplementary income by way of pensions, and other social service payments, receipts from lodgers, &c.; and that the income required depends on the size, sex and age constitution of the family. While, then, Booth's method gives only indirect evidence of poverty which needs supplementing by more precise investigation, it is nevertheless very valuable for obtaining a picture of the distribution of income. For various reasons in Southampton it proved easier to begin with the larger enquiry on the Booth plan.

THE enquiry was confined to families with dependent children, or strictly, children of all ages up to school-leaving age, information being obtained in respect of 21,538 families and 43,519 children. It is thought that this census was practically complete. The date of the investigation was August, 1928. The information available included the occupation of the head of the family and the number of children under five years of age, and of school age. The differentiation into income grades was made on the basis of an assessment of the earnings or other direct income of the responsible head of the family, no account being taken of the earnings of other members. Precision and uniformity of assessment being essential, either full statements or samples of the

*For one such attempt, see Newsholme, VITAL STATISTICS (new edition), pages 521, 596. In this case the aim was to show the alteration of indices through time for the same area, and not to compare different areas at the same date.

actual wages paid were obtained for some industries, and these proved useful in keeping the assessors to common principles. This information was not used as an exclusive test for grading, but enabled the assessor to ask himself, " Granted that this type of occupation on an average yields this specified income, to what extent does my knowledge suggest that this case deviates from it ? " Allowance could thus be more clearly and consciously made for various personal and other factors, such as idleness, misfortune and efficiency, which affect an individual's income. In any case, wage rates and even earnings for large classes of workers are determined by standard agreements between employers and trade unions, or by the State, so that the range of variation between one individual and another following the same occupation can, apart from purely personal factors, often be determined within fairly narrow limits. The size of the area surveyed proved to be of advantage. In a large area like London, it is practically impossible for any one person to have even a slight acquaintance with all its varied districts, but Southampton is just small enough for one individual by personal visit to get a general knowledge of nearly every street. By making visitation of this sort part of the method of survey, it was possible to raise queries as to the accuracy and uniformity of assessment, any cases of serious disparity being dealt with at a joint meeting of assessors. The information so obtained has been placed on two maps. The first, published in the Civic Survey, shows the proportion of the total number of families in each ward which were in the lower income grades, while on the second, streets were coloured on an impressionistic scheme akin to that used in Booth's famous maps, to show their general income character.

BOOTH's scheme of eight income grades was found convenient, but the ranges of income were adapted to the requirements of Southampton. The table below shows the kind of occupation found in these grades, but it should be observed that personal as well as occupational facts were taken into account in the grading.

Class.	Description.	Income (Shillings).	Examples.
I.	Loafer		
II.	Casual	20 and under 30	Fringe of dock and shipyard labour, hawker.
III.	Intermittent and Seasonal	20 and under 40	Ice cream vendors.
IV.	Low regular ..	30 and under 42	Labourer.
V.	Regular standard ..	42 and under 50	Blacksmiths' labourers, firemen, railway porters, riggers, seamen.
VI.	Skilled	50 and under 80	Joiners and other tradesmen, tram motormen.
VII.	Supervisory labour and clerical	80 and over ..	Foremen, some clerical.

(Date—Autumn, 1928.)

THE following table shows the percentage of families enumerated in the various income classes in each ward. The percentages could have been based also on the number of children in each class. The difference between the results obtained for the whole town is as follows :—

	I.-IV.	V.	VI.	VII.	VIII.
Families	12.5	24.1	43.5	15.7	4.2
Children	13.8	26.1	42.4	14.2	3.5
Mean	13.15	25.1	42.95	14.95	3.85

IN connection with these figures, it is interesting to observe the average number of dependent children per family for each income class.

I.-IV.	V.	VI.	VII.	VIII.	All.
2.2	2.2	2.0	1.8	1.7	2.0

PERCENTAGE OF FAMILIES WITH DEPENDENT CHILDREN IN INCOME CLASSES.

Total families surveyed—21,538.

	Income Class.				
Ward.	I.-IV.	V.	VI.	VII.	VIII.
Town	20.1	34.9	33.1	10.1	1.8
St. Mary's	44.7	17.5	27.6	9.4	0.8
Northam	16.0	41.2	37.4	4.3	1.1
Trinity	30.0	21.6	40.2	6.7	1.5
Newtown	1.6	26.8	54.5	13.3	3.8
All Saints'	6.5	19.6	49.2	22.0	2.7
Bevois	2.0	27.6	43.0	14.9	12.5
Banister	1.1	7.6	40.6	34.7	16.0
Freemantle	10.5	18.7	49.6	18.6	2.6
Millbrook	18.0	16.7	48.1	16.0	1.2
Shirley	8.6	17.8	46.6	22.1	4.9
Portswood	2.8	17.2	32.5	28.9	18.6
St. Deny's	1.4	21.4	52.4	23.1	1.7
Bitterne and Pear Tree ..	11.4	23.0	48.2	14.5	2.9
Bitterne and Sholing ..	9.8	48.2	35.2	5.7	1.1
Woolston	9.7	20.3	55.4	12.5	2.1
St. Nicholas	9.0	22.1	50.5	15.3	3.1
Total	12.5	24.1	43.5	15.7	4.2

(B) RELATION OF INCOME DISTRIBUTION TO POVERTY.

WHAT incidental light does this enquiry throw on the problem of poverty ? The classification is based on the direct income of the head of the family, and not upon family income. Comparison of the income grade of any given family with a Southampton " poverty line," would show if it were in poverty, *on the assumption that there was no contribution from any other earning members of the family, and no liability to support them ;* or stating it in another way, the income grade can be used to measure poverty, if one assumes that the other earners contribute exactly what it costs the family to maintain them and no more. Now this is very far from giving a definite measurement like that obtained by Bowley's minimum need enquiries, but at least it is of value for the purpose of general comparisons of ward with ward, and may perhaps be regarded as a first approximation.

In drawing a poverty line, the minimum need standard as set forth in 1924 in Has Poverty Diminished? was used, and the diet worked out in Southampton prices at the date of the Survey. Though afterwards modified, allowance for clothing, lighting and cleaning was at first made as in that standard. Owing to the great inequalities between the tenants of corporation, controlled and uncontrolled houses, fixing a standard sum for rent was difficult, for it has not been possible for families to pick and choose in such a way that equal incomes and equal needs have in fact paid equal rents. The cheapest corporation house costs over 9/- weekly, and in the light of all the facts a rent of 8/- was assumed.

This standard can be criticised both as to its scientific validity and its relation to the actual habits of the working class. The diet, though scientific in the sense of being based on a calculation of calorific content would be unlikely to secure the unreserved recommendation of a modern dietician who is interested also in chemical constituents and vitamins. It is probable that he would enlarge the amount consumed at the age of 12 years rather than make the break at 14 years, and he would criticise the absence of green vegetables, fruit and fish. It is in these points that the standards also depart from the actual practice even of the poorer working class. They patronise, however little, the hawkers' barrows and stalls; they rely on getting economical meals when large catches of fish are going cheap, and in this southern town the oatmeal diet would be notable for its absence.

The items most open to doubt are the estimates for clothing and fuel. A group of working-class men and women, which included a Councillor, a Guardian, insurance agents, and canvassers—all with an intimate knowledge of working-class life, were inclined to regard an allowance of 60/– per annum for clothing for an adult as likely to be in excess of the facts for low borderline incomes. Those on the poverty line rarely purchase new clothing, and indeed a donkey and cart can be seen going the rounds with second-hand suits priced at 7/- to 10/-; while unredeemed pledges and jumble and Salvation Army sales are other sources of cheap clothing. One estimate placed the expenditure of an adult male on this meagre income as unlikely to exceed 30/- per annum. The fuel allowance could be reduced from 3/- per week to 2/6, if account be taken of the fact that poor coal is purchased in buckets from the wharves at cheap rates. A standard of life based on a monotonous diet, and on wearing only the cast-off clothing of the more fortunate, seems severe enough to justify the title of "poverty line."

ALTHOUGH any theoretical standard must be somewhat arbitrary, Bowley's minimum need standard, whether revised or not, is as he claims, an intelligible one. The cost of securing it was, at the date of the survey, as follows :—

	Bowley.	Revised for fuel and clothing.
For a man and wife and one child under 5 years	32/-	30/-
one child under 5, and one between 5 and 14	37/2½	34/8½
two under 5, and one between 5 and 14	41/1½	38/2
one under 5, and two between 5 and 14	42/5	39/9
three between 5 and 14 ..	43/8½	40/9

In comparing these figures with actual earnings, allowances must be made for compulsory insurance deductions, and in some industries, for trade union subscriptions, since without a union card there might be difficulty in obtaining work.

ON the assumptions made, i.e., ignoring both the contributions by and the expenditure on children who are earning, the following conclusions are probable. A family in Class IV. was in poverty, i.e., had insufficient income to obtain this standard, if there were three children, unless one were an infant; it was certainly in poverty if there were four children. If the family were in Class V. and receiving the maximum income of that grade, it was in poverty if there were five children, two of them under five years, and was running things close, if there were four, who had passed the age of five and had not reached earning age.

THESE comments assume steady employment and steady income. In periods of reduced income from whatever cause, whether sickness, short time or unemployment, the family would be able to keep itself above the poverty line only by resort to the social services, since the poverty standard makes no provision for saving. Alternatively, it could ensure that there was a margin available for emergencies by reducing its normal expenditure on rent and sharing the house with another family. In this sense overcrowding, pernicious as its consequences are, is only an act of common prudence.

SUMMARY OF RESULTS.

(1) INDICES OF SOCIAL CONDITIONS.

THE following table sets forth the indices for each ward. The infant mortality rate has been selected as representative of health conditions.

WARD.	Population, 1921.	Estimated Population, 1928.	Increase or decrease.	Persons per room, 1921.	House density per acre of housing land, 1928.	Population per acre of housing land, 1928.	Persons per acre of public open space.	Per cent. of Families in Income Classes, I.—IV.	Average Infant Mortality, 1919-28.
Town ..	11,733	11,100	− 633	1.11	16.3	99	2,340	20.1	95.1
St. Mary's ..	12,989	12,800	− 189	1.13	21.9	169	1,075	44.7	82.5
Northam ..	11,594	11,000	− 594	1.11	8.9	58	†	16.0	68.0
Trinity ..	9,065	8,600	− 465	1.00	20.9	112	†	30.0	67.6
Newtown ..	8,759	8,700	− 59	0.82	19.6	94	3,955	1.6	57.9
All Saints' ..	9,706	8,700	−1,006	0.85	10.5	48	264	6.5	54.5
Bevois ..	8,331	7,700	− 631	0.75	10.7	47	888	2.0	65.5
Banister ..	8,318	8,400	+ 82	0.63	7.4	32	33	1.1	41.3
Freemantle ..	8,239	7,900	− 339	0.83	9.2	45	†	10.5	50.2
Millbrook ..	10,843	12,100	+1,257	0.91	8.3	39	852	18.0	47.8
Shirley ..	11,182	13,900	+2,718	0.88	6.5	26	1,569	8.6	55.6
Portswood ..	9,771	10,700	+ 929	0.77	6.9	26	160	2.8	52.1
St. Denys' ..	9,095	9,900	+ 805	0.84	5.4	23	1,388	1.4	44.0
Bitterne and Pear Tree ..	8,960	10,000	+1,040	0.96	7.1	37	417	11.4	*56.1
Bitterne and Sholing ..	9,882	11,200	+1,318	0.98	3.5	18	571	9.8	*57.2
Woolston ..	8,187	8,100	− 87	0.86	6.3	29	558	9.7	*45.4
St. Nicholas	4,340	9,100	+4,760	0.79	5.9	20	†	9.0	*49.5
Totals ..	160,994	169,900	—	0.85	7.5	37.6	374	12.5	61.2

*Average for 8 years only, 1921—28. † No open Space

(2) NOTES ON THE WARDS.

THE following notes on the separate wards, taken from the data collected for the income survey, will indicate the nature of some of the social and occupational conditions in them. In the extracts from the records of typical streets, all names of streets and of persons, and all house numbers have been omitted, but it is hoped that the bare record will convey to the social worker with imagination something of their life, work and social atmosphere. The entry "two families" or "three families" means that the house is shared by families with dependent children. There are, of course, houses shared with childless families or single persons, but of these no record was made.

THE first four wards, Town, St. Mary's, Northam, and Trinity make distinctly the worst showing, in health, overcrowding, and with one striking exception, house density. For the first three the average number of dependent children per family is greater than the figure for the whole town (2.0), being 2.2, 2.3 and 2.3 respectively. Three of the wards abut on to the water front and contain docks, wharves and shipyards, &c.

TOWN Ward presents an interesting problem. It has the repute of being the worst of the wards, some of its old courts being scheduled for clearance, and its infant mortality rate is consistently the highest; yet in rooms per person, house density, population per acre of housing land and the percentage of families in the low income classes, its conditions are more favourable than those of St. Mary's, the other ward adjacent to the docks. The difference does not seem to be due to lack of uniformity in grading. The quality of ante-natal and post-natal attendance was suspected as being deficient, especially as the clinic is rather distant for many of the mothers, but inspection of the addresses of those attending it does not suggest any notable failure to attend. The average figures for the ward conceal marked differences, and if the data concerning the insanitary courts and other bad areas could be isolated, part of the contrast would be removed. Besides the slum areas east and west of High Street, there are council houses inhabited by workers of better incomes, numbers of lodging-house keepers providing for seamen and resident shopkeepers who make a tolerably good living. Many of the dock workers in Town Ward have higher and steadier incomes than those in St. Mary's, and although they sometimes live in poorer accommodation, this is due not so much to lack of means as to the desire to live near their work. If Classes I. to V. are compared, instead of I.-IV. only, the contrast between the two wards is softened.

	I.-IV.	I.-V.
Town	20.1	55.0
St. Mary's	44.7	62.0

THE large proportion of families in Class V. in Town Ward is due to the numbers of firemen, seamen and labourers of Class V.

TYPICAL Streets in Town Ward are as follows.

————Street. Four families with children in one house; Coal Porter, Class III., 1 child, Fisherman, Class III., 2 children, Boiler Scaler, Class V., 5 children, Boiler Scaler, Class V., 5 children. Widow, Class IV., 4 children. Widow, Class IV., 1 child. Labourer, Class V., 5 children. Boiler Scaler, Class V., 1 child. Two families, Labourer, Class V., and "Woodman," Class V., both one child. Two families, Widow, Class IV., with 2 children and a Labourer, Class V., with 4 children. Boiler Scaler, Class V., with 2 children. Rest of street similar. Six families below poverty line and others marginal.

————Street. Better class street. Widow, Class VI., with 2 children. Seaman, Class V., 4 children. Stevedore, Class VI., 3 children. Fitter's Mate, Class V., 5 children. Small Shopkeeper, Class VI., 1 child. Commission Agent, Class VI., 4 children. Stevedore, Class VI., 2 children.

ST. MARY'S contains some of the labouring population of the docks and shipyards as well as seafarers, but many of the labourers have less regular work than those of Town Ward, where permanent men and tally holders are found in larger numbers.

ONE of the poorer streets contains a total of 54 families, with no skilled workers of Class VI. and only three families in Class V., all the rest being of lower income grades. Sixteen families were in Class II. (casual work). There were 162 dependent children in the street, an average of three per family as compared with 2.0 for the whole town and 2.2 for the whole of income classes I.-IV. throughout Southampton. One section of the street reads as follows. Beerhouse, Class VI., 2 children. Labourer, Class II., 2 children. Stevedore, Class IV., 5 children. Three families, one with school children; Dairyman, Class IV., 3 children, Seaman, Class III., 1 child, Labourer, Class II., 2 children. Three families, a Painter and two Labourers with 2, 3 and 2 children. Two families, Widow, Class I., 3 children, and unmarried, Class I., 1 child.

————Street. Even poorer, contains 13 families and 39 children. There are no cases of regular labourers of Class V., all being Class I.-IV., and nearly one half of

Classes I. to II. Are hostile or indifferent to suggestions that they should move to better surroundings.

A CONSIDERABLE proportion of the families in these two streets are under or on the margin of the poverty line.

NORTHAM. A low lying ward adjacent to the river, with wharves, shipyards, timber yards, gas works, &c. There are no public open spaces in the ward. The population is very homogeneous, no less than 78.6 per cent. of the families being in the two income grades, V.-VI. The ward has a social atmosphere of its own, many families never having lived outside it, a condition of immobility due partly to the fact that most of the ward lies between the river and the railway line. The light house density figures are a surprise to those who have seen only its long streets and small houses with narrow frontages, but often they have fair sized gardens, while many of the streets are comparatively wide. The bad feature of the housing situation is not heavy house density, but the crowding of families into houses—one house has eleven voters on the register! Judging by the reduced number of children in the schools, there has been a considerable relief of overcrowding by transfer to council houses. The records of some streets show a dreary regularity of shared houses.

————Street. 29 houses, 44 families with children, 40 children under 5, and a total of 101 children up to school leaving age. Eight families in poverty in the sense defined. One portion of the street reads—Labourer, Class V., 4 children. Three families, Invalid, Class III., 1 child; widow, Class II., 1 child; Labourer, Class V., 1 child. Widow, Class III., 1 child. Small shop, Class VI., 3 children. Three families, Seaman, Class V., 3 children; Labourer, Class V., 1 child; Widow, Class II., 2 children. Two families, both Labourers with 4 and 3 children. Two families, Pensioner, Class V., 4 children, and Labourer, Class V., 2 children.

————Street. 74 families of whom 59 are in Classes II.-V. There are 193 children of whom 78 are in Classes II.-IV. Probably 14 families are in poverty in the sense defined. Examples from this street:—two families, Labourer, Class V., 3 children, and Labourer, Class VI., 1 child. Widow, Class II., with 1 dependent child but 3 older children. Two families, Labourer, Class IV., 2 dependent, and 4 older children, and a Steward, Class VI., with 1 child. Three families, Widow, Class II., Labourer, Class IV., with 1 child, and Billposter, Class V., with 2 children. Two families, Labourer, Class V., with 6 children, and Ships Fireman, Class V., with 1 child. In successive houses 5 families, one Class III., one Class IV., and three Class V., with 10 dependent children.

TRINITY Ward. This has a relatively heavy house density per acre, partly by reason of its many narrow streets. Some of the streets are very poor, being occupied by labourers with irregular work.

————Street. 65 families, 40 of Class IV. and under, with 133 dependent children, of whom no less than 53 are graded Class II. In one section, 8 houses have 10 families, all labourers or hawkers, Class III., except a seaman, Class V. A common feature is the sharing of houses by related families. One section of the streets reads:—Three families, all labourers, IV., III. and II., with 5, 3 and 1 respectively. Two of the families are related. Widow, Class III., 1 child. Two families, both Class II., and related, with 3 and 2 children. Labourer, Class II., 1 child. Labourer, Class II., 2 children. Dock Worker, Class VI., 1 child. Two families related, one Class IV. and one Class VI., with 1 and 3 children. There are 8 streets of this kind in the ward.

CENTRAL Wards. These do not call for detailed comment, the principal facts being apparent from the tables. Newtown is dominantly

Classes VI. and VII., i.e., skilled artisans, Foremen, Clerks, &c. Bevois includes two diverse sections, a well-to-do residential district, in which the houses are occupied by the owners and managers of town businesses, professional men, &c., and a working-class area. The infant mortality rate seems higher than is warranted by the other indices and may be due to a heavy incidence in the poorer area. For example :—

———Street, contains 116 families with children, of whom one half are in Class V. and 8 in Class IV. There are 278 children, or nearly 2.4 per family. One section contains 13 families with 39 children, two of them certainly below the poverty line.

BANISTER Ward makes the best showing in most of the indices, only a small fraction of its population being graded Class IV. or under. On the coloured street map of its two-score streets no less than one quarter are coloured for the highest grade and fourteen the next highest.

PORTSWOOD Ward is mixed, containing areas of well-to-do persons, and a series of streets occupied by the upper grades of clerical and supervisory labour. St. Denys' Ward, which stretches across the river on either side of Cobden Bridge, includes two diverse groups, the western side being inhabited by railway and other transport workers, and the eastern side including also commercial and seagoing workers of higher income grades.

THREE western wards, Freemantle, Millbrook and Shirley include part of the old Urban District of Shirley, and they have a life of their own centred around Shirley High Street and Road. FREEMANTLE is a built-up ward and its population is probably not increasing, but there is danger that the extension of the docks proceeding along its frontage will lead to a demand for house room near them and so cause overcrowding per house. This situation will need careful watching. Of its forty streets only two are dominantly Class VII., and all except 12 are dominantly Class VI.

MILLBROOK is a boundary ward with all the characteristics of a partly developed area. It includes groups of large houses, some old large houses now depreciated and inhabited by working-class families, council houses, ordinary working-class streets and new houses of a size purchasable by better-off working people. Of its poorer streets the following is typical :—

———Street. Labourer, Class IV., 3 children. Steward, Class V., 3 children. Carman, Class IV., 2 children.

MUCH of SHIRLEY Ward consists of fairly modern houses inhabited by the upper grades of dock and shipping company employees.

ONE street includes the following entries :—Steward, Class VII., 1 child. Steward, Class VII., 1 child. Steward, Class VI., 3 children. Bank Clerk, Class VII., 1 child. Steward, Class VII., 1 child. Steward, Class VI., 1 child. There are older areas of poverty and congestion. A portion of ———street reads :—Separated, Class IV., 3 children. Watchman, Class V., 1 child. Spinster, daily work, Class III., 1 child. Labourer, Class IV., 7 children. Widow, Class IV., 3 children. Basketmaker, Class IV., 5 children. The street has 13 families with 34 children, and of these 6 were in poverty in the sense defined.

THREE wards across the River Itchen, Woolston, Bitterne and Pear Tree, and Bitterne and Sholing, were either included in Itchen Urban District, and brought within the Borough in 1920, or taken in from the county. The ward boundaries cut across the natural grouping of the population. In 1928 there were three nuclei of population separated by partly developed land, two spreading out fanshaped from bridge ends, and one based on old Bitterne village. These groups of population are divided between four wards, one of which stretches on both sides of the water. In two of the wards the average number of dependent children per family is considerably greater than the average for the town, being 2.4 for Bitterne and Pear Tree, and 2.25 for Bitterne and Sholing, the former being the highest for any ward in Southampton. This is partly but by no means exclusively, due to the building of council houses in the area, for before the war the census of 1911 showed that the average census family for the Urban District (not then incorporated in the borough) was 4.6, as compared with 4.2 for Southampton.

————Street containing 27 families with 79 children. It includes the following entries :—Scaler, Class VI., 7 children. Seaman, Class VI., 7 children. Caulker, Class VI., 5 children. Labourer, Class V., 6 children. Several of the families are probably under the poverty line. One section includes 10 families with 33 children at least 3 being in poverty.

BITTERNE and Sholing is an undeveloped boundary ward. Its extremely light house density is partly due to the fact that road and street acreage with undeveloped frontage has of necessity been included in "land used for housing." Although one might expect a large element of semi-rural occupations, the docks and shipyards make their influence felt even in the places most distant from them.

FOR example :————street, a Carrier and Market Gardener, both Class V., with 3 children living alongside a Crane Driver, Class VI., 3 children ; Seaman, Class V., 1 child ; Steward, Class VI., 2 children, and an Engineer, Class VI., 2 children. It is said that there are more seagoing men (other than stewards) in this ward than in any other, the occupation being traditional for many families. The incomes in the ward are on a lower level than would have been expected, nearly 30 streets being dominantly Class V. Families tend to be large, the average being 2.25. Even recently built houses are shared between two families. For example :————street. Two families, Labourer, Class V., 1 child ; Chargehand, Class V., 1 child. Two families, Class VI., 1 child ; Labourer, Class V., 1 child. Two families, Labourer, Class V., 2 children ; Carpenter, Class VI., 1 child. One suspects that in these cases overcrowding is not due entirely to inadequate income, but possibly to unwillingness to pay an adequate rent, since some of the families are not exceedingly large. In a portion of another street, are seven seamen in successive houses with 8, 4, 2, 3, 4, and 1 dependent children respectively. Here 17 families have 55 dependent children, an average of 3.2.

ST. NICHOLAS Ward covers the whole north boundary of the town and was an undeveloped fringe with groups of houses for the well-to-do. Development of council estates has added to the population and increased the number of children. Low house density is due partly to length of roads with undeveloped frontage. The Survey showed the existence of a number of small pockets of semi-rural bad housing which need attention.

LIST OF SUBSCRIBERS TO THE SERIES

Individual

Alexander, Miss M., M.A., 63 Common Lane, Titchfield, Farnham.
Bonnard, B., The Twins, Le Petit Val, Alderney, Channel Isles.
Bunker, B.A., 32 Radford Ave., Wallington, Surrey.
Butler, Ms C.B., B.A., Ph.D., 121 Bernard Street, Bitterne, Southampton.
Casson, M.C., 6 Wayside Green, Woodcote, Reading.
Chandler, J.H., B.A., Ph.D., Jupes School, East Knoyle, Salisbury.
Connor, W.J., Marigold Cottage, Galphay, Ripon.
Cook, Mrs J., 7 Plaitford Walk, Southampton.
De Grouchy, P.J.W., 1 Khartoum Road, Southampton.
Diaper, Mr C., 36 Kellett Road, Southampton.
Douch, R., M.A., 46 Wilton Crescent, Southampton.
Douglas, Professor A.E., M.A., The University, Birmingham.
Emery-Wallis, F.A.J., D.L., Froddington, Craneswater Park, Southsea.
George, A., M.A., D.A.A., 33 West Road, Southampton.
Gibbons, Mrs D., 26 Bronte Way, Southampton.
Hammond, J.R.P, Durley Mill, Durley, Southampton.
Harwood, Mrs E., 3 Lauriston Drive, Chandlers Ford, Southampton.
Hawes, T.L.M., 8 Keswick Road, Cringleford, Norwich.
Henton, J.C., 23 Welbeck Avenue, Southampton.
Hicks, Professor M.A., Ph.D., University College, Winchester
Hind, Ms. L., 21 Shaw Close, Andover.
Hodson, Professor F., B.Sc., Ph.D., F.G.S., The University, Southampton.
Hutton, Professor S.P., D.Eng., Ph.D., The University, Southampton.
James, J.F., 3 Sylvan Close, Hordle, Lymington.
James, Professor T.B., M.A., Ph.D., Sydenham Lodge, Cranham Road, Cheltenham.
Jones, Ms S., Ph.D., 20 Tennyson Road, Southampton.
Kaye, J.M., B.C.L., M.A., The Queen's College, Oxford.
Keene, D.J., D.Phil., 162 Erlanger Road, Telegraph Hill, London.
Key, D.M., 171 Cranbury Road, Eastleigh.
Lawton, Ms L., 23 Foyes Court, Shirley, Southampton.
Leonard, A.G.K., M.A., 10 Radway Road, Southampton.
Lewis, Ms E.A., B.A., 9 Hope View, Shipley, Bradford.
Mather, Mrs P.H., M.A., 3 Monks Road, Hyde, Winchester.
Morris, Rev. Professor C., F.R.Hist.S., 12 Bassett Crescent East, Southampton.
Morris, M., 80 The Butts, Alton.
Morton, A.D., 32 Graham Road, Southampton.
Ogier, D.M., Le Monnard D'Aval, St. Andrews, Guernsey, Channel Isles.
Pain, J.H., 68 Summit Way, Southampton.
Pinhorn, M.A., B.A., F.S.G., Norman's Place, Newport, I.O.W.
Platt, Professor C.P.S.P., M.A., Ph.D., The Old Rectory, Littlehempston, Totnes
Riseborough, D., 24 Glenn Road, West Road, Hants.
Rothery, Mrs E.A., 32 Hill Place, Bursledon, Southampton.
Ruddock, Miss A.A., B.A., Ph.D., F.R.Hist.S., Wren Cottage, 10 Heatherwood, Midhurst.

Selby, Mrs V.A., 32 Oakley Road, Southampton.
Smith, A.A., M.A. Ph.D., The University, Southampton
Spicer, A., M.A., Ph.D., Oxford Brookes University, Oxford.
Stevens, P., 6D Arthur Road, Southampton.
Stewart, Mrs S.C., 58 Upper St Helens Road, Hedge End, Southampton.
Sturman, C.J., 30 Broadbank, Louth, Lincs.
Thomson, Ms S.D., 51 Alfriston Gardens, Southampton.
Wagstaff, Professor J.M., Ph.D., The University, Southampton.
Welch, Dr C.E., 7487 Forest Turn, Lantzville, British Columbia, Canada.
White, A.J., 2 Swift Close, Winchester.
Woolgar, Mrs S.L., B.A., D.A.A., 16 Stinchar Drive, Chandlers Ford.

Institutions (Great Britain and Ireland)

Aberystwyth, National Library of Wales (copyright library).
Belfast, The Queen's University Library.
Birmingham, City Library.
Birmingham, University Library.
Bognor Regis College, West Sussex.
Brighton, University of Sussex Library.
Bristol, University Library.
Cambridge, University Library (copyright library).
Coventry, Warwick University Library.
Dublin, Trinity College Library (copyright library).
Edinburgh, National Library of Scotland (copyright library).
Edinburgh, University Library.
Exeter, University Library.
Glasgow, University Library.
Hull, Central Public Library.
Hull, University Library.
Leeds, Brotherton Library, University of Leeds.
Liverpool, University Library.
London, British Library (copyright library).
London, British Library of Political and Economic Science.
London, College of Arms.
London, Goldsmith's Librarian, University of London.
London, Guildhall Library.
London, Inner Temple Library.
London, Institute of Historical Research.
London, London library.
London, Public Record Office.
London, Royal Historical Society.
London, Society of Antiquaries of London.
Manchester, University Library.
Newport, I.o.W., County Library.
Norwich, East Anglia University Library.
Nottingham, University Library.
Oxford, Bodleian Library (copyright library).
Oxford, The Queen's College Library.
Portsmouth, Central Public Library.
Portsmouth, Frewen Library, Univeristy of Portsmouth.
Reading, University Library.
St Helier, Jersey, Channel Isles, Société Jersiaise, Countanche Library.
Sheffield, University Library.
Southampton, Central Library.
Southampton, Civic Record Office.

Southampton, King Edward VI School.
Southampton, New College Library.
Southampton, Tauntons Sixth Form College Library.
Southampton, St Joseph's Church.
Southampton, Southern Newspapers Ltd.
Southampton, Hartley Library.
Swansea, University College Library.
Wetherby, British Library – Document Supply Centre.
Winchester, City Library.
Winchester, Hampshire County Library.
Winchester, Hampshire Record Office.
Winchester, University College.
York, University Library.

Institutions (Overseas)

AUSTRALIA

Adelaide, University Library.
Brisbane, Queensland University Library.
Canberra, Library (Chifley), Australian National University.
Melbourne, Victoria State University Library.
Perth, Western Australia University Library.

CANADA

Edmonton, Alberta University Library.
Kingston, Queen's University Library.
Toronto, University Library.

CHILE

Santiago, Sociedad Chilena de Historia y Geografia.

DENMARK

Copenhagen, Det Kongelige Bibliotek.

FRANCE

Paris, Bibliothèque de l'Université.

GERMANY

Göttingen, Niedersachsische Staats und Universitätsbibliothek.
Munich, Bayerische Staatsbibliothek.

ISRAEL

Jerusalem, Jewish National and University Library.

POLAND

Torun, Towrarzystwo Naukowe w Toruniu.
Warsaw, Institute of History.

PORTUGAL

Oporto, Biblioteca Pública Municipal.

SWEDEN

Uppsala, University Library.

UNITED STATES OF AMERICA

Albuquerque (N.M.), New Mexico University Library.
Ann Arbor (Mich.), Michigan University General Library.
Ann Arbor (Mich.), Michigan University Law Library.
Athens (Ga.), Georgia University Library.
Atlanta (Ga.), Woodruff Library, Emory University.
Austin (Tex.), Texas University Library.
Berkeley (Calif.), California University Library.
Cambridge (Mass.), Harvard College Library.
Cambridge (Mass.), Harvard University Law School Library.
Charlottesville (Virginia), Alderman Library, University of Virginia.
Chicago (Ill.), Chicago University Library.
Chicago (Ill.), Newberry Library.
Cincinnati (Ohio), University Library.
Columbia (Mo.), Missouri University Library.
Dallas (Tex.), Dallas Public Library.
Durham (N.C.), Duke University Library.
Eugene (Oregon), Oregon University Library.
Iowa City (Iowa), Iowa State University Library.
Ithaca (N.Y.), Cornell University Library.
Los Angeles (Calif.), California University Research Library.
Madison (Wis.), Wisconsin University Library.
Minneapolis, Minnesota University Library.
Nashville (Tenn.), Vanderblit University Library.
New Haven (Conn.), Yale University Library.
New York (N.Y.), Columbia University Library.
New York (N.Y.), Public Library.
Poughkeepsie (N.Y.), Vassar College Library.
Princeton (N.J.), Princeton University Library.
Providence (R.I.), John Hay Library, Brown University.

LIST OF SUBSCRIBERS

Rochester (N.Y.), Rochester University Library.
Salt Lake City (Utah), Genealogical Society.
San Marino (Calif.), Henry E. Huntington Library and Art Gallery.
Stanford (Calif.), Stanford University Library.
Stonybrook (N.Y.), State University of New York.
Tucson (Arizona), Arizona University Library.
Urbana (Ill.), Illinois University Library.
Washington (D.C.), Library of Congress.

THE SOUTHAMPTON RECORDS SERIES

Volumes already published:

I. *Italian Merchants and Shipping in Southampton, 1270–1600,* by Alwyn A. Ruddock (1951).

II. *The Third Book of Remembrance of Southampton, 1514–1602.* Vol. I (1514–1540). Edited, with an introduction, by A.L. Merson (1952).

III. *The Third Book of Remembrance of Southampton, 1514–1602.* Vol. II (1540–1573). Edited by A.L. Merson (1955).

IV. *The Brokage Book of Southampton, 1443–44.* Edited, with an introduction, by Olive Coleman. Vol. I (1960).

V. *The Local Port Book of Southampton, 1439–40.* Edited , with an introduction, by Henry S. Cobb (1961).

VI. *The Brokage Book of Southampton, 1443–44.* Edited, with an introduction, by Olive Coleman. Vol. II (1961).

VII. *The Local Port Book of Southampton, 1435–36.* Edited, with an introduction, by Brian Foster (1963).

VIII. *The Third Book of Remembrance of Southampton, 1514–1602.* Vol. III (1573–1589). Edited, with an introduction, by A.L. Merson (1965).

IX. *Southampton Maps from Elizabethan Times.* Twenty-four facsimiles, with an introduction by Edwin Welch. Published by the City of Southampton (1964) and made available by the courtesy of the City Council to Records Series Subscribers.

X. *A Selection from the Southampton Corporation Journals, 1815–35, and Borough Council Minutes, 1835–47.* Edited, with an introduction, by A. Temple Patterson (1965).

XI. *A History of Southampton, 1700–1914. Volume I: An Oligarchy in Decline, 1700–1835,* by A. Temple Patterson (1966).

XII. *A Calendar of Southampton Apprenticeship Registers, 1609–1740.* Compiled by A.J. Willis and edited, with an introduction and notes, by A.L. Merson (1968).

XIII. *The Admiralty Court Book of Southampton, 1566–85.* Edited, with an introduction, by Edwin Welch (1968).

XIV. *A History of Southampton, 1700–1914. Volume II: The Beginnings of Modern Southampton, 1836–1867,* by A. Temple Patterson (1966).

XV. *The Southampton Terrier of 1454.* Edited by L.A. Burgess, with an introduction by L.A. Burgess, P.D.A. Harvey and A.D. Saunders (1976).

XVI. *Southampton Notarial Protest Books, 1765–1810.* Edited, with an introduction, by Geoffrey Hampson (1973).

XVII. *The Beaulieu Cartulary.* Edited by S.F. Hockley, with an introduction by P.D.A. Harvey and S.F. Hockey (1975).

LIST OF SUBSCRIBERS

XVIII. *A History of Southampton, 1700–1914. Volume III: Setbacks and Recoveries, 1868–1914*, by A. Temple Patterson (1975).

XIX-XX. *The Cartulary of God's House, Southampton.* Edited in two volumes, with an introduction by J.M. Kaye (1976).

XXI. *The Southampton Mayor's Book of 1606–1608.* Edited, with an introduction, by W.J. Connor (1978).

XXII. *The Third Book of Remembrance of Southampton, 1514–1602.* Vol. IV (1590–1602). Edited, with an introduction, by T.B. James (1979).

XXIII. *Minute Book of the French Church.* Edited, with an introduction, by Edwin Welch (1980).

XXIV-XXV. *The St Denys Cartulary.* Edited in two volumes, with an introduction, by E.O. Blake (1981, 1982).

XXVI. *Southampton Sources: 1086–1900.* Edited, with an introduction, by T.B. James (1983).

XXVII. *A God's House Miscellany.* Edited, with an introduction, by J.M. Kaye (1984).

XXVIII. *The Brokage Books of Southampton for 1477–8 and 1527–8.* Edited by K.F. Stevens (1985). The Book of 1477–8 translated by T.E. Olding (1985).

XXIX. *Dilapidated Housing and Housing Policy in Southampton, 1890–1914.* Edited, with an introduction, by Martin Doughty (1986).

XXX. *Henry V and the Southampton Plot of 1415*, by T.B. Pugh (1987).

XXXI. *Minute Book of the Pavement Commissioners for Southampton 1770–1789.* Edited, with an introduction, by Jan Stovold (1990).

XXXII-XXXIII. *The Port Book of Southampton, 1509–10.* Edited in two volumes, with an introduction, by T.B. James (1990).

XXXIV-XXXV. *Southampton Probate Inventories 1447–1575.* Edited in two volumes, with an introduction, by Edward Roberts and Karen Parker (1992).

XXXVI. *The Southampton Port and Brokage Books, 1448–9.* Edited, with an introduction, by Elisabeth A. Lewis (1993).

XXXVII. *The Book of Examinations and Depositions Before the Mayor and Justices of Southampton* 1648–1663. Edited, with an introduction, by Sheila D. Thomson (1994).

XXXVIII. *The Southampton Steward's Book of 1492–93 and the Terrier of 1495.* Edited, with an introduction, by Anne Thick (1995).

XXXIX. *The French-speaking Reformed Community and their Church in Southampton, 1567-c. 1620*, by Andrew Spicer (1997).